THIS IDENTITY BELONGS TO:

me
↓

who ——→ CORY ANTHONY PAMPALONE

i can be funny
ha ha ha

THE
IDENTITY

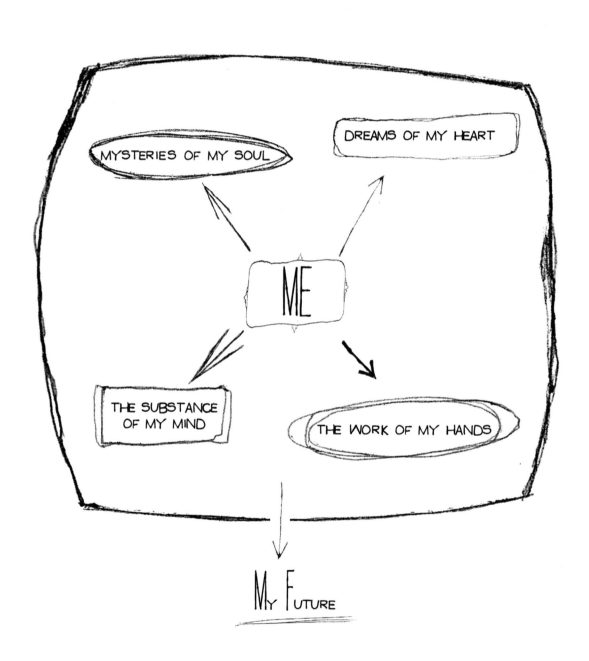

PROJECT

BY Patrick Dodson

WITH Blue Bradley

{ pause for effect }

Other titles by Patrick Dodson:

Stuff My Father Never Told Me About Relationships

Psychotic Inertia: A book about calling and confusion

Copyright 2011 © Patrick Dodson

Published by Pause for Effect Limited
709 New North Road
Auckland, New Zealand 1022

Pause for Effect books are available through most book stores and are also available in a variety of electronic formats. To contact Pause for Effect directly write to:
info@pauseforeffect.co.nz

ISBN **978-0-473-19235-8**

With thanks to Meredith Cochran, Emma-Kate Hall, and Videne Dodson for their inspired editing. Thanks also to the Mosaic crew for letting me write at Crave Cafe

Book design by Patrick Dodson
Illustrations by Jasmine May Dodson

Printed and bound in the US, UK and Australia by Lightning Source.
Lightning Source UK Ltd. Chapter House, Pitfield, Kiln Farm, Milton Keynes, MK11 3LW.
Email: enquiries@lightningsource.co.uk
Voice: 0845 121 4567. Fax: 0845 121 4594

National Library of New Zealand data
(Te Puna Matauranga o Aotearoa):

Title:	**The Identity Project**
Author:	**Patrick Dodson**
Publisher:	**Pause for Effect**
Address:	**709 New North Rd, Mount Albert, Auckland 1022**
Format:	**Hardback**
Publication Date:	**08/2011**
ISBN:	**978-0-473-19235-8**

First Edition

THIS BOOK IS DEDICATED TO Heather BECAUSE SHE IS INDUSTRIOUS, CARING, HOSPITABLE,

FAITHFUL, AND DEEP... TO Josiah BECAUSE HE IS HONEST, GENEROUS, INGENIOUS, LOVING,

AND SMART... TO Jordan BECAUSE HE IS VISCERAL, ANCIENT, VISUAL, DRAMATIC, AND

KIND... TO Jasmine BECAUSE SHE IS ARTISTIC, MUSICAL, OLD, ARTICULATE, AND STRONG...

TO Levi BECAUSE HE IS LINGUISTIC, KINESTHETIC, CREATIVE, EPICUREAN, AND SHY...

TO Joseph Foote BECAUSE HE IS EXTROVERTEDLY INTROVERTED, AN ENCOURAGER, A

THINKER, A SON AND BROTHER, AND ABSTRACT... TO Heather Svensson BECAUSE SHE

IS QUIET, A CREATIVE MOTHER, RESOURCEFUL, A RESEARCHER, AND A MIDWIFE... TO Gert

Jan BECAUSE HE IS A DREAMER, A PROBLEM SOLVER, AN ADVENTURER, A LISTENER, A

TRAINER, AND A CREATOR... TO Rebecca Greenwood BECAUSE SHE IS RESTLESS, Gods

MASTERPIECE, INSECURE, BEAUTIFUL, AND SEARCHING... TO Tiffana LeMaster BECAUSE

SHE IS STRATEGIC, A LEARNER, FASCINATED BY IDEAS, INQUISITIVE, AND AN ACTIVATOR...

TO Lauren Kulp BECAUSE SHE LOVES HORSES, IS HEALTHY, IS AN ENCOURAGER, LOVES

PEOPLE, AND ADVENTUROUS... TO Isaac Chatterton BECAUSE HE IS A SON, A CREATOR, A

WORSHIPPER, A LEADER, AND AN ARTIST... TO Emma—Kate BECAUSE SHE IS REDEMPTIVE,

A CREATOR, WHIMSICAL, INTRAPERSONAL, AND ARTICULATE... TO Sarah—Anne Jackson

BECAUSE SHE IS A CREATIVE SOUL, AN ADVENTURER, A JOURNALER—WRITER, A HEALER,

AND A FRIEND... TO Des Rountree BECAUSE HE IS CONSIDERATE, AESTHETIC, EMPATHETIC,

AN AGENT, AND OPEN... TO Dino Biaggi BECAUSE HE IS IN NEED OF CHALLENGES, A

BUILDING BLOCK, AN INTIMATE WORSHIPPER, TEACHABLE, AND IN NEED OF STRUCTURE

WITH FREEDOM... TO Zadok Wartes BECAUSE HE IS A PROVOKER, A DREAMER, IDEALISTIC,

A SKEPTIC, AND A PROCESSOR... TO Colin Hewitt BECAUSE HE IS A NETWORKER, AN

EXPLORER, A DREAMER, A HUSBAND... AND A CHANGE AGENT... TO Kay Morten Aarskog

BECAUSE HE IS A FATHER, PROTECTOR, AN ADVENTURER, TEACHABLE, AND A WARRIOR... TO

Margie Jansen BECAUSE SHE IS A NATION—BUILDER, CREATIVE, A DRAWER OF PEOPLE,

A LOVER OF TRAVEL AND CULTURE, AND DISCERNING... TO Heidi O Sullivan BECAUSE

SHE IS A MUM, A, SERVANT, A LOVER OF CRAFT, PART OF A GREAT FAMILY, A WIFE TO

A GREAT MAN... TO Meredith Cochran BECAUSE SHE IS TEACHABLE, PATIENT, STRONG

INSIDE, WISE, AND GOOFY... TO Arie Gort BECAUSE HE IS ARTISTIC, ANALYTICAL,

RESOURCEFUL, A PEACEMAKER, AND COLLABORATIVE...TO Kathryn Hewitt BECAUSE SHE IS

A JOYFUL FACILITATOR, A TRUTH—SEEKER, SENSITIVE, TACTILE, AND A COLLABORATOR...

TO Ben Story BECAUSE HE IS A FATHER, A BUILDER, A NURTURER, A PHILOSOPHER, AND

IS WORTH KNOWING...

Table Of Contents:

Patrick Dodson is:

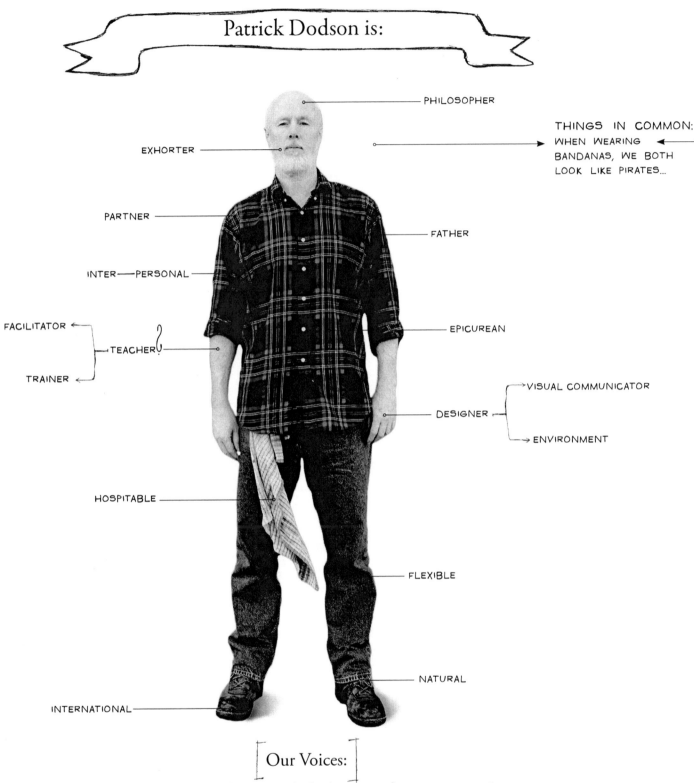

PHILOSOPHER

EXHORTER

THINGS IN COMMON: WHEN WEARING BANDANAS, WE BOTH LOOK LIKE PIRATES...

PARTNER

FATHER

INTER—PERSONAL

FACILITATOR

TEACHER!

EPICUREAN

TRAINER

VISUAL COMMUNICATOR

DESIGNER

ENVIRONMENT

HOSPITABLE

FLEXIBLE

NATURAL

INTERNATIONAL

Our Voices:

Blue Bradley and I are collaborating on this book to cross-reference our perspectives on coaching identity development. We have very different approaches but very similar end goals. Our diversity suits this project perfectly because we're not about prescribing solutions, we're about discovery and—hopefully for you—creation. To differentiate between our voices, we'll use different typefaces: Patrick's voice will look like this:

"Our soul knows what it wants, we just need to let it breathe."

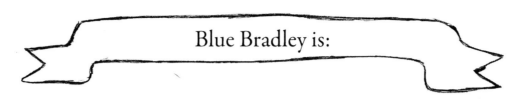

Blue Bradley is:

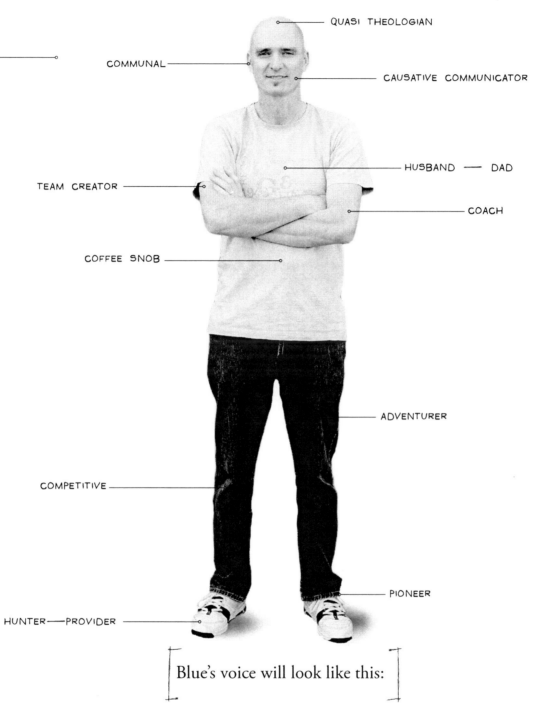

QUASI THEOLOGIAN

COMMUNAL

CAUSATIVE COMMUNICATOR

HUSBAND — DAD

TEAM CREATOR

COACH

COFFEE SNOB

ADVENTURER

COMPETITIVE

PIONEER

HUNTER—PROVIDER

Blue's voice will look like this:

"In short, we didn't react to our environment, we created it..."

Vocation does not mean a goal that I pursue.

It means a calling that I hear. Before I can

tell my life what I want to do with it, I must

listen to my life telling me who I am. I must

listen for the truths and values at the heart

of my own identity, not the standards by

which I must live , but the standards by which

I cannot help but live...

[Parker Palmer]

I WAS BORN

to write

THIS BOOK

Not in the pre-determined sense that God had planned it, the stars willed it, or that vague idea that it was 'just meant to be...' These notions reduce me to a mere puppet with pre-programmed abilities, just waiting for the right time to start my routine. There's no real creativity in being made to be or do something, at least none on my part. Like you, I was born with distinct abilities which could be molded into all kinds of outcomes. Things like the desire to communicate, the ability to assess needs and trends, and a certain intelligence that can formulate words in a meaningful way. I was born with the substance of a writer, as many others are, but I had to acknowledge it and *make something of it.*

I was

also born to take pictures from a certain perspective, father my children in a unique way, and cook the most amazing huevos rancheros you've ever had.[1] From the hard wiring of my intelligence (the working of my neurons) to the softer areas of my dreams (the workings of my soul), I was born with a vast array of things which I meld together every day of my life. The gift I was given was not a plan, but the diverse raw material with which to make something new. My destiny is not based on 'what I was meant to do'—my destiny happens as I co-create—and the fireworks begin there.

What all of us were born with is a unique identity. This is spread across the distinct range of our intelligences, personality traits, physical attributes, and the more ethereal areas of our soul. What we do with that amazing mix of potential is largely up to us. But there's a twist in life that's worth noting. I believe most of what we've been given to work with is natural, or our nature, and therefore our life choices should also be natural. But there's also a nurturing part of our lives that has to be both appreciated and reckoned with. Because for most of us, the way we were 'nurtured' has become a point of departure. A departure away from our potential and towards a kind of conformity that may have left us a little deformed.

For instance, some of the nurturing I was given came in the form of an 'education' which harshly judged me by my poor math skills. That same education also taught me to read and write, but then harshly judged my poetry assignments (I once got a failure mark on a poetry assignment for allegedly copying, which I hadn't). Had I not got in touch with my identity later on, the 'nurture' part of my life would have dissuaded me from my nature, or from seeing myself as a potential writer. Thankfully, the other parts of my nurture / context, like examples in the culture that I grew up with (books / film / ads), the inspiration of a few friends who were amazing communicators, and then later in life, opportunities to speak in 30 countries over 30 years, all countered the earlier experiences in school by inspiring my communication skills. This larger nurturing context (the world around me) is the mass effect of curriculum developers, media men, my parents, and some 7+ billion other beings all contributing to the context of my development as I contribute to theirs.

This environment has a plan for our lives. Agendas which are very tricky to navigate. My parents had plans for my upbringing, my schools had curriculum, and my bosses had ideas about work, all of which affected me in ways that were largely distracting to my soul's development. It was hard being me with someone else's plans always in play. And I had it easy. What happens to your identity when you're a six year-old girl in India being dedicated to temple prostitution (devadasis) or a twelve year-old boy soldier being commanded to burn villages in Sudan? Sometimes other peoples' plans are virtually impossible to break free from.[2] But even in the worst case scenario, using your identity may be the only way to escape these kinds of hellish situations. Which is exactly what Emmanuel Jal did. Recruited by the SPLA at the age of nine to fight in Sudan, Jal later escaped, developed his music, and is now a leading

---

1 My leetle secret for this Mexican/Kiwi fusion is to add fresh Kaffir lime leaves, fresh Heirloom tomatoes, and home grown chilies to the base. Then poach the eggs in the mix with some crumbled halloumi cheese sprinkled on top. Everything else I humbly borrow from my brothers south of California.

2 It's estimated that only 1 in 20 devadasis escape prostitution into other careers due to the fact that they begin as prostitutes soon after reaching puberty. Source: Nine Lives by Wimmiam Dalrymple. Page 70, Bloomsbury Publishing London 2009

artistic voice against poverty. <u>Identity is amazingly resilient</u>. It can lay dormant or suppressed for years, but like a tulip bulb in the right conditions, it pops back out of the ground in a beautiful way. <u>Sometimes though, these seeds require a crisis, like a forest fire cracking a redwood cone</u>. Jal had to trek for three months through southeastern Sudan to escape, but in the end found help at a refugee camp. From there he began another journey, one where he created a musical language to process his past and change his future... If Emmanuel Jal can be dealt a crap hand and still do well, it should be a breeze in Northern California where I grew up, right?

Kind of. I know this is a little bit emo in comparison to child slavery, but <u>when the world around us gets very complex it's easy to defer to others and let them drive</u>. For the addict, it can be to let the addiction take over. For the mother, it can be to let the kids take center stage. For the bored, computer games... Each of us has a way of tossing the keys to someone else when life gets too hard. For people of faith (like myself), who believe that one God made and loves the universe, <u>it can be to give back to God the authority given to them, namely their free will.</u> This results in fatalism and it's this kind of deferring that's the scariest of all. At least the addict and the workaholic know their point of departure. But the religious person slowly convinces themself that someone else is actually in charge.[3] And once this happens, that person can no longer see what they were born to do because the world they now inhabit is unreal. The trance they call faith blurs the place identity plays in their calling. They miss the forest for the trees because the path they're on is being determined by someone else. Or so they think, and so they act, or don't.

Recovering from these points of departure from your identity takes time. Breaking free from the inertia of a self imposed fatalism takes time. Loosening the grip of fear in order to take risks again also takes time. Shaking yourself out of the malaise of laziness takes time. <u>I've found that it took me around 20 years to shake off negative nurturing by developing a true understanding of self</u>. I hope your journey wastes less time and that this book will really help. But going from a place of being kinda stuck to moving fluidly with your real identity is a process that was designed to grow over years. If you pro-actively give yourself that time, you'll probably avoid the traps of past efforts that stalled because maybe you <u>wanted too much too soon.</u>

For me, those years were spent developing a solid sense of what I was given to work with. I needed to articulate and experiment with the substance of my soul, mind, and strength. I needed to make commitments to develop my identity alongside other people so I could build on my real strengths, in community. A road map would have been really helpful (which is why I'm writing this for you), but as I delved into this area (knowing who I am in order to create my future) I found that the process was largely organic. <u>Meaning, that it was obvious once I put down the other toys or lost the weird world-views that led to my lazy fatalism</u>[4] Even putting a little effort into developing what was already in me created a kind of momentum or inspiration that led to investing even more time. All of this grew into a better understanding

---

3 I won't labour this point as I've already covered it in another book called Psychotic Inertia - A book about calling and confusion. Have a read if you are really stuck on this point.

4 I think all forms of fatalism are lazy. It's our way of getting out of having to weed the garden. If I call whatever happens God's will or fate, then I don't have to be responsible... If you follow the effects of fatalism you will find our gardens turn into deserts, and our prosperity collapses into debt. And worst of all, our true identities as co-creators lapses into a clone-like existence.

13

of what I'd been blessed with which then formed ideas, plans, and (eventually), books. I found that I was born with an identity that could, among other things, write this book, or a screenplay, or poetry, or lyrics, or whatever I was committed to communicating. As a spiritual person, I think God celebrates this kind of creative diversity, and wouldn't want to pre-design it's outcome and thus ruin the unfolding.

From what I know of Blue, he was born to be a

team player / coach. The diverse range of his identity allows him to connect with a wide range of people and yet go deep with the individual. His empathy forms bonds while his intuition sees issues and opportunities. Blue can challenge people with the strength of his intelligence and passion, and yet cry alongside them with the same gifting. All these attributes form a basis for the people in his life to connect with each other, and thus make the team...

Like most of us, Blue Bradley seems like an enigma. To look at certain angles of his identity (such as his passion for hunting or running camping retreats), one could get the impression that his life is about a truck, rifle, and a dog... However, Blue happens to be well engaged with the urban scene of his neighborhood including it's art, food, sports, and dare I say it, scooter culture. He has that Kiwi down-to-earth realism matched with a fierce intelligence for philosophy and truth. And like all of us, when you look closer at the intersection of these abilities, you see that seeming contradictions actually make up the beauty of the man.

Which is exactly why I've asked Blue to write this book with me. He's taken the time to train in and understand the deeper aspects of the most popular identity metrics (which I haven't), and suss out the essential elements to be truly relevant for his friends. His hands-on approach for immediate application is matched by his patience and understanding for how long life in the real world takes to unfold. There are many aspects to Blue's identity which I think will help you articulate and then facilitate your identity. Because as far as I can see, this is one of the many things he was born to do.

So that's us. What were you born to do?

You, sent out beyond your recall,

go to the limits of your longing.
Embody Me.

Flare up like flame

and make big shadows I can move in.

Rainer Maria Rilke
— Das Stundenbuch or The Book of Hours

{ INSTRUCTIONS }

Whenever you learn *something interesting* about yourself, add a bit to the front page where you've written your name.

Write stuff everywhere, treat this like your **journal**. *Paste in your own pictures*, write in your own ideas...

This book is about *movement* (yours), and the tools to keep you moving. There is a flow, but only if it's helpful towards your own initiation and creativity. So start anywhere you need to, go anywhere that's helpful.

Scan first, get a feel for the flow. Work on the important issues as they arise or become obvious. *Build good foundations*.

Then work / **customize** the entire process with a friend to create some structure and take action together.

The **random portraits** are friends of mine with their identity statements. I suggest you *paste in pics* of yourself and your friends and write in some identity statements that line up with the portrait.

To go through all the exercises properly, to process all the ideas, and to apply what this book is about could easily take a year. *Pace yourself* but don't slack off.

⌐ Ignore all instructions if you like. ⌐

Oh, and **a word** on *motivation...*

Two things I've learned in life: positive change only occurs when you make it happen and guys hardly ever journal... The information found in this book only facilitates action when you're ready to act. The problem is, our will has become inept and we're not really sure what we want to do with the days we have. This means I can lead you to water, but you may just stare at it for a while, unsure if you want to drink or not... So in order to sort this out, I suggest you let the first few chapters sink in. Think about all the times where you've been inspired but unchanged. Or about all the tools you've wielded and yet so little was actually made... At the core, you have to find those inner motives, or the soft voices of your soul, and not only take heed but be ready to act on them. I could threaten the slow death of not knowing your identity, but we don't really grow through threats. You and I need to get back in touch with both the value we possess and the felt needs of our hearts (not our wallet).

Growth happens when we're:

1: Committed to change, then we need to

2: Educate our selves, which must be followed by

3: Applying what we learn.

So in terms of identity, what do you want to:

commit to?...

....

....

learn about?...

....

....

apply?..

....

....

*THE RISE

?

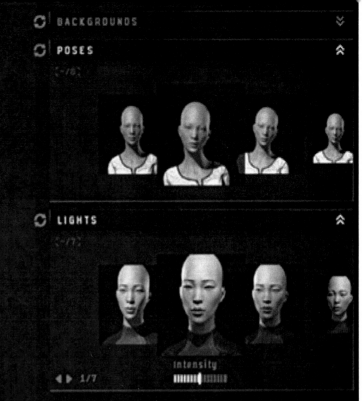

BACKGROUNDS

POSES

LIGHTS

Intensity

1/7

*Second Life is populated by alter egos while Grand Theft Auto has wannabe gangsters posing all over a virtual LA. Aliases dominate the digitally masked communication landscape where 40 year-old men act like children on Neopets and 15 year-old girls fight like ancient warriors on WoW. It's a heck of a lot easier to be someone else, especially when that someone else can **instantly** dress up or smack down in a seemingly amazing way. It's not that these virtual ID's don't have some connection to the real person and their abilities, it's that the pretending is becoming a viable surrogate to life. I mean, why bother struggling to develop and reveal your real self when the fake one can take over the world, or rather, your world, with a mouse?

CLICK!

OF AVATARS

IS A TELLING TALE

Back   Finalize

Part One

Are you ready?

Stuff we're going to try and wrestle with in this section:

- *your motivations*
- *your commitment*
- *your ownership of the process*

This ain't *The Secret*. This book is not a simple set of ideas to make your life easier or show you the road to success. Odds are, it'll create a lot of hard work for you. I will not play on the common need to over simplify a complex process which means you'll need to get comfortable with owning your half of this book.

Figuring out your identity, and thereby your future, has become a great business opportunity for authors. There are stacks of books on the subject and a lot of them, in various ways, are a helpful part of the journey. One thing I've noticed though, is that they tend to capitalize on the assumed need to get a fast answer because the clock is ticking. The educational timer is demanding we fill in the school application and choose a subject. The financial tic-toc is that annoying tension between jobs we don't like and the need to pay bills. The biological bell tolls reminding us that we're not getting any younger and we must make relational / life choices—**NOW!**

In response, well meaning and talented authors have tried to meet this 'need' with what I consider to be quick fixes. In classic modernist style (machines fix things), personality tests move from living conversations to algorithmic tests; computerized processes leading to a simple set of letters in quadrants, five strengths, or a few love languages... All of which are still helpful towards understanding the larger story (except for that love language crap), but self-defeating in the short term. Here are a few reasons why:

1. Algorithmic tests, where you are asked a series of questions and have to make simplistic responses (like on a scale of 1 -10, or more like this, less like that...), lead to a quantitative result. You're placed in a general sphere of personality types, or intellectual strengths. Which happens to be very helpful for putting you in the right part of the factory... You, however, are an extremely complex person with nuanced differences from everyone else on the planet. At best, these tests can only give you a very general impression of identity. In my opinion, horoscopes aren't much better.

2. Due to the apparent need of the subject (you must choose the right school, job, or woman...), modern responses have focused on delivering an outcome. Meaning, if you are this kind of person (you and 1,000,000 others like you), then you should choose that kind of job, or relate to those kinds of people... These methods tend towards **predicting** your future based on your personality / identity which sounds like a nice idea, but is an impossible promise. Our anxiety for answers has created a market for **typical** solutions. Fortune cookies aren't much better.

3. Having done a test like Myers-Briggs, then another like StrengthsFinder, and then possibly another, a lot of people still feel like they're no further along in terms of a clear path to a fulfilling life. At some point they feel like it's just a bunch of words and so develop a 'been there, done that' mentality towards identity altogether, giving up on the process. This is why I say a lot of these methods become self-defeating in the short-term. It's also why religious people just ask God to tell them what to do.

Again, in my opinion, it's not the author's fault. A lot of these ideas are well researched pieces of a larger puzzle that can be really helpful over the long-term. Some have been developed over centuries and have real merit in their approach. I particularly like what Andreas Ebert says about personality tools, that "Signposts show the way, but we have to take the way ourselves."[5] However, it's the way these tools are approached (based on our nervous needs) that leads to either wrong expectations on the readers side, or over-promising on the author's. Our need for an answer to life's questions overshadows the real need to understand what we've been given to create life's solutions. The predictive nature of a church sermon, a facebook quiz, or even a horoscope, has become an addictive search for our destiny. What we should be looking for is **the substance** we've been given to create that destiny. Then, everything from StrengthsFinder to the Enneagram can be put into the mix from which we create (not find) that future.

So the main difference between this book and others you may have read, is that we will not predict your future, or find you a match (to a school, job or person), or give you a boiled down list of anything. You will not be given easy answers, but rather tools to articulate your identity. We will attempt to help you know yourself a lot better by seeing the **wide spectrum of your identity** and the **creative potential of synthesizing** it's various aspects. By seeing what fearfully and wonderfully made really means for you, you may also see your potential to create something that doesn't even exist yet. We hope this qualitative approach helps you find new ways of learning, working, and relating that are truly you. Which takes time and effort, but at the end of the day is a wonderful thing.

Getting to this place has tons to do with your attitude towards the process. For instance, I have a love hate relationship with the story of Jack & the Beanstalk. On one hand, I hate that Jack is looking for a quick fix to poverty and sells the family asset for a few beans. On the other hand, I love that having planted those beans, he has to climb this massive stalk, find treasure, escape death, and return home in

---

5 Richard Rohr. *Discovering the Enneagram* (The Crossroads Publishing Company, New York, 1999), p. XV.

nothing short of a life changing experience. And maybe this is us. We pick up a book like this hoping there's a better (and oh please, faster and less painful) way to being whole, fulfilled. And we plant the few things offered hoping for a fast return, only to find that we have some massive challenges / opportunities to take on. But this time we find they're OUR challenges, suited to OUR passions and abilities, and that we're capable of doing things we never imagined. But it still requires work, meaning you have to climb up the thing you plant.

And so I ask again, are you ready for all this? Are you ready to overcome the discouragement of a lousy situation at home or in school? To acknowledge the expedient approach you may have taken to previous attempts at figuring things out? To overcoming the fear of failure or an obsession with money? To embrace complexity instead of simplicity? To working hard, but this time in a way that's actually natural to you and therefore completely doable? You may have to reckon with past pains and present fears which make us seek a quick-fix, drug based approach to a harsh world.

A lot of us have lost the energy to create our own way and have become super vulnerable to other peoples' plans for us. Which begs a huge question: **what is your present energy level like**? What kind of encouragement do you need to get back on that bike and try again? Who's in your life that can help you and you them? So much of the success of this journey depends on your motivation and energy to proceed. Sheer will is for the worst case scenario. What we need, daily, is a will energized by a constant source. I think knowing your identity is that source, but the 'catch 22' is that you need energy to rediscover what may have been suppressed. What we need is a caring community to help us catch our second wind by holding forth an idea of ourselves that's worth recovering. Can you find two or three people in your community to help? It'll make all the difference.

I've found through the years that this whole identity thing was originally designed for, and still works best in, a family / community setting. So maybe the best way to start this is to look at the key relationships amongst your family and friends, grab a couple of them, and do this together? Even if you're doing well and just wanna refine the future you're already creating, I suggest you get someone close to you and share your energy to support each other in this journey.

Again I looked and saw all the oppression that was

taking place under the sun:

I saw the tears of the oppressed

and they have no comforter;

power was on the side of their oppressors

and they have no comforter.

...

Two are better than one,

because they have a good return for their work:

If one falls down,

his friend can help him up.

But pity the man who falls

and has no one to help him up!

Also, if two lie down together, they will keep warm.

But how can one keep warm alone?

Though one may be overpowered,

two can defend themselves.

A cord of three strands is not quickly broken.

... Ecclesiastes four—ish ...

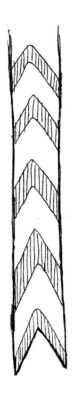

Chapter One Seeing

the *future*

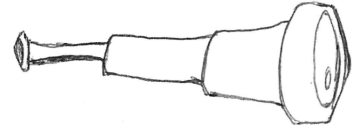

The difference between the person achieving their potential, or at least following their dream, and the one who's stuck, is that the dreamer already sees themselves as living out their identity. They don't think "one day I'll be a musician", **they already are that musician** as far as their heart's concerned. The expression of that gift will mature throughout the years, which to them is about *when* not *if*. The rest is simply a timing issue.

What do you see in your future?
Wanna use this space to draw that out?

I have an annoying habit of asking most people I meet what they'd like to be doing in 10 or 15 years. One in a hundred (the outlier[6]) has a clear idea, and they're usually already pursuing it. The rest struggle to reveal a clouded view of the next six months, or maybe even two years. I understand their pain. Who gets to choose their own path? And if you can choose, are you able to do what you really want? And who can say what's going to happen tomorrow, right? How does anyone know what will happen, especially if we think **life is what happens to us?**

Some people sketch out 'a very practical path' because their parents have willed it to be so. Others throw in a dream or two as potential hobbies in an otherwise factory view of their future. They have a faint glimpse, a cameo of their identity which they'd love to put into action, but it's been put down so often that they slowly agree with how implausible it would be. So when pressed, as in "if you could choose, what would you really like to be doing 10 years from now?", most people say they don't really know. And when they say 'I don't know', they mean 'I don't know, or forgot, who I am'. And so they wander off, as in a daze, reacting to those daily financial or relational prompts only to wake up in some mid-life cold-sweat wondering what the hell just happened to their last 40 years.

The outliers are different. Something inside of them has not been

extinguished by misguided curriculum or social norms. They maintain a kind of clarity even when their abilities haven't quite caught up with their dreams. Their soul knows something that makes the world around them conform to their will instead of the other way around. They're not necessarily type-A personalities either; I've found that these people are all over the personality spectrum. So it's not sheer drive or a 'can do' mentality that moves them. It's something deeper and stronger than will, something that moves their will. A great example of this is spoken word poet Sarah Kay. She describes how her will journeyed through three phases. "I can" was the moment she saw that she was capable of being a poet (at the age of 14) through the encouraging word of one very tall girl in a hoodie who had been touched by what Sarah said. "I will" was the point she determined she would continue taking the steps to do what she loved by returning to New York's Bowery Poetry Club week after week, despite the fact she was a decade younger than everyone else there. "I am" was when she learned that her version of spoken word poetry had to be uniquely her own, because her version was a way to discover identity as much as it was expressive of it. Sarah learned that the third phase was an ongoing process of "infusing the work you're doing with the specific things that make you you, even while those things are always changing."[7] It's this kind of clarity that marks the outliers; they glimpse their identity long before anyone else even notices. All of us have this capacity and our soul has been trying to reveal those glimpses since our earliest years. The trick is to pay attention to it.

I have a video clip of my nine year-old son Josiah explaining, in intricate detail, the inner workings of a game called Sim City. He's poised next to a '94 blue and white iMac, screen flickering in the background, talking about how the water-

---

6 An outlier "is the one that appears to deviate markedly from other members of the sample in which it occurs." Barnett, V. and Lewis, T.: 1994, *Outliers in Statistical Data*. John Wiley & Sons., 3rd edition.

7 From a presentation Sarah gave at TED 2011 in Long Beach. It's well worth watching because of her amazing poetry and the unfolding of her own journey. http://www.ted.com/talks/sarah_kay_if_i_should_have_a_daughter.html

pipe infrastructure needs to keep the simulated city's inhabitants happy, so it can grow... It's a little trippy to watch this curly haired child outline the workings of a computer game with such clarity, as though he designed it himself. In fact, being able to design worlds within Sim City is why the game was so appealing to him. So, it shouldn't have been a surprise to us that he went on to design his own board games the following year, and then 10 years after that, to work on Halo 3. Josiah knew something about himself that he was trying to show the rest of us. Something innate. Something that was so natural to him, it not only defined how he spent his time growing up, it was designing his future from the inside-out. What I learned from him was this: that at the root of a person is their identity, and that identity, if unhindered, will motivate their will to make choices which will create their future. Simple as that.

I SEE A BIT OF WHO I AM VIA EXPERIENCES

—FIG. A

JOSIAH MAKE BELIEVING IN THE FOREST, FASCINATED BY GAME INFRASTRUCTURE...

I EXPERIMENT

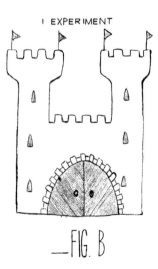

—FIG. B

HE STARTS CREATING HIS OWN BOARD GAMES

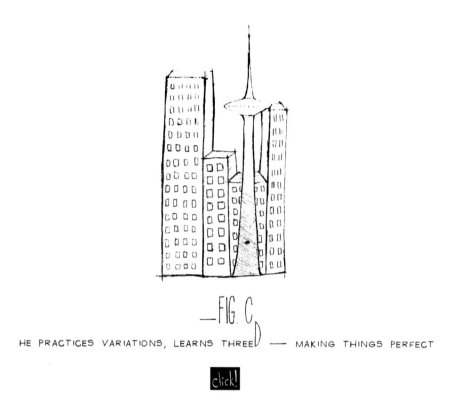

— FIG. C

HE PRACTICES VARIATIONS, LEARNS THREE — MAKING THINGS PERFECT

click!

I CREATE THE FUTURE

— FIG. D

JOSIAH ENTERS THE FIELD OF GAME DESIGN

The 1 in a 100 who know what they want to be and do 10 years from now have this kind of clarity, and have usually had it since they were young. Their profession may be a moving target, but not their identity. Meaning that Richard Branson may end up running 50 different companies, but he'll always be an entrepreneur, an innovator, and a rebel. Identity outliers know the difference between an interest (as in 'I like music') and a passion (as in 'I am a musician'). And they know that their passion is not a matter of **if** it will happen, but rather **when** it'll happen. So they fill their hours, all 10,000 of them,[8] developing what they **already know about themselves**. And so they fill their days, and their weeks, and their decades, until they're doing pretty much what they saw in themselves years prior. In effect, from the vantage point of their own identity, they had already seen the future and they just kept walking towards it.

The other 99

think that the outlier is different from themselves. They think the outlier has more luck, talent, opportunity, money, or some amazing trait they themselves don't possess. The 99 will judge the outcome of the outlier's process rather than analyze the actual process itself. But if we look closely at the real life of anyone who is being themselves, we'll see that their lives are pretty much like ours. Some have had exceptional opportunities to break out, but I think the main difference is that the outlier is looking for **their** opportunity and seizes it. The rest of us aren't even sure what we're looking for, and therefore miss the fleeting moments of opportunity or inspiration. One such inspiration was delivered to Dan Barber in the form of scrambled eggs whipped over a double boiler with French butter. His aunt was helping him recover from tonsillitis, and revealed a whole new kind of cooking which was in direct contrast to his father's typical rubbery eggs. This seemingly small thing became an opportunity for Dan's identity to speak up and reveal an awe for the pleasures of great food. He is now a widely renowned Chef, who not only runs two amazing New York restaurants (one of which is Blue Hill at Stone Barns), but is also changing the way restaurants do food all together. This kind of transformation is the result of his unique approach and his identity speaking through his craft. Mr. Barber is not unlike you or I. Something triggered what was already there. He was just brave and hard-working enough to follow it through.

I've described these world-views in my previous book (*Psychotic Inertia*) as either living from the outside-in, where the world predicts your behavior, or living from the inside-out, where you live from your identity and create the restaurants you want to eat in. For the most part anyway, because you can't create or control everything around you, and wouldn't want to, but you can transform and affect a lot more than you tend to think you can. Still, the industrial revolution continues to have an adverse effect on how we view our futures or careers—constantly distracting our ability to see and live from our identity. In her book *The Future and Its Enemies*, Virginia Postrel describes our dilemma:

> *"How we feel about the evolving future tells us who we are as individuals and as a civilization: Do we search for stasis—a regulated, engineered world? Or do we embrace dynamism—a world of constant creation, discovery, and competition? Do we value stability and control, or evolution and learning? [...] Do we consider mistakes permanent disasters, or the correctable by-products of experimentation?*

---

8. 10,000 hours is the average amount of time it takes to master any given subject according to Daniel J. Levitin, PhD, a neuroscientist at McGill University. Malcolm Gladwell posits a similar theory in his book *Outliers*

Do we crave predictability, or relish surprise? These two
poles, stasis and dynamism, increasingly define our political,
intellectual, and cultural landscape."[9]

So how about turning the model on it's head? Instead of looking at what
the world has on offer in terms of education or work, how about starting from who
you are and what you could create with that? Instead of comparing yourself with
other peoples' success, how about celebrating their identity development and seeing
where a similar dedication could be your own? Instead of reacting to the very real
pressures (like needing to sustain yourself), how about taking a few steps back and
looking for creative solutions to your problems as well as the problems of others?
Similar perhaps to how Steve Jobs re-imagined computing, then film making, and
now mobile communication. Because when you're truly being yourself, you not only
get to pay the bills, you start helping your whole community to prosper.

Living from the inside-out projects a doable future on the path of your life. Which
has the added benefit of changing your day to day circumstances. Letting your
identity inform and reignite your passion grows a clarity inside of you, which leads
to ideas, dreams, plans, and then choices that become a daily reality. This reality
eventually affects your relationships, the community you live in, and hopefully
the world in need all around you. Over time, and looking back, you'd see that a
reactionary life would've only led towards a self-fulfilling negative prophecy of
surviving from day to day. And you may also see that you largely had control all
along. It's this perspective I want to offer you now, so that you avoid becoming a
clone. I want to help remind you of the faint glimpses you've had of yourself—
playing out the dreams of childhood, those performing moments on stage, or taking
things apart in your grandfather's tool shed... I want to help you expand those few
glimpses of the past into a wonderfully broad array of truths you can sew back into
the fabric of your intelligent, natural being. I want to help you project that into
possibilities and ideas, into stories only you can tell of yourself and the future as you
see it. But I can't do this without your dedication to the process. In fact, I can barely
be involved at all. You have to find the stamina, courage, and will to regain this
future, because armed with that perspective everything can help you, even those who
still want you to just get a job.

And you do need a job. But while everyone needs to work if they want to eat, we
have to be aware that industrial dead-end, low-end labour is often the result of
typecasting identity. Cookie cutter industries extract the last energies of people who
haven't had the opportunity or ability to delve deeper into their internal resources.
Martin Luther King said that "Capitalism is always in danger of inspiring men to be
more concerned about making a living than making a life."[10] So every time you see
bad news about the economy, or your dad asks you to put down your dreams and
get a real job like he had to, let it drive you deeper into your identity. Because it's in

---

9 The FUTURE AND ITS ENEMIES: The Growing Conflict Over Creativity, Enterprise, and
Progress, Free Press, 1999, page xiv

10 The full quote goes on to say "We are prone to judge success by the index of our salaries or the size of our automobiles,
rather than by the quality of our service and relationship to humanity-thus capitalism can lead to a practical materialism
that is as pernicious as the materialism taught by communism." *Strength to Love,* Augsburg Fortress Publishers, First
Edition, 1981, page 103

that creative tension that you may end up revitalizing cities. Our world thrives when a few guys invent Google and invite millions of others to build on that innovation. Each person needs to shine / co-create along side of their neighbor in order to create a better and more sustainable future. There are a lot of hard jobs that need doing, but my assumption is that even then, if people are walking in their identity, they'll create a better way to deal with all the garbage, literally.

But isn't the future gonna be horrible?

Maybe. Right now in the US 3 out of 10 students are dropping out of high school and less than a third of American youth are finishing college. Internationally, the economy has been a disaster and crisis looms on a number of fronts... So what can your identity do with that? Here are a few ideas from Reihan Salam's Time Magazine article entitled *The Dropout Economy -10 Ideas for the Next 10 Years* where he says, "the millennial generation could prove to be more resilient and creative than its predecessors, abandoning old, familiar, and broken institutions in favor of new, strange, and flourishing ones...

- Imagine a future in which millions of families live off the grid, powering their homes and vehicles with dirt-cheap portable fuel cells.

- As industrial agriculture sputters under the strain of the spiraling costs of water, gasoline and fertilizer, networks of farmers using sophisticated techniques that combine cutting-edge green technologies with ancient Mayan know-how build an alternative food-distribution system.

- Faced with the burden of financing the decades-long retirement of aging boomers, many of the young embrace a new underground economy, a largely untaxed archipelago of communes, co-ops, and kibbutzim that passively resist the power of the granny state.

- Rather than warehouse their children in factory schools invented to instill obedience in the future mill workers of America, bourgeois rebels will educate their kids in virtual schools tailored to different learning styles.

- Private homes will increasingly give way to co-housing communities, in which singles and nuclear families will build makeshift kinship networks in shared kitchens and common areas and on neighborhood-watch duty."[11]

Salam's take on the near future is a plausible response to the very real problems you're about to face. His ideas focus on your strengths, values, and the possible connections you can make with present resources (like using your home as a studio/office) and relationships (where "Buddhist vegan militia members and evangelical anarchist squatters trade tips on how to build self-sufficient vertical farms from scrap-heap materials").[12] To some these ideas may be really scary, while to others they may resonate some tangible hope. In any case, what I mean to say here is that the future, including the scary bits, is largely what you and your identity is willing to create of it.

---

11 *Time Magazine,* Wednesday, Mar. 10, 2010.

12 ibid

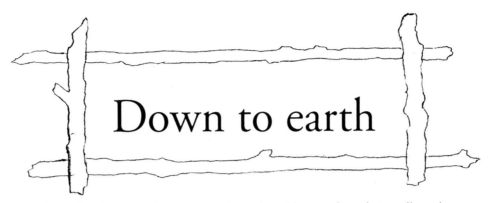

Down to earth

I've asked a few friends to let me know how these ideas work in their really real world. At the end of most chapters one of these people will share a slice of their lives to add some balance, challenge, or new perspectives on the chapter above. To start off with, here's Blue's take on Seeing the future...

"**When I was 22** I didn't want to live in a flat with a bunch of random people simply to cover the rent. I wanted to have deeper friendships that were really meaningful. I had a sense that in order to understand who I was becoming, I'd need to work it out in the context of relationships. I discovered that it wasn't by chance that I lived in houses full of people, I actually loved the dynamic of interaction and self discovery. It's also no wonder that when we got married my wife and I bought a really big house with lots of bedrooms. We filled the rooms up with all sorts of people; some were doing well and others had some real hurts and needs. Whatever it was, everyone had a story and our home became a place where you could discover who you were and take the next step.

We started getting involved in other households from time to time via weekly meals, giving support and encouragement, sharing resources etc., we even formed a community action group. When my family moved cities we didn't leave these experiences behind, we found others who were like minded to continue this journey. We joined another family and bought a building with two apartments on the top floor with retail spaces on the ground floor in a residential / commercial area with very little community interaction. We now host a weekly cooking club in our kitchens and a monthly 'cigars and philosophy' talk-fest on our deck. We built a kick-ass café in the retail space where local artists display their creations, local businesses meet up regularly and community groups are forming around special interests etc. It's not just a café, it's a third space where our community feel they can belong and engage (as well as have the best coffee ever). Honestly, at times the café feels like an extension of our home.

In short, we didn't react to our environment, we created it. When you discover who you are, you don't need to ask permission to live in a way that reflects it. You see the future by seeing your self. As I saw with my natural love of community, I can project where that naturally wants to go... If you can imagine the possibilities, like your place in that café development, you can create it by putting steps in place to make that future a reality. I've found the cool thing about all this is that when you live out who you're meant to be, you actually help others find out who they are right along side of you."

Praxis:

To help process this future business, I'd like to throw some practice your way. The idea is to draw out and create your own vision of life, work, and creativity. In some of the chapters, there will be some practice pages which are designed to help articulate what's going on inside of you, and hopefully, what you can do about it. Again, these are not prescriptive tools that will get you the perfect job or wife, they're reflections on the substance you've been given and how that's been either messed with or facilitated... I would suggest that you get a good friend, or some family, and go through these questions together (*maybe get some wine and cheese too? A Chardonnay perhaps with a very dry cheddar and some cashews, dried muscatels even?*). The idea is to know yourself better and articulate what's been floating around in your head. It really needs to be said, and heard, and then acted on. Putting things to paper and getting them in the light allows you to see and work with what's subtly guiding or misleading you.

1. Watch this (http://www.youtube.com/watch?v=A3oIiH7BLmg) and describe your time perspective? Are you:

❑ past positive

❑ past negative

❑ present hedonistic

❑ present fated

❑ future creative

❑ future after death

Most of these are general headings, how would you describe your particular attitude towards the future?

....

....

....

....

....

....

....

2. Up until now, how have you perceived your ability to create the future? Are you mostly:
❑ reactive - *meaning you react to what's going on around you*
❑ creative - *meaning you create opportunities for yourself and others*
❑ a mix of both - *how would you describe it?*

....

....

....

....

....

....

....

....

....

....

....

3. If I asked what you want to be doing in 10 years, how would you respond? Why?

....

....

....

....

....

....

....

....

....

....

....

4.

If you took at least one thing you know that you know about yourself, and projected that thing into the future, what would it look like?

For example: *I know that I love kids and sports. I could coach a softball team that's a place of safety and growth for my community. And they'd win, a lot.*

....

....

....

....

....

....

....

....

....

....

Chapter Two

What do you WANT?

The grass is always greener where you water it.
Dave Andrews

I like talking about my kids and what they're doing. I'll often share with students during my talks, or with friends in a cafe, about Josiah's adventures working in the computer game industry for the last five years, or Jordan's exploits in making movies over the same period. Or I'll talk about how Jasmine published her first children's book as a teenager and then show some of the illustrations... Basically, I like talking about what kids can do in an environment unhindered by major dysfunction.[13] In response to my parental oozing (read: pride / bragging), a lot of people will often let me know that they'd also love to work in the film industry, or that their cousin would die to be able to design computer games... At which point I often ask what's stopping them? As the conversation unfolds, so do the reasons why those people are not doing what they love. It's hard to get into film school in Germany, or there's no opportunities to create games in Ohio, or there's so few people who can actually make a living from of their art, etc. All of these are good reasons about how hard it is to do what you love. Which I relate to completely. When my dad left us (I was nine), my world fell apart and my confidence took a huge hit. There wasn't much hope in my heart about pursuing my dreams... So if our world *is* distracted by dysfunction, or just a lack of resources, can we really pursue what we want? Eventually I had to ask which is stronger; my will or the memory of my pain?

Anyway, being an encouraging guy, I'd often introduce people to my friends in the industry they're interested in and see if they could help with an internship or some advice, etc. But in doing so, I would often catch some flack, especially from my passionate and hormonally imbalanced son Jordan, who would rake newbies over the coals for their lack of commitment and focus. I'd usually say, "Give 'em a break Jordan, they're just starting out". And he'd say, "If they are not willing to die for this, it'll never happen for them." What he, and many like him, are measuring is the person's commitment to what they want. They know everyone has ideas, and some talent, and one day the person may actually get somewhere—if they're committed. But they also know that wanting to isn't enough.

Having only a few hundred seats for film students in Germany is a good problem. It tells the thousands of people who were dabbling with the idea to go play elsewhere. In fact, a lovely and determined friend of mine in Frankfurt applied to her design school there three years running until she finally got in. She didn't let external circumstances stop her from being herself. And if school didn't work out, she would have found another way to be the designer / photographer / storyteller she is. The reasons we give ourselves about why we can't act on our ideas often become self-fulfilling prophecies. They are no more substantial than we make them to be.

For instance:

I don't have enough money to... means you've probably made money the indicator of your success. And so it will be. You'll probably limit yourself to the resources you presently have instead of finding a better way to create those resources, or do something that doesn't require so much money, or learn to save and discipline

---

13 We've got plenty of dysfunction as a family, but in the main the kids have had a pretty sweet ride so far. So says me anyway.

your spending. You don't need a college loan to work in primary health, or to do interior design, you could just start working with what you have and build from there.

I'm too old to... means you've made your age a pre-requisite. Comparisons with younger people and fast-track processes dismiss you from the game. You lose sight of the benefits of age and maturity, and the years it takes to make something really well.

I'm not good enough to... means you've locked yourself into place based on your present skills. You're judging your long-term ability based on a very short-term experience, and therefore will not put any effort into what it takes to be very, very good at something.

Yes, it's really hard to be yourself in a world that doesn't play nice. Where encouragement and opportunity seem so thin. But the hurdles placed in front of you are actually really important. They sort out what is just an idea you're playing with, and what you are super committed to being / doing. I saw this truth played out on a film set in Vancouver one night talking with the second unit AD on a major feature film. He was telling me about all the cool kids at film school, with their berets, and cigarettes, and film theories... all of which were being paid for by their parents. He, however, had to work his arse off to get through school—which he did because he **owned it**. He was passionately committed to working in that industry and he rarely saw any of his alumni on the set. They were still hanging out in cafes pontificating about films while he was out making them.

Your soul knows what *it* wants

Growing up, I was a bit of a loner. Seemed like there were no other kids on my block and pretty early on my dad kinda checked out. I processed everything internally and was quietly observant of human nature. I was also very stubborn. And while I never did well in school, I helped my older brother and sisters with their home-work... Looking back, I can see how these emerging attributes were the early signs of identity trying to express itself. For instance, the pain of not having a dad around seemed to get translated into an awareness of the pain in others. I remember getting into my first (and last) fight because somebody made a racist comment about my friend. When there was an opportunity to stand up for something, or come alongside someone in need, my soul wanted to respond.

As children, our soul doesn't have to fight its way through layers of distractions to be seen or heard. Those little inspirations (like when your foot connected with the ball and it went exactly where you wanted it to, or when you sang out a tune and smiled at what came out of your mouth) popped out unrestricted. Your soul kept showing you what was natural, and if given the room, powerful. Over time though, expectations (educational standards) and distractions (peer pressure) form veils over the soul, making it really hard for it to shine. It becomes hard to hear, hard to know what it's saying, and hard to know what it wants. But if you travel back and watch for those enigmatic moments when your soul told you what it wanted, what would you hear?

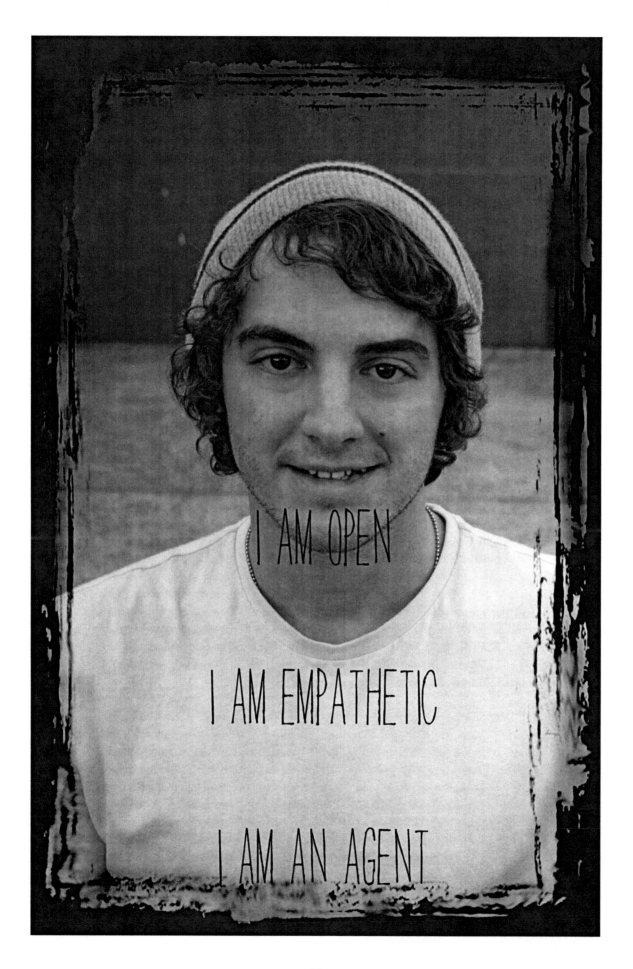

Would it be something like:

- Nobel laureate (for literature in 1981) Elias Canetti's fascination with the words on his father's newspaper, and his sisters books. He saw them as magical, and would inhale the smell of his father's newsprint, or chase his sister around the yard simply to glimpse her alphabet book...

- Israeli Prime Minister Golda Meir's passionate political skills calling her to action in the fourth grade. At 11 years old, she organized protest groups in her Milwaukee public school to expose issues of inequality for poorer students.

- Master film maker Ingmar Bergman's love of the mysterious and his willingness (at age 9) to trade his set of tin soldiers for a battered laterna magica (a primitive projector). As a child, he would fashion all the scenery of his puppet plays, create lighting effects, and read all the parts, creating a world where he felt completely at home.[14]

Sometimes the soul breaks from it's prison as it shines in adversity and pounces on crises. Winston Churchill developed his intellectual strengths during a time in his life where he was laid up from massive physical injuries, and J.M. Barrie learned to tell stories while trying to distract his mother who was grief stricken over the death of his older brother. When life gets hard, the layers of distraction get put aside and the soul finds purpose. The poet W.H. Auden once said that, "The so-called traumatic experience is not an accident, but the opportunity for which the child has been patiently waiting—had it not occurred, it would have found another, equally trivial—in order to find a necessity and direction for its existence, in order that its life may become a serious matter."[15] Our soul knows what it wants, and whether it's through cajoling our memories or hitting the wall, it needs to be heard again.

So what are you committed to?

I've found there are lots of people of good will and capacity who really want to help others move forward. But these same people have developed a sort of grid / gauntlet that helps them determine who they will invest in. It's like this: Once upon a time some blind guys were calling to Jesus for help, and oh yeah, they were blind. And so Jesus asks the blind guys, who He knows are blind, what they want. So to clarify, the guys are blind and everyone knows Jesus can heal the blind. So why in God's green goodness does Jesus ask them "What is it you want me to do for you?"

You have to look deep inside yourself and find that connection between your identity and your will. Your identity is capable, your soul knows what it wants, but your will has to put all it's strength into the unfolding. I know a lot of us have been so beaten up by external rejection that we've picked up the same stick and taken over the doling out the abuse. It's hard to find the internal commitment that will help

---

14 Bergman's father was a Lutheran minister and chaplain to the King of Sweden. This world created a rich context for Ingmar's soul to communicate what it wanted. As he wrote in his autobiography *Laterna Magica:* "I devoted my interest to the church's mysterious world of low arches, thick walls, the smell of eternity, the colored sunlight quivering above the strangest vegetation of medieval paintings and carved figures on ceilings and walls. There was everything that one's imagination could desire – angels, saints, dragons, prophets, devils, humans."
Pan, 2004, 332 pages

15 *Traumatic experience in the unconscious life of groups*, Jessica Kingsley Publishers, 2003, page 65

us endure the pain and time involved in becoming ourselves again. But find it you must. Nothing else will give you the grace required to overcome all the obstacles ahead. Your will is an amazing thing. The human capacity to endure with resilience is tied directly to that will. If you can look past self-defeating statements and engage your will to act on what you already know about yourself, you'll be putting to work the same strength that enabled people like Martin Luther King to move social mountains. Because when you think about it, there's no real difference between you and anyone else on the planet fulfilling their call in life, except for the will to do it.

Personalities may be hugely different from one person to another, but the thing that pushes all of us forward is the will. A friendly extroverted type with a nice body may seem like they're getting more opportunities than the next person, but is that holding the shy one back? People who come from wealthy backgrounds may seem like they can do anything they want, but does that mean you can't because you don't have the same resources? Not necessarily. In fact, the ones who seem to have the great looks and all the money aren't necessarily happy people fulfilling their identity. Fulfilled people answer the question about what they want with each and every choice. They engage their will in such a way that reaching their goals is just a matter of time. They'll learn more about themselves as they go, and even change course at times, but they're not playing around. Knowing what you want develops ownership of the process, which is exactly what Jesus, good mentors, or guiding friends are about; helping us own our lives. Great facilitators don't ask you what you want thinking they'll supply it, they ask you knowing that **you need to know** in order to engage your identity. They know that your faith and abilities will soon follow, eventually turning your ideas into reality.

 # Praxis:

By the way, if you don't really know what you want, the rest of this book will be useful in helping you to work that out. Just explore the questions below and see if that helps.

1. What have you (or your soul) wanted in the past and what stopped you from pursuing it? I mean, what really stopped you. Was it truly money or opportunity? What exists inside for those externals to matter?

....

....

....

....

....

2. What has your soul cried out when you were growing up? Remember any instances where your child-like heart broke out with something inspired, for any reason? *I find this question a hard one. I have to really look back at moments of bliss or passion or intense focus on something. Fascination is a good clue, something you couldn't let go of...*

....

....

....

....

....

....

....

....

....

3. What have you been putting your energy (your will) into lately? We're always doing something with our will, even if it's selling out. Where's yours pointed these days and what do you think about that?

....

....

....

....

....

....

4. When it comes to passion, where's yours at? Were you passionate about something in the past and lost it? Why? Are you passionate about something right now? What could you do to rekindle inspiration and kick your will back into action?

....

....

....

....

5. If there are really hard circumstances in your life making this more difficult than it should be, what are some creative things you could do to get around the limitations? Who is there in your life right now, or who you could recruit, to help you overcome obstacles?

....

....

....

....

6. What would you be willing to fight for? It may be an issue like human trafficking or better school lunches for kids... When you look at what motivates you and what YOU could do about it, you start to get in touch with what you actually want in life.

....

....

....

....

Down to earth
with my friend Aaron

I asked Aaron, who works in the film industry, if he'd write this chapter's ending. His response:

"I am so sorry, but I have not written anything. I just read the chapter "What do you want" last night and then sat looking at the screen for ages. I'm currently struggling with each of your criteria. I am in one of those cliched 'valleys', and it is really hard right now to see the value of my experiences over the last 13 years. I realize this is the last thing you want to hear right now when you are under a deadline, but I don't want to write a few paragraphs of bullshit when that's not where I am at. I'm struggling with what I want and what I'm committed to. Not to mention, the last couple of weeks have been full on for us, as I am trying to wrap up the film while moving our family... All that to say, I don't have anything for you."

In my opinion, Aaron is in the thick of it. He knew enough of what he wanted 13 years ago (when he moved to L.A.) to start working in an industry that spits out most people in the first 90 days of their adventure. He's learned a lot about himself over those years, and yet the growing challenge of applying that knowledge as the bar keeps getting higher can be brutal. Aaron is familiar with the making of 200 million dollar films and is a very capable producer / director. But in the middle of following your passions, life can still go blurry on you...

We ask ourselves, Who am I to be brilliant, gorgeous, talented, fabulous? Actually, who are you not to be? You are a child of God. Your playing small does not serve the world. There is nothing enlightened about shrinking so that other people wont feel insecure around you. We are all meant to shine, as children do. We were born to make manifest the glory of God that is within us. It is not just in some of us; it is in everyone. And as we let our own light shine, we unconsciously give other people permission to do the same. As we were liberated from our own fear, our presence automatically liberates others.

Marianne Williamson

from A Return to Love

Chapter Three

Loving your neighbor

↑↓

as your self

Some of my Christian friends think I've gone way overboard on this identity stuff. I've got a bit of criticism, which can be summed up as: "tone down all this talk about self, God's in control, we should just ask what He wants and obey", or "talking about yourself too much leads to pride and maybe even idolatry, so we should sacrifice our gifts on the altar of service to God"... I think this kind of language is a throwback to the middle ages, where the institution of the church maintained tight control over the 'flock' by having access to scriptures the common man couldn't read. It therefore determined what that man thought about what God wanted him to do... And I don't think this is just a Christian problem. Any institution that tries to maintain control for its own ends will always find a way to suffocate individual identity, or determine the path people should take as a reflection of its own image. Bugs me to no end.

Jesus, however, was not about the institution and warned us about our propensity to control one another. His alternative is concise and revolutionary. When He says we should love our neighbor as ourselves, it means we should and will love ourselves, and that we should love our neighbor in the same way. Thus, I cannot ignore my self, its identity and its potential. I cannot put my personal abilities on some altar of sacrificial service when it's that same self that defines how I can truly serve my neighbor. I can't shut my intelligences, passions, and skills off to blindly listen for some abstract direction. Galileo framed this beautifully when he said: "**I do not feel obliged to believe that the same God who has endowed us with sense, reason, and intellect has intended us to forgo their use and by some other means to give us knowledge which we can attain by them.**"[16] I mean why would we be given distinct intelligence, a wide emotional capacity, unique identity, and our particular physical skills, only to set them all aside and wait for other instructions? And wait we shall, because when you trash everything God's given you to function and then ask the giver of those gifts for something else, you may just be waiting a long time - in crazyland.

Now, I understand the argument that pride puffs a person up. Or that if you're really good at something, things can get real strange—like that whole Elvis thing. But automatically connecting the proper love of self with a prideful downfall is downright paranoid. There are plenty of examples of pride leading to a fall, but if you look closely, they're not often because that person was following God's advice to love self AND neighbor. Typically, people who wig out via their own talent are not functioning in the wider range of their identity and are out of balance in some way. What the true love of self should result in is an appreciation of the dynamic range we've been given. That same appreciation turned towards our neighbor can then create an equal appreciation for who they are, their value and potential. This is also true for the beauty of the world around us. As we see the universe inside, and all it's wonderful complexity, we understand the beauty in nature and the people of that nature differently. We should therefore want to take better care of them, find our place with them. So, when we know and function as our complete selves we become collaborators, and move away from our propensity to act as the center of the universe. Or as Simone Weil says: "May I disappear in order that those things that I see may become perfect in their beauty..."[17] Self without neighbor is a hedonistic trap, but love without self is servility. Jesus was definitely onto something. Here's Parker Palmer's take:

> "Contrary to the conventions of our thinly moralistic culture,
> this emphasis on gladness and selfhood is not selfish. The
> Quaker teacher Douglas Steere was fond of saying that the
> ancient human question "who am I?" leads inevitably to the
> equally important question "Whose am I?" — for there is no
> selfhood outside of relationship."[18]

---

16 Letter to the Grand Duchess Christina (1615) Essay published in 1615, in response to enquiries of Christina of Tuscany, as quoted in *Aspects of Western Civilization : Problems and Sources in History* (1988) by Perry McAdow Rogers, p. 53

17 *Grace and Gravity,* Routledge Classics, 2004, page 42

18 From *Let Your Life Speak,* Jossey-Bass, 1999, page 17

So firstly, how are we doing when it comes to loving our selves? I understand this on two levels. The first is self-preservation and care, similar to the lower levels of Maslow's hierarchy. Seeing yourself as made in the image of God and as an eternal being should make you brush your teeth twice a day. I mean at least, right? Even without the spiritual view, watching the miraculous behavior of white blood cells at the cellular level should make you wanna dress better. This kind of self-love doesn't form a prideful / protective stance—it creates praise, wonder, and joy, regardless of whether you look like Christian Bale or not.[19] Loving yourself for the tapestry that you are is the first step in being able to do so for others. Self love is not about protecting yourself and then a few more in your family. It's understanding what you've been given and then celebrating that with everyone around you (read: internationally).

The second level, and true joy, of loving your neighbor as yourself, is **loving them your way**. We have the privilege of loving the people around us with our unique and diverse expressions of self. We don't staff soup kitchens simply because we want others to survive, we develop outstanding foods to enrich peoples lives because we're designers, nutritionists, or entrepreneurs. This amazing breakfast granola may come from your deep appreciation of agriculture and your unique experiences in different countries... You could create an outstanding blend of morning goodness (your brand name) which you could sell, give away, or whatever, at the local farmers' market (or the soup kitchen, as you like). Loving your neighbor with your self, your unique expression, unlocks all kinds of ideas and opportunities which is exactly what they need. In doing so, you'll be modeling something they themselves can be: a person in touch with their identity and potential. This creates sustainable relationships which can grow into a true community. When self goes communal you're on the right path.

Another dimension of loving self / neighbor is the therapeutic side. I've found that the times I've not been loving or understanding towards myself, when I've been depressed and immobile, are the best times to love my neighbor. Doing something for those around me, with what little I have or know about myself, has been the best medicine in terms of getting me out of a rut. And once out of the rut, the effort of meeting needs creatively draws out even more of my identity. My intelligences find a context and my soul has something meaningful to work on. My body gets active by engaging more of my internal gifting through tangible expressions—like AD'ing on a short film or helping someone get their art sold. When my identity finds a healthy connection to the world around me, my internal world gets healed to the same degree.

Loving other people gets us moving, while just loving ourselves turns us introverted in a negative way. When you use your gifts for others, for their sake, something amazing happens; you discover an unconditional flow. Your identity gets unfolded and unleashed when it connects with the needs of others and their identities. The result is the kind of collaboration of which symphonies, or crowd-funded indie films, are made. Identity on its own is a dead end process. You'll never know your own depths unless you're in concert with others. But when you give the loving of your

---

19 I have, however, been compared to Ed Harris, a nice compliment but it's not going in my facespace pics because *my doppelgänger is non existent.* There's no one quite like me, or you.

neighbor equal weight to the love of self, you enter into a spiritual dynamic that can move mountains. One of my favorite examples of this is the work Cate Blanchett and her husband Andrew Upton are doing with the Sydney Theatre Company (STC). They both clearly understand and celebrate their identity as storytellers (Cate as actress and Andrew as playwright / director), but they've also acted on their wider values for community and the environment at large. They've engaged the state government, businesses, and the general public to revitalize the heritage building ('The Wharf') which houses the STC by installing Australia's second largest rooftop solar energy array and an impressive rainwater harvesting system (among other things). But what's really outstanding about their lives, and the resulting project at The Wharf, is how they synthesize their artistic sensibilities with their environmental concerns. "Theatre, we don't believe fundamentally is there to educate; we believe it's there to illuminate." says Blanchett. "People, particularly adults, don't respond well to being told what to do, but they can be inspired by something."[20] This brilliant application comes from their creativity, not despite it. They're loving the 300,000 people who come through the STC each year with **their style of love**. They're 'illuminating' the 30,000 students who will observe the Blanchett / Upton effect and may just grow up thinking a bit differently about the creative spaces around them. This famous couple could do the odd soup kitchen appearance, or throw money at some local drug problem, or just ignore the outside world all together; what Upton calls "disappearing up your own arse".[21] But instead, they apply the rich expanse of who they are to the world they live in. This is creatively loving your neighbor as your self.

I'd call this dynamic 'the neighbor effect'. Instead of putting your passion on the altar of service, it becomes the motivator of service. Neighbors force us out of our myopic trance into meaningful action in a way that draws out the range of our identity. I'm sorry I can't find the source of this quotation, but I think it beautifully sums up my meaning here:

> *The way to know your calling is to ask 'what is the pain in the world that I want to heal and what's my solution to that pain?'*[22]

What needs exist around you that you passionately connect to? There's a connection with that need and your identity. It's speaking to you, drawing you out. Once you've made the connection, can you then see what your unique solution is, or the creative synthesis of your abilities that can alleviate that pain? This simple question can be a powerful motivator away from depression, rejection, laziness, or whatever is binding us to inaction. We're all called to heal that part of the world with which we identify. Not exclusively, because there's always a toilet to be cleaned whether we like it or not. But in the main, your daily activities can be a healing connection between your soul and the needs around you.

---

20 *MINDFOOD Magazine: The Power of Two*, By Pip Cummings, October 2010 issue

21 ibid

22 Frederick Buechner may be being paraphrased here. He once wrote: "The place God calls you to is where your deep gladness and the world's deep hunger meet." *Wishful Thinking*, Harper & Row, 1st edition (1973), page 95

Which brings me to the last point I want to make about this.

Since we're meant to work our identity in concert with others, we need to find those others to work with. 21 year-old design student Veronika Scott started her search by trying to meet a basic need: bring warmth to Detroit's 20,000 homeless during its brutal winters. In response, she designed a coat that doubles as a warm, waterproof sleeping bad. But her real goal was, "to empower, employ, educate, and instill pride." Because as far as Veronika is concerned: "The importance is not with the product but with the people."[23] She now contracts cutting edge material designers to work with the homeless women who manufacture these coats creating both innovation, and employment...

We need to identify our own tribe, or team, or crew... Loving our neighbors means finding or creating a neighborhood of people to work with. Sometimes we just live / create with those around us, but I think over time, we should be developing a dimension of community that lines up with our identity, or compliments it in a solid way. This does not happen by accident. You have to intentionally know what you're looking for, speak it out, and develop these relationships over many years. And don't think flitting from place to place will do the same thing. You may need a bit of movement in the beginning of your development, like moving to find a good school or searching for the right job / community mix. But once you get a clue, get a house, or anything that will ground you to a place. It's unlikely you'll find a community that gets you and wants to make great stuff with you. You'll probably have to create such an environment by committing to people over many years, because during those years, you'll network, discover, and then co-create the very place you've been looking for.

23 Check our Veronika's project at: http://detroitempowermentplan.blogspot.com/

Praxis:

There's a good reason 'the golden rule' is in the scriptures of all major faiths. It not only addresses all the core spiritual needs we have, it spans out into all areas of life. From better products and services to cleaning up all the plastic bottles in the ocean. The relationship between identity and treating others as yourself will always have a beneficial impact. So:

1. What are some ways you've already been loving your neighbors as yourself?

....

....

....

....

....

....

2. Who do you know that's doing some amazingly loving / creative things and how has this inspired you? Why? *I'm fired up by how Ebay co-founder, and now storytelling-social entrepreneur, Jeff Skoll makes films about life in Afghanistan (The Kite Runner) and then starts 87 libraries across the country with the profits.*

....

....

....

....

....

....

3. What are some ways you could be loving your neighbor as you, that you're not right now? What could you do about that today?

....

....

....

....

4. How are you caring for your self (personal well-being, time management, educating your passions?) and what needs developing so you have more to give away? *For me, that means disciplining myself to work on the raw gifts I have (writing, photography, working with food) so they can mature into something really useful.*

....

....

....

....

5. What is the pain in the world you want to heal? What baby steps could you be taking right now to get involved? *For me, it's both micro finance through KIVA and helping local artists sell their work. It's not a big thing, but it's in the right direction because it calls out my strengths into the service of others.*

....

....

....

....

Reference:

For those who want to take a more radical approach to what Jesus said about loving our neighbors, I would suggest the super practical book by Mark Scandrette called *Practicing the Ways of Jesus.* He and his friends have undertaken some really cool and very stretching practices in the Mission District of San Francisco, and they've offered their stories and suggestions to us in this super challenging book.

MEDITATION:

THE LIFE THAT I TOUCH FOR GOOD OR ILL WILL TOUCH
ANOTHER LIFE, AND THAT IN TURN ANOTHER, UNTIL WHO
KNOWS WHERE THE TREMBLING STOPS OR IN WHAT FAR PLACE
MY TOUCH WILL BE FELT.

FREDERICK BUECHNER
THE HUNGERING DARK

Down to earth

with Nigel Cottle

As the son of a pastor, I thought I understood the idea of loving my neighbor. But the path I wanted to pursue was about making large amounts of money and then being generous. As I considered this future, I eventually realized that my personality could be consumed by the processes of making money. Even while trying to be generous, I knew that in the end my focus would adversely affect my humanity.

So, after finishing my business degree I went into youth work for 10 years. But that didn't quite fit, as it became clear that I wanted to experiment with some new expressions of faith and community. I'd spent years 'going' to church, but I wanted to work out what it meant to 'be' the church myself, be in the community in a meaningful way. After connecting with Blue, our two families looked at where we could make a difference locally, and hopefully be ourselves along the way. It's been very positive for the most part, but being a good neighbor comes with it's challenges. Since we want to be hyper-local, one of the difficult things for us as a family has been putting our kids in the closest school, which happens to be the worst school in the area. It's proving very difficult to make a positive difference there. While holding to a philosophy of community it seems we're making our kids miss out on the best education available. But when you look closer, maybe that's not the case. For instance, the school is culturally diverse and our kids are now friends with kids from many different nationalities and religious backgrounds.

Kingsland (the part of Auckland we live in) is a very diverse neighborhood with no real geographical or social boundaries. So, to establish an old-school sense of place, we committed to the people whose houses or work places we can walk to in less than 10 min. We also set up Crave Collective to get some projects off the ground within this locality (including a café providing some kick ass coffee and a solid sense of place for our neighbors). Since most people don't talk to their neighbors over the back fence any more, we draw them into the cafe and gallery with a really comfortable environment and some really good food. One of our guys in the Collective lives in a building across the street with 86 apartments in it and in six months has only had a handful of conversations with other residents. But in the café I can't get any work done due to all the chats with people from the same building.

It seems that in our context, baristas are the barmen of yesteryear. If you come into the café and we know your name, and we know your order, you feel like you belong. I'm now looking forward to taking our community on a coffee journey which connects them with growers in the developing world, helps them know what different coffee regions in the world bring to the palette, and aids them in discovering different brewing methods. In this process, our community will connect with each other, new friendships will be birthed, new initiatives will get going, and oddly enough, the neighborhood gets better. Which is what I was looking for all along. The journey has showed me that it's not care vs. the money, but the proper mix of all my motivations, and my identity, held accountable to the idea of loving my neighbor as my self.

LISTEN TO YOUR LIFE. SEE IT

FOR THE FATHOMLESS MYSTERY

IT IS. IN THE BOREDOM AND

PAIN OF IT NO LESS THAN IN

THE EXCITEMENT AND GLADNESS:

TOUCH, TASTE, SMELL YOUR

WAY TO THE HOLY AND HIDDEN

HEART OF IT BECAUSE IN THE

LAST ANALYSIS ALL MOMENTS

ARE KEY MOMENTS, AND LIFE

ITSELF IS GRACE.

FREDERICK BUECHNER

NOW AND THEN

Chapter Four

What's become of you?

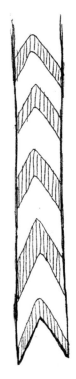

As a ramp-up to the next section (where we'll dive deep into the details of your identity) I want to look at few questions:

1. In terms of your identity, which bits are naturally you (your nature) and what's attached itself (yuck) through your environment (your nurture)?

2. How do you differentiate between an interest and a true ability? Meaning, you wanna do 15 different things, but which ones can you actually achieve?

3. What do you already know about your identity from your past experiences, personality tests, and your present situation?

We all have preconceived notions of ourselves which could use a little objectivity. And we desperately need to make some time to go deeper on the issues we rarely take the opportunity to process. This chapter will require a bit of introspection, but it won't hurt—much.

If you pay attention, you can learn a lot about someone in a few minutes. Their body language, actions, style, and spirit all give a constant flow of information. If you spend a few hours with someone, that stream of data starts to go exponential. And so it is when you know someone for a few years or more, the universe that is them starts to seem endless. Which makes sense if we truly are eternal beings. This eternity is reflected in the universe within us, with every one of our cells holding millions of miles of DNA code... The seemingly endless creativity we're capable of is highlighted by the billions of neurons we possess, all firing off different ideas, concepts, and connections every millisecond of our lives.[24] Our personalities are growing ever deeper with each new experience, and each opportunity to interact with other eternal beings. Altogether, we are an amazing tapestry, and a morphing one at that.

The ironic thing, is that although upon close examination we can observe seemingly unfathomable biological and intellectual depths within our species, as individuals of that species many of us barely know ourselves. And what we don't know about ourselves affects our capacity to be whole. This lack of knowledge results in partial people living in a way that William James describes thus:

> *"Every one is familiar with the phenomenon of feeling more or less alive on different days. Every one knows on any given day that there are energies slumbering in him which the incitements of that day do not call forth, but which he might display if these were greater. Most of us feel as if we lived habitually with a sort of cloud weighing on us, below our highest notch of clearness in discernment, sureness in reasoning, or firmness in deciding. Compared with what we ought to be, we are only half awake. Our fires are damped, our drafts are checked. We are making use of only a small part of our possible mental and physical resources."* [25]

Most of us haven't even tried to understand our various intelligences, physical makeup, or the vast diversity of our souls. And while we may not have been given the opportunity to do so up until now, we must stop and take a closer look. Our well-being, our neighbor's welfare, and our futures depend on it.

We may, at different points in this adventure, have to look back and deal with the roadblocks of our development and the resulting myopia. But my sense is that if we press ahead and unfold a deeper knowledge of our diverse selves, we'll have the grace, wisdom, and a sense of direction to deal with the blockages of our past. The wow factor of knowing the intricacies of identity, will energize us to move through all kinds of crap.

---

24 When I say creativity, I mean all of us are creative, but not all of us are artistic. Please don't confuse creativity with painting or writing music. Take some time to reflect on your kind of creativity. What do you like making and why. What do you enjoy working with... Understanding your distinct kind of creativity helps you to stop dismissing yourself as uncreative.

25 From the essay, *The Energies of Man:* First published in Science, 1907. N.S. 25 (No. 635), 321-332.

The challenge is where to begin. If you start with your biology, reading through *You the Owners Manual* by Dr. Oz Mehmet for instance, you'll revel in the fantastic design of your physical self. If you take the time to absorb all the literature on our multiple intelligences (emotional and otherwise) you'll start unpacking our complex neurological makeup.[26] And if you study the scriptures, and the accompanying 10 gazillion books about them, you'll start to understand all kinds of spiritual truths. Each one of these routes could take decades, and you'll probably get to the point where you see **that you are an eternal person of unfathomable depth**. This is both very cool and very frustrating. Frustrating because today we feel retarded in our knowledge of self, but very cool in that we have both a ton of potential to unveil and the time in which to do it.

So, as we start to look at the complexity that is your self, I'd like to start by teasing out the question of nature and nurture; or what exists in our identity that's actually natural to us, and which part is the product of our environment (our nurturing). To some degree it doesn't really matter, like whether you prefer Jazz music because your parents did... But to a large degree it's very important, like whether you're a teacher because you **naturally** impart wisdom to people, or you're stuck in a classroom because in your family girls who like being with children should be teachers (unless of course you're really smart, in which case you should be a nurse... or if you're really not that smart you should be in retail...). The dumbing down of our futures is often the result of our environment (family, socioeconomic, and cultural conditions) transposing itself on top of our nature, often suffocating our identity. Growing up in this space can leave us unsure as to whether we're in corporate finance because we're amazing stewards, or because we happened to score highly on our math exams. A nurture based environment (read: outside-in) creates identities that when asked **who they are,** often respond with **what they do**—a regretful acknowledgement that we've become a product of the conditions around us.

A nuance of this question (am I a product of my nature or nurture?) is distinguishing between a preference we develop from our environment, and a true ability to be what we envisage. For instance, a person who loves food may or may not become a chef. Same for music, business, or any field where you form a preference but may not have the inner ability to do anything about it. I grew up with jazz fusion influences which I'd love to participate in. But when I look closer at my nature, there's no real musical intelligence, physical ability, or a soulful ability to create it with. That doesn't mean I have zero musical ability, but in order to take this preference further I'd need a deeper reference to build on. I need to know more about my true identity (or the complex range of soul, mind, and strength we'll explore through this book) to see what I can really do with music. For instance, in seeing my **lingual and interpersonal strengths** (two of the nine intelligences we'll talk about), I may want to try writing lyrics or use my understanding of story to put soundtracks to film. In this way I can overcome discouragement (both external and internal) or the lack of faith that often accompanies chasing a foolish dream, and put my efforts into something I may actually have a shot at.

---

26 I suggest reading Daniel Goldman's *Emotional Intelligence* and Howard Gardner's *The Unschooled Mind.*

Cross-referencing identity

So, you have to ask the question; which part of my life is really me and which part exists because of my reactions to the world around me? When you look at the results of any personality test like Myers-Briggs or StrengthsFinder, you'll see things that are true about yourself but only in certain situations. Is that nurture or the result of your work environment (where the tests are often taken)? Are the results showing you your nature? When you look at the particular course of study you're pursuing or the job you're in, you have to ask which parts of these pursuits are really you and which parts are just expedient. The good news is that wherever you are today, I believe you can extract the precious (your nature) from the worthless (negative nurturing) by cross-referencing identity with the range of your life experiences. Here are two ways to do this.

First, if you look at your identity based on the choices you've made so far, you'll see at the root of those choices lay certain strengths. Even in super negative environments we survive hardship by using our strengths. They're actually quite obvious when we stop demonizing them (which is simply a natural response to seeing their overblown nature acted out in crisis). For instance, the intra-personal boy may shy into a corner when the parents start yelling, but end up processing that pain via social work or poetry. The social work may have been the result of certain opportunities, and may not even be a good job fit, but that child's strengths will continue to come through regardless. At the same time, his older sister may have come out swinging every time things got tense, and continues to do so as a competitive physical person who ends up in team sports, or maybe an aggressive corporate type. Again, the present situation may or may not be a good fit for her, but if you look closely, she's still functioning, or surviving, with her strengths. You will be yourself one way or another. The way we survive or thrive in our childhood is by using these core identity strengths, or our natural abilities. Sometimes they become overblown monsters because it's the only way to survive. At other times they become real assets in our lives by keeping us focused on what we're really good at. But if you look at how you've managed your childhood, and what continues to show up daily in your reactions and choices, you'll see those strengths coming through. For me, it's communication, processing, being with people, and dreaming of what could be instead of accepting what is. Being able to cross-reference all these experiences helps me to know the difference between a reaction to nurturing or a true identity response in my nature.

Q. *What are some of the ways you reacted to your environment: Can you extract some identity statements out of that?*

....

....

....

....

The second way to cross-reference your identity is to map out the extensive range of it's expression via your soul, mind, and body. We'll get around to this later in a practical way, but the idea for now is that if you can see 20 things that are true about your nature, you'll also see the difference between a simple preference (I like coffee) and a true identity statement (I develop third space cafe environments). The similarities keep popping up in what I call identity themes. For instance, among other things I am a father, coach, trainer, chief, counselor, cook, encourager... When I look at this combination I can see a thematic approach towards people (from being with my kids to being with total strangers at a writers group) which helps me differentiate between a typical approach to helping people (as a psychologist for instance), and **who I naturally am** with them (a friend, trainer, exhorter). Cross-referencing this broad range of identity statements helps me see the difference between a typical job description (counselor) and the more nuanced opportunities I may be able to create that don't even have a name yet. This is really useful in defining between a preference and my true potential.

Cross-referencing my identity gives me a clear way to make better choices, especially in what to say yes or no to. It helps me spend my energies developing my own job description instead of spending six years in school to become 'qualified' for something I may never enjoy or ever follow through with. Knowing the dif between **what I'd like to be** and **who I really am** also helps me deal with the fear of rejection or failure. If I'm not a musician, I won't waste time trying and comparing, etc. Instead, I'll spend a lot of my time enjoying music and maybe coaching a few friends in their lyrical development. Refined choices based on my cross-referenced identity moves me out of a make-or-break mentality (rock star or nothing) toward a beautifully nuanced development with my true abilities. And the really good news? There's no real competition for what only I can do.

Identifying identity

So what have you learned so far about your identity? If you and I are eternal beings, coming up with a list of 20, 50, or 100 things that are true about us should be simple right? Not necessarily, not with all the misdirection we've been subjected to. Many of us simply haven't been given the room or encouragement to even go there. Even when you overcome the narrow casting of your past, you still face the oversimplification of identity developed by the present array of tools on offer. Some identity systems try to peg your personality to a short list of attributes or 'types'. Others give you five strengths among many (again, this is largely because we want the simple definitions rather than create out of the breadth). Even the complex ones like the Enneagram only hint at our diversity by boiling us down to a No. 5, or a No. 9...

However, I still think that this over simplification is due to our own expedient approach. So just to make sure we don't throw the baby out with the bath water, Blue and I would like to explore with you how a few of these systems can actually expand the identity map we're going to build throughout this book / journal. Just do me a favor: as we go through and review what you may have already learned through these tools, remember that they don't define possible job descriptions etc., rather see them as helping to articulate the growing list of raw materials you get to create from later on.

Over the next few pages Blue will summarize a few of the tools on offer today (except for SIMA, which I'll cover) and give you some space to journal what you may have already gotten out of them. Or if you want to take some of the tests online or whatever, you can write your results here. Which will be helpful as we combine and synthesise all the info later on in the book.

A few notes about personality / identity testing:

During the process of writing this book we had a bunch of our friends give us some really useful feedback about their experience with personality tests. Especially:

A) what they thought about the tools available today
B) what they got out of using them
C) what they actually did with the information to enhance their lives (or not)

There were some common themes which came through and I'd like to give a few tips on how to get the best out of what you may have already invested in.

In my opinion, not all tools are created equal. It's really important to use the ones that have been around a long time or have some decent research behind them done by reputable organisations. For instance, the Myers-Briggs tests are used internationally because of their scientific rigour and the proven results. The Enneagram has been developed over hundreds of years and has a massive base of testimony across time. StrengthsFinder is based on Gallup University's extensive research with hard data to back up their findings; called viability and validity reports. I researched and trained in both Myers-Briggs and StrengthsFinder and found that when done well they can be very accurate and super helpful. There are lots of other tools we don't mention in this book—some are lightweight and others are much more in depth. I'll cover the ones I know and have used.

The feedback:

A lot of people commented about how the tools differ in results depending on how they felt when they did the test. This has a lot to do with the environment you're in or the 'head space' you had at the time. For instance, I often coach people who've been tested as part of their job (or even as a way of being considered for a job). The results often favoured their bosses expectations over a true reading of the employee. These tools are easy to manipulate if you really want to. People who do the test in a neutral environment with a simple commitment to know themselves better have found even standard tests hugely beneficial. So to get the best out of tools like Myers-Briggs, StrengthsFinder, and the Enneagram, I suggest you find a quiet place at home and get in the right headspace to allow your soul to speak up.

Another thing we noticed in the feedback was that very few people, if any, actually had coaching involved in their process. The results in this case can be largely hit and miss. Coaches help you to understand how to interpret the results by resonating via relationship those parts of the data which you can actually use. They provide a direct and objective sounding board to help interpret and apply what you're learning. Having other people as part of your process (as we'll delve into as the book progresses) connects well with my third observation.

Most people who do these tests seem to focus on self awareness. It's a good start but to get the most out of these tools I'd recommend more of a communal approach. When your friends and family are involved they can use these tools as a starting place for discussion, collaboration, and hopefully everyone knowing themselves a little bit better. You don't need a trained coach to work through the information you're getting, but you do need people that love you and are willing to have a go with furthering your understanding.

Finally, although many commented that they found some of these tools very insightful in helping them understand various personal attributes which shed some light on some of their motives and relationships, very few commented on how they applied the insight in their current situations or future planning scenarios. We hope the rest of this book sheds further light on the application of identity, but at this point I'd like to share my basic approach to any identity insight.

The first thing you usually get from typical testing is an awareness of a **talent/raw identity** piece. This could be a personality trait (like being Intuitive) or a strength (like Ideation or Empathy). In them selves, they're raw identity truths which remain unformed until you add **skills, knowledge, and a plan to develop them** on the one hand as well as **character / moral fibre** on the other. Adding these attributes to the talent / raw identity piece enriches that part of you, but there's another dimension which is essential to stay whole. When you orient your life plans and activities—including work—around a **range of talents / identity statements** you'll find yourself working out of your passions. **Passion** is the element which draws these various pieces together into a unified creativity, whether that's in a job, or whatever. It moves the whole process forward and over time, your core talent matures into a solid expression of self. When this happens across the range of your identity statements, it's a wonderful thing to behold. Over time, these elements develop that raw thing into a true strength or a beautiful personality expression. Working this out in community and, as we'll discuss later, in the loving of your neighbourhood brings the entire process full circle and makes any investment in these tools well worthwhile.

So just to bullet point the above:
• Do the test in the right frame of mind and in the right environment.
• If possible, find a coach or a course.
• Make it a communal process.
• You are more complex than just one tool to reveal. Don't get boxed in.
• Not all tools are created equal, the best ones have solid research behind them.
• Use the information as the foundation to add skills, knowledge, and character to over time.

SIMA:

The System for Identifying Motivational Abilities

started as a personalized process which later became a computer algorithm. The core idea is actually really good and has a lot of depth to it in terms of unpacking motivations and therefore identity.[27] The shortcoming in my mind is that SIMA ends up boiling all this down to top-line and secondary motivations, as though these two identifiers are the most important things about you. Not cool as far as I'm concerned, but here's what it's basically about: SIMA asks you to tell eight stories of success in your life. Things in which you thought you did well. From those stories they unpack repeating circumstances, values, and motivations. While they summarize this in a single sheet to show you what seems to be your 'top-line motivation', they also give a lot more feedback to help you understand the nuances involved in what you thought was successful. If you go through those eight stories and look at various identity statements that pop up, I bet you could come up with 30 or 40, no problem. My wife Heather did the test and came out with a 'top-line motivation' called "**Bring to completion**". This is totally true about her. If she starts something, she has to finish it, and it's one of the many qualities her hard-working self blesses all of us with.

SIMA didn't show her what she could do with that motivation but it gave her a lot of affirmation regarding how she ticks. I think this is true of most personality tests— that they affirm things about you that you may have stigmatised or misunderstood.

If you want to look into SIMA and see what it may reveal, start here:
http://www.simainternational.com/
And if you did, can you write some of your findings here:

....

....

....

....

....

....

---

27 We'll develop this later, but I've observed that if you look closely at what motivates a person - identity or 'I am' statements are not far behind. For instance, I am highly motivated to make really good food for people and create a welcoming, safe space for them. You could convert that motivation into 'I am a host' or 'I am a father' or 'In myself, I *am* a home'. The more you tunnel down on these motivations, the closer you get to some bedrock identity statement that you can further develop and act on.

JoHari Window:

We'll switch back to Blue here as he's much better in both understanding and applying the next four sets of tools.

When I was a panel beater's apprentice

I had a tool kit. The more tools in the kit, the more I was equipped to deal with. But even still, it didn't really matter how many tools I had if I didn't use them well. They might get the job done, just really badly. The same goes for identity / personality tools. So, what I'd like to do is go through a few of the tools I've used over the years, describe them, and see how they may be helpful or redemptive for you.

Seeing yourself:

This is a great tool. It's quick, easy to understand and remember, and can be very insightful. If time is an issue and you want something cheap / free with a group of friends to start you out on this journey, then this is a great place to begin.

The tool was developed by **Jo**seph Luft and **Har**ry Ingham back in the '50s. The idea behind it is that you have a list of 55 adjectives of which you pick five or six that you think best describe yourself. You then put those words into two of the four quadrants, the *arena* or the *façade*. (If you place any words in the façade it's up to you whether you choose to tell others about them). Then it's your friends turn to **identify you**. They get to select five or six words from the list that describe you and place them in the quadrants of the *arena* or the *blind spot*. The unknown quadrant exists for adjectives yet to be discovered: identity that's unknown to you and others largely because it hasn't had the context (a death in the family, sudden wealth...) to be seen or understood yet.

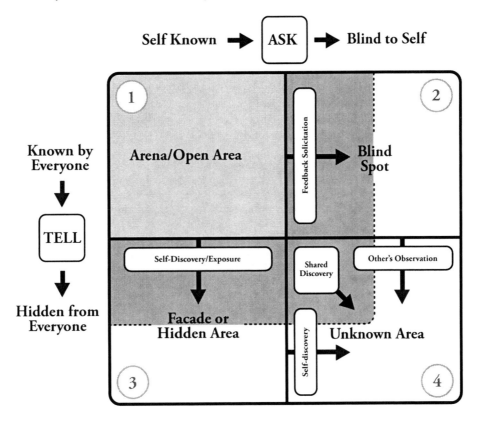

Understanding the four quadrants:

The first quadrant/area is called the **Free / Open area** or **Arena**. It's the obvious stuff known by your friends, your family or your workmates. It's where the good, the bad, and the ugly parts of you come out to play all the time. It's all there, like it or not, smiles and pimples, gut busting laughing times and sulking moody tantrums. We know this part of ourselves and so does everyone else. All quadrants are not created equal. The overall size of this quadrant in your life will depend on your self awareness. The idea here is to make the **Open Area** the biggest quadrant out of the four (the dotted line in the diagram shows that the size moves with how *open you are*). When we can honestly look at ourselves in the mirror, warts and all, and know where we can celebrate with others and say 'yeah, I'm doing some good stuff here', or know the areas where we could lift our game, where we can start to have a healthy perspective on who we are and a greater sense of wholeness. This quadrant might not start off being that big for you, but if you keep working on it, talking it through with friends and fam, you'll see it grow.

The second quadrant is called the **Hidden Area** or the **Façade**. It's the place where you alone are aware of it's contents. If the descriptions you put there are positive and affirming then cool, but you'll have to ask why they wouldn't be noticed by others and put in the *free/open area*. The idea behind a façade or mask is that you're trying to hide something right? If we're honest, we all have stuff going on in our lives we're not too proud of. This quadrant is sometimes called the shameful self, the hidden self, the self that you might say 'If they only knew what I was really like I'd want the ground to open up and swallow me'. I've often called it the place of the secret self.

For some, this quadrant might be really big so you'd want to reduce this over time. The way to do this is to simply tell someone about it. When I say simply, I know that this could actually be really difficult. It could be quite painful for a while. Being vulnerable is really scary; I mean we keep things hidden for a reason right? But how's keeping secrets hidden all this time working out? If the answer is 'not so good' then can I encourage you to find someone you can trust and start the journey of moving from the *façade* to the *open / free*? We grow by shrinking that quadrant.

The third quadrant is called **The Unknown**. We all have stuff in our lives that we don't really know about or understand and neither does anyone else. It's really hard to work with that. So, when life throws a curve ball at us or we go through a relational break up, encounter a huge success or win the lottery, something in the unknown quadrant comes to the surface. It usually surfaces as a reaction and we have to decide what to do with it. We can put it in the *façade* if it's a self discovery or put it into the *open arena* quadrant (especially if it's a public discovery).

The last quadrant is called **The Blind Area**. It's the area of our lives everyone else knows about except for us. It's kind of like every day I wake up and start the movie of my life. It's a great movie, it's about me! The lenses I view this movie through are my eyes. By the way, I'm the main character in my movie and of course I'm stone cold good looking! The movie is obviously an action packed adventure full of romance where I'm a Super Dad saving the world one person at a time. You by the way are just a character in my movie, you're not the star. I see you differently through my lenses... But here's the rub—you also have a movie about me going on through your lenses and I'm just a character in your movie. You actually get to see more of me than I do. I might think 'I'm all that' through my lenses but I can't see what's behind me, you can. You get to see my blind spot, and this is where you can point out, for instance, that I have a bald spot:-). The problem is no one wants to tell you that you need to take a shower or that you really aren't as nice to people as you think you are. But if you really want to learn a thing or two about yourself you need to ask somebody about the movie they're watching, as in: 'Hey, I always thought of myself as _____, what do you think?' Start the conversation, change the window.

You can download a list of adjectives from the online Johari Window tool http://kevan.org/johari[28] By the way, you're not limited to the lists of words they give you, they're just a good starting point to get on the same page with others, but feel free to create your own that are more specific. My rule of thumb is that the journey towards wholeness / self awareness is an exciting and rewarding one, and we should have some fun with it. If we're honest, there's usually enough stuff that surfaces as a result of the process to work on without trying to dig too deep.

Wanna try it yourself? Go to the web site for the lists and use this template here:

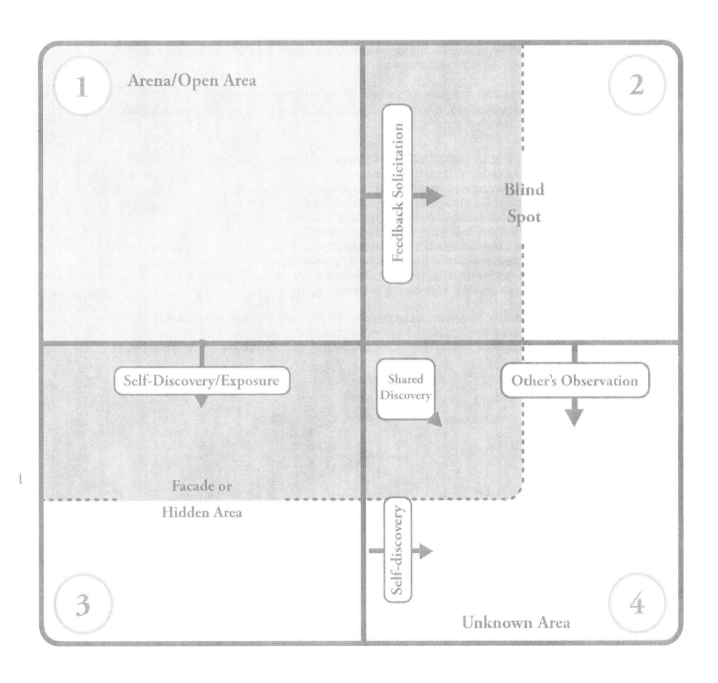

---

28 Online Johari & Nohari tools are written by Kevan Davies. There are other sites to download pictures of the window or a list of adjectives, for instance: http://en.wikipedia.org/wiki/Johari_window

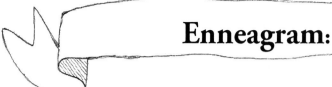

Enneagram:

I first encountered the Enneagram back in the '90s when my wife Katey and I went to a course lead by an amazing Catholic woman. No one knows where the Enneagram concept really came from. There's many ideas ranging from the symbolism of a philosopher called Pythagoras (500BC)[29], the oral traditions of the Sufi, the influence of different religions brought together by a guy called Oscar Ichazo in the '60s and developed further into what we have today by Don Riso and Russ Hudso.[30] So yeah, a lot of people have either added to or laid claim to the core idea, but here's what I've got out of it:

There are nine different personality types described in the Enneagram. Each of us have attributes of all nine types within us, but we all have one we could call a **home base**.

The nine basic personality types:
One: this place is called 'Good' or the reformer.
Two: this place is called 'Loving' or the helper.
Three: this place is called 'Efficient' or the achiever.
Four: this place is called 'Unique' or the individualists.
Five: this place is called 'Wise' or the investigator.
Six: this place is called 'Faithful' or the loyalist.
Seven: this place is called 'Joyful' or the enthusiast.
Eight: this place is called 'Powerful' or the challenger.
Nine: this place is called 'Peaceful' or the peacemaker.

You may come across other names given to these 'types' when people view this through the lens of spirituality, passion, relationships, and work etc. Don't get too confused with these terms, they're just exploring the different aspects of the types.

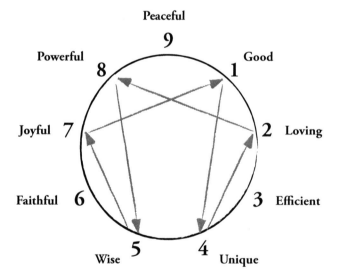

WINGS:
While it's true we may call one type or number our '**home**', it's also true that we can see ourselves in other types or numbers. (Remember, we are all of the types in some way at some time, it's just that we operate out of our home base more than

---

29 http://en.wikipedia.org/wiki/Pythagoras

30 http://www.enneagraminstitute.com/history.asp

others). It would stand to reason we would often see this most worked out in the type's right next to us. These are called the wings. So, the wings for the type one (The Good) would be the type nine and type two. The wings for five would be four and six, and so on. You may find that you have a dominant wing or that you are more balanced. You may also find you don't use wings much as you work out of your home type best. You may find that as you get older you move your focus from one wing to another. For example, my home base is a one / good and I'll always feel very comfortable with my two wing (loving). My nine wing (peaceful) has been overshadowed for years by all the activity of life. However, there's more of the peacemaker (my nine wing) coming out as I slow down a little and give it time to breathe. Some would say its just because I'm getting less ornery!

Health and unhealth

As I said, the Enneagram is a very old tool that many people have been involved in creating over time. Somewhere along the way someone has figured out that there are aspects of health and unhealth for any of the nine types. All nine types look great on a healthy day and the Enneagram will give you examples of what a great day might look like for you, what drives you and motivates you etc. For instance, a healthy day for my being type one (the Good) would be when I give myself to a worthy cause or project. I'll exercise my type to rally everyone to that cause, lock arms and work really hard to bring it to life. But if I let myself become too driven, or overwork myself, I'll turn to the unhealthy aspect of my type; a perfectionist who demands more of myself than I should. I then usually demand the same from everyone else... I've found the Enneagram helpful in these situations because it shows me these positive and negative aspects. Seeing the unhealthy expressions of my personality encourages me to make adjustments and move towards wholeness.

The journey towards integration and disintegration.

We can build on this idea of health for our type by **integrating** the health of our connecting type, or **disintegrating** to the unhealth of our connecting type. This is where those weird arrows in the diagram fit in. For example, when my type one (Good) gets stressed and over worked I will naturally follow the direction of the arrow down to the type four (Unique). This process is called **disintegration** as it leads to the unhealthy place of the four (I'm not just unique, I'm all alone...).

I'm not sure if anyone really knows why the one (the Good) slides down to the 'four' (the Unique) and uncovers the darker side of that type. At times, I've felt like the whole world is against me, that life's not fair, and I want to give up on it all. At times like this I have found it useful to read about the unhealthy aspects of the four and ask myself if this is really how I'm feeling. If it sounds about right then I know I need to do something about it, I need to go a place of integration. So when I get a bit obsessive and become the perfectionist (the unhealthy One, or Good) my path to health or **integration** would be to go against the arrow and head over to the healthy side of type Seven (the Joyful). I'll let go and give myself a break, not take things too seriously and have some fun, or watch a movie, or go hit a little white ball around a some nice grass.

When you find your number on the diagram, look at the areas of integration and disintegration, read what they have to say, and see if there's anything going on there that you can relate to. You can find out what the numbers mean here: http://www.enneagraminstitute.com/descript.asp Write some notes in here for later reflection?

....

....

....

This is an important step because it helps to broaden our understanding of ourselves on both good and bad days, giving us productive pathways to find health as well as solidify the number we call home.

The head, the heart, or the gut.

There are three centres in the Enneagram and each centre has three numbers associated with it. The 2 (loving), 3 (efficient), and 4's (unique) come from **the heart center**. The 5 (wise), 6 (faithful) and 7's (joyful) come from **the head center** and the 8 (powerful), 9 (peaceful) and 1's (good) come from **the gut center**. For instance, have you ever been in an emergency situation where you found yourself acting in a way that was different to your friends and were left wondering why? I've had mates come across accidents on the road, where one of them has gone into the wreckage while someone else is calling an ambulance. It's the typical movie scene: someone is jumping into the carnage, someone is on the phone calling the police, and someone is always saying to everyone it will be alright.

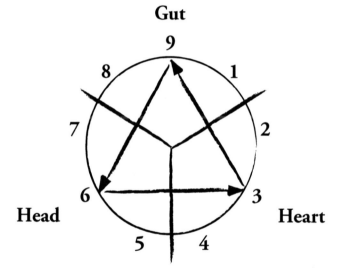

I once led a group of about thirty teenagers into the NZ bush on an overnight trip. We came across part of the track that had slipped away into the river. I cautioned everyone and carried on around the path. I stopped when I heard someone scream that one of the girls had fallen down the slip. An action hero emerged from my being as I unclipped my pack while running towards the slip, jumped over the path and landed on the downward face, slid as fast as I could to the bottom, clutched onto a hanging branch, grabbed onto the pack of the girl who was dangling about 3 metres above the river and pulled her up to safety. As I said, very heroic, but all I felt climbing back up the bank was how **enormously stupid** I'd just been. When I'd jumped off the bank I'd passed all the people who had their hands over their mouths or were calling out directions etc. and I'd wondered what do they know that I didn't? As I'd slid down the bank I'd passed two guys who were carefully making their way down. What had they seen that I hadn't? I may have saved the day, but that event left me feeling like an idiot for years. It wasn't until I understood that we all see things differently that I finally got it. The guys on the top of the bank were saying, "Heck, I hope things turn out alright, I can help with some really good suggestions here." They were using their **heart center** to respond to the situation. The two guys who were making their way down the bank were thinking, "if we're not careful there'll be three of us down their needing to be rescued". They were using their **head center** to respond to the situation. Then comes me, bat-outa-hell, in boots and all. I was using my **gut center** instinct in response to the situation. There's no right or wrong here, we are all the hero, or comforter, or analyst... somewhere at some time. The take home from this is that we need to work out where we primarily operate from; the head, the heart, or the gut. We use them all, it's just that we start from one of them, and it's pretty useful for us to know which one—especially if you need to take out some more insurance.

Your center?
If you found yourself in a building that was on fire, would you get out as fast as you can and then consider your options? Would you think about who else might be in the building before you get out? Would you wonder about how the fire might have started and have a crack at putting it out?

....

....

....

....

....

Putting it all together:
Once you've done one of the tests mentioned below, read through the results, and looked into the aspects of your wings, you can follow the arrows and read about the areas of health and unhealth. Finish by thinking through the different centres of the head, heart, and gut. All of this will help reinforce your home base type and may provide some really useful insights to help you understand how you tick.

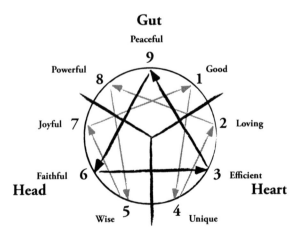

Remember, where possible, its always more fun and insightful to do this self discovery with a group of friends. If you want to do a course like I did, jump online and find one nearby or try the websites below. There are a few options in different countries to try:

http://www.enneagramaustralia.com/

For general info for what's going on around the world check out this website:
http://www.enneagramworldwide.com/

If you want to check out some online options you could try any from the list below.
http://www.9types.com/
http://similarminds.com/test.html
http://www.personalityonline.com/tests/engine.html?testid=2

If you want to buy a book about the Enneagram there are heaps out there.
Like anything, there are a lot of whacked out versions that can take you down a
number of rabbit holes if you let them. I'd suggest *The Wisdom of the Enneagram* by Don
Richard Riso & Russ Hudson or *Discovering the Enneagram* by Richard Rohr & Andreas
Ebert.[31] Rohr is a solid guy when it comes to the inner journey.

Got any Enneagram results you want to journal here?

Myers-Briggs:

"Whatever the circumstances of your life, the understanding of type can make your perceptions clearer, your judgements sounder, and your life closer to your hearts desire."
(Isabel Briggs Myers)

Way back in the 1920s a guy called Carl Jung published a
book on Psychological Types. His idea was to help you learn about your preferences and how you perceive the world around you. Your decisions are an outworking of those perceptions. His work was later picked up by a woman called Katharine Briggs and her daughter Isabel Briggs Myers. In the '60s, they developed the tool that has become the Myers-Briggs Type Indicator (MBTI). It has become one of the more widely used personality assessment tools in the world today.

The basic idea behind this tool is trying to help you determine what personality type you have a preference towards. There are four possible dichotomies, or opposing mental functions, you get tested on which results in sixteen distinctive personality types. Remember, although the test is designed to help you fit into one type or the other, it doesn't mean you can't function in the opposite type. It's just that you have a preference, like the Enneagram, where you feel at home... 'Best fit' is a descriptive term from the MBTI but I don't care if we don't use it:-). Here's how the whole MBTI has helped me, and maybe could be helpful to you?

I remember when I was working for a large automotive firm. I was good at my job and I loved the challenge but something was wrong. I was always sick (as in my body was doing weird stuff), I felt anxious, tired and at times lethargic. I still loved my job and it's many challenges, so one day I took the Myers-Briggs test with my wife (adding another tool to the toolbox of life). But it took me about 40 minutes to answer the first four questions, which was really frustrating. I could clearly see myself in both answers to the questions. I was confused until it clicked that I could see myself answering the questions one way if I imagined myself in my working environment, then answering the question in the complete opposite way if I imagined myself at home, with my family, hanging out with my friends, or even pursuing personal interests. Taking this process back to my vocational question (working at the car yard) I finally understood I was working in an environment that was not natural to who I was and it was making me sick. As I said, its not that I couldn't do the work, I was good at it. It just wasn't working out of my preferences / identity, which over time was taking all my energy and motivation away. The writing was on the wall. I resigned not long after and moved my focus to people instead of product.

As you pursue your identity through Myers-Briggs, please don't misunderstand the letters as being boxed in (like Patrick does:-). It's just a way of understanding your preferences whether they're slight bents or strong ways of being... The more at home or secure I am in my **extraversion**, the more I allow myself to walk in my **introversion** for a while without freaking out...

For instance:
Attention / Energy: E – I Dichotomy (Extraversion – Introversion) is a dichotomy that focuses on how you get your energy.
• Do you feel energised by being around people and talking things out? You might be an **Extravert** and if so you may focus your energy on people and objects. Extroverts really **like to party** and are often the last ones standing.

- Or after being with people do you need to have your own space for a while and think things through or process. You might be an **Introvert,** and if so you may focus your energy on concepts and ideas. Introverts often **need to fire gaze** or **have some cave time.**

I'm the kind of guy that can go to a café and strike up a conversation with a stranger and lose a couple of hours. If I go camping, I always want to invite the neighbourhood. I like to hang out with people and spend a massive part of my life in contact with others. A few years back, I was working hard leading up to Christmas and missed out on all the hype and shopping. Fine by me, but when Christmas Eve came around I just needed to go up town and be part of the craziness. I didn't buy anything, I just wanted to be amongst it all, soaking up the energy. I'm an **E** (extravert) and get energised by people. There are times when I'm hunting and want to sit out on a ridge alone in the wilderness and bathe in the solitude... but after two hours I want a campfire and a crowd. Death comes to me in the form of a silent retreat.

I flatted with a guy named Mike who would come home from work and grunt 'hi' on the way to his room. After about an hour he would come on out and join in whatever was happening in the life of the house. When we would ask him if he was alright he'd say, "I'm fine, I just need to wind down for a while". We grew to understand and expect this from him, and when others would ask where he was we would just say he was 'fire gazing'. At different points of the day he needed to collect his thoughts and internally process. He's an **I** (introvert). Mike has grown to be one of my closest friends in life. We have loads of fun when we're together and he's not that shy at parties. It's just that he's always better equipped to engage with life when he's grounded. I can imagine him saying, "a day alone with my thoughts.... bliss". As long as we don't try to change each other we'll always be great mates.

Internal World / Order: S – N Dichotomy (Sensing – Intuition). This dichotomy focuses on how you order your internal world and interpret information. To put it simply:
- Do you focus on the 'now' of life, the concrete information or the facts? **Sensing** people use their five senses to interpret their world. You might be Sensing if you're factual and realistic. **You** really like **the details.**
- Or do you spend time thinking more about future possibilities? You might be **Intuitive** and if so you might see the connections and patterns or interrelationships. **You don't sweat the small stuff** or **you work from the gut.**

My wife Katey is an **S** (*sensing*) and I am an **N** (*intuitive*). I'm constantly amazed at her attention to detail. For example, when the kids and I can't find something at home she tells us to have a 'mummy look' for it. Honestly it can take me three attempts to look for a book in the bookshelf or find that flight confirmation on my computer. I get a little panicked with large amounts of detail sometimes while she can have all the info I need in what seems like a nanosecond. On the other hand, when I run large events or speak to large crowds, I can see the big picture well and can deviate in a nanosecond, or pull things together in order to bring the thing to life. Katey often asks me how I do that because it would terrify her... Most of the time it's better for me to not know too much detail (it just hurts my head). I thank God we're wired so differently as there's never a dull moment in the house. Another plus is when we make important decisions together, they are often super sound.

Information / Process T – F Dichotomy (Thinking – Feeling). This dichotomy focuses on how you decide things or make judgements.
- Do you think about cause and effect? Do you value logic and analysis? You might use **Thinking** as your primary way of making decisions, and if so you might

be an objective person who may be able to detach themselves from a particular problem. Like: '**I think through my feelings**'.

- Or do you base your decisions / values on asking questions about how this decision might affect others? You might use **Feeling** as a way to inform your decisions and if so, might have people and relationships in mind as you process. Like: '**I feel through my thinking**'.

Please don't confuse a thinking orientation with being void of feeling. In the same way, don't confuse feeling with emotion as a lack of thinking. It's just the process we go through to make our decisions.

I remember making some fundamental changes to the direction of a youth work I was part of some years ago. This resulted in closing down and re-branding an organisation that had been functioning for over 50 years! Although I felt it was the right decision, it weighed very heavily on my heart. I thought I'd share the process with my predecessor who would be a great guy to lean on through this burdensome time. But something went terribly wrong. As I sat at the breakfast bar and unfolded the layers of process I had gone through to make my decision, I was overcome with emotion and wept. I was ending something that had been going on when my Dad was a kid. I felt terrible and excited about the possibility at the same time. I remember looking at him through misty tears, and his face was like stone—in my mind he didn't seem to care. Some thoughts went through my mind, like "Why aren't you upset? Don't you care??? Say something damn it! HAVE YOU NO HEART MAN @@##^^##@!!!!!"

I didn't say any of this out loud, and after a while when I calmed down a bit, he then quietly affirmed my decisions for change pointing out why he thought these changes were good and where they could lead. I was amazed at his perspective. He also expressed the deep sadness he felt as he remembered the wealth of history which the organisation had, including all the people involved over the years... It was the first time I'd really encountered a situation where two people were obviously working through a process from such different points of view. I was obviously working from my heart to my head. My friend was working from his head to his heart. At the end of the day the outcome was the same, it's just that we had different processes to get there. As I said, the head is not void of the heart and vice versa.

External World / Executing J - P Dichotomy (Judging - Perceiving). This dichotomy focuses on how you deal with the world you live in.

- Do you like to be well organised? Well planned? You might use a **Judging** approach to living life with an attitude towards getting the job done, and if so you might be decisive, ordered, and tasks oriented. You're about '**done that, finished! What's next!**'

- Or do you like flexibility in what you do? You might use a **Perceiving** approach to living life and if so you will tend to be more open-ended and spontaneous. Like: '**Yeah I'm on it, I'm finishing it now!**'

Note that judging doesn't mean judgemental and perceiving doesn't mean aimless, its just the way you may interpret the world around you.

My friend Alan is a pretty onto it kind of guy; he's a **J** (*Judging*). If it's not in his diary it's not real. He's very organised. We have been mates since time began and have worked together with different organisations creating different events. At the moment we are on a team that runs a camp of over 4000 people each year. Al is the Chairman of the Board and writes the agenda for our meetings, asks about time-lines etc. He loves to get things done and is the backbone for the camp's organisation. I'm the Director of the camp and sometimes I need to have stuff finished, but mostly I'm kinda always getting around to it... I go to a lot of meetings with an idea of what I'd like to see happen and that's really how I run the camp. I'm a **P** (*Perceiving*) so my underpinning question is what NEEDS to be done so that it won't fall over? The rest we'll work out when we get there... Which is why I'm often asking Alan "What's next"? For instance, I remember talking to him about the report that needed to be done. For days I talked about all the items needed in the report and I danced around the work I should have been doing... but I didn't actually write anything down. He summed it up brilliantly by saying to me "the freakin things not going to write itself you know!" It was the kick start I needed to get the job done. Guy's like me need Alan's in our lives to remind us about the stuff that needs to happen. Guy's like Al need people like me in their lives to help them embrace the possibilities of what could be. It's always a stronger result when we work together as the chart below shows:

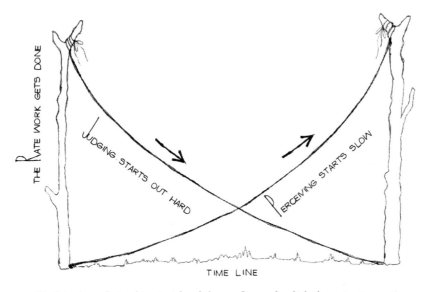

'Judging' people tend to start hard then refine and polish the output over time
'Perceiving' people tend to gather, build their resources, and escalate over time.
We need other people's personalities to both stretch us and compliment our efforts.

So how do I do the test?
To do the Myers-Briggs Type Indicator (MBTI) go online and find a site to do the test. There are plenty of free ones (Facebook has one too). I've listed a couple in the footnotes. Be warned though, as with most tests, you get what you pay for. If something is cheap and nasty it'll yield a rough result. The more options you have for answering and the more thorough the process, the more in-depth the result will be. You could also look for a workshop or course that's being run nearby, grab a bunch of friends, and let the unfolding begin.
http://www.teamtechnology.co.uk/
www.myersbriggsreports.com Costs money to do this one.
http://www.humanmetrics.com

What's your Myers-Briggs stuff look like?

....

....

....

....

....

StrengthsFinder:

There are many tools out there that will describe you with a colour, a mood, an attribute, or even as a particular animal (like a hawk or beaver... but I've never met a self professed turkey, even though there are plenty around). I've shown you a couple of tools that use numbers or letters to describe you. But I often come across people who hate the concept of being 'boxed in', as in 'I'm more than just a nine on the Enneagram...'—and they're right. As I said, there's no tool that can fully get you and all your complexities. Having said that, I really like StrengthsFinder for the following reasons:

StrengthsFinder was developed in the '60s by a couple of guys called Clifton and Gallup. When they looked around at the tools available at the time, they noticed that current counselling and psychology was geared towards what's wrong with us. They asked what it could look like if we worked on what we do well, 'what's right with us'. This doesn't mean that we don't have things that we need to work on. It's just not where we should stay, because we're still really good at some other stuff—which by the way, helps us deal with the crap. It's more productive to give attention to strengths rather than weaknesses...

A few years ago I came across StrengthsFinder and thought it was fantastic. My group of friends and I couldn't stop talking about it that day, and then into the week as we started to discover more. The idea is pretty simple: buy any of the books listed below,[32] and somewhere in the book there's a web address with a code you can use to access the online test. Word of warning, the code is a once only deal; you can't reuse the code in the book. The book also acts as a reference with collections of stories, experiences, and action points to help flesh out the core idea. As with any of these tests, it's a good idea to find a place where you can concentrate, where you're relaxed and can just be you. If you're doing the test under pressure—like in a working environment in a 'work mindset'—it'll influence the result towards what's expected of you in that place. It's more important to understand who you are in your broader life than who you are in a particular job. So grab a cup of coffee, switch your cell phone off, close your Facebook page for a half an hour or so, and do the test in a neutral place. The world won't stop without you.

Once you've logged in there are about 180 questions you need to answer and you'll have about twenty seconds to give one of five possible answers. Don't over analyse the questions as just the 'top of your head' answers are needed. You'll get a report that gives your "Top 5" talents. A talent is a thing you do well naturally without having to think about it. The idea here is to understand these talents, add skills and knowledge to them, and work on them until they become known to you and others around you as your 'Strengths'. In my opinion, the best way to gain a fuller understanding of your top 5 is to meet up with a qualified Strengths Coach. They're trained to offer insight to the tool, as well as help you work out a plan of applying your top 5 to your life. I've listed a few websites in different countries in the footnotes. Contact them or search the web if you want to be coached.[33]

Again, you might say 'but surely I'm more than my top 5'. The answer, of course, would be absolutely. There are 34 talents and you potentially have way more than five, it's just that you have them in a different order than the guy or girl next to you. And that order influences how you live. I have a list of all my thirty four because I trained, and I can tell you that I am very different to my friends who have something called **Harmony** in their top 5 (it's my 34th). I don't think like they do, or act like they do, because it's high on their radar and its pretty low on mine.

---

32 *Living your Strengths. Now discover your Strengths. 2.0.*

33 Trans Pacific. www.cys.org.nz Gallup University.

StrengthsFinder is a great tool because it doesn't just tell me what I'm good at, it helps me work out how to be kick-ass at it. Most other tools tell me about myself without helping me to grow in the area. 'Strengths' talks to the inner motives behind the talent and leaves you feeling quite unique, not boxed in. Think about it, we're surrounded by voices in society that are often telling us where we need to lift our game, fix that flaw in our lives, be more organised etc. Which may be kinda true but it's not the whole truth. There are things that we do really well, and when we outwork the things we're passionate about, we can order our life according to those strengths instead of always spending time correcting weaknesses.

You'll find the book and test provide some valuable insights, but it sticks better when it's worked out with a group who are all talking the same language. Living my life out of who I am, from what I know about how I am wired, is not arrogant, it's quite freeing. It's freeing because I know what I have to offer the world. If I know who I am it can help me to understand how others are really different from me. Instead of feeling insecure about my difference or yours, I can seek to understand who you are and work together for good, rather than having to compete or conform.

What's have you learned about your strengths?

....

....

....

....

....

....

Summary:

These tools may have already been part of your journey. There may have been some speed bumps on the way. You may want to reconsider their place in your overall process. Using these different approaches is like opening up a doorway into a room in your life. You can choose to take a peek inside the room or fully dive in and discover all the cool nooks and crannies. The rest of this book can add volumes to these initial tools if you care to spend the time.

Any other observations or notes you wanna make at this point?

....

....

....

....

....

....

Three dimensions of identity

I think by all means, we should use all the tools we can to go deeper into the long tunnel of our identity. Most of the ideas we've looked at so far in this chapter give you a decent summary of your personality. But while summarizing our strengths may be helpful to affirm our quirky nature, or narrow down job opportunities, the snapshot isn't enough to build a new world from. Fulfillment is not based on a simple connection between one ability leading to one job. You've probably already tried that. Holistic living comes from living out the broad range of our whole being, and needs to be expressed in a much wider spectrum than just our work.

In order to see this broader spectrum, I've created a few questions of my own. Again, not to develop a short list or simplify the issue, but to broaden it. Over the years I've asked myself three questions that further an internal conversation about identity. They're based on a natural storytelling method which draws out individual nuance and diversity. We'll work on these questions a lot more in later chapters, but I want to introduce them here to get you processing and journaling a bit more (unless you're a guy, in which case I guess you'll just think about them). So just have a quick look, note what comes naturally, and keep the overview in mind. It'll come in handy in Part Two.

I see our overall identity as the complex mix of three
human dimensions. The first is **your spiritual identity**, the second is **your social / familial identity,** and the third is **your personal identity**. There is, of course, much more to you including your intelligences, physical makeup, and personality traits, but I find these areas are largely expressions of these three dimensions. For instance, you use various intelligences to process and make things that originate from your social identity. Your sense of style and personality is an expression of your soul, etc.

In listing these three aspects of identity, I am not trying to narrow the field. But I have found them to be excellent starting points, or foundations, in a conversation that unlocks tons of 'I am' statements. An 'I am' statement is an identity statement which summarizes things you know about yourself. For instance, I really like culinary art and making people feel welcome. So, if I take the time to pursue these interests and apply myself over time, I may see that 'I am hospitable' or potentially, 'I am a chef'. These statements come from simple questions that draw out stories, circumstances, memories, and present day examples of you being yourself. And since the process is based on your story and experience, the names you use to describe yourself are a lot closer to the true you than a pre-defined list some website spits out. In this way, you move away from quantitative identity statements to qualitative truths that resonate deeply inside of your heart. At least, that's the goal.

So, here's what I ask myself and my friends to get the names flowing, or to add to what they already know through other methods like the ones listed above:
1. Who are you spiritually?
2. Who are you socially?
3. Who are you personally?

What I'm listening for through these questions are stories that reveal the person. Events, dreams, circumstances, etc. that allow me to see who people are **being** in their stories. The questions I ask to get the conversation going are something like this:

(Note: I'll leave room for you to jot some things down, but don't treat it like a test. Just write down whatever comes to you if the question is relevant. We'll give more depth to the questions and room to process later, this is just to warm you up a bit.)

1. For your *spiritual identity*, what have you heard in your spirit that you resonate with?

a. What scriptures have meant a lot to you and why?
b. What words of encouragement have been spoken over you that stuck?
c. What conviction have you felt, especially of things you need to correct or work on in your life (*often, this is getting the crap out of the way for the true self to come through*)?
d. Has there been any significant spiritual event that you recall and what does that say about you?

....

....

....

....

....

....

....

....

2. For your *familial / social identity*, what is your name?

a. Meaning, what are you called by those close to you based on who they see you as?
b. What kind of neighbor or fellow worker are you?
c. What do you love about your culture, or your part in it, and can you put a name to it?

....

....

....

....

....

3. For your personal identity, what do you love, and what's natural to you, and why?

a. Just shoot from the hip here, list a few things you love, ask why you love them, and then try to write an 'I am' statement from that. Like, *I love food, because I love to create art and hospitality with it, so I am a chef, or host...*

....

....

....

....

....

....

....

....

Overall, we want to move away from a narrow view of self to a broad, expansive, even scary, look at the huge range of identity you possess. The few examples given from other peoples' methods and the ones I add to the mix, still only get the party started. There's still so much more to unfold by looking at your intelligences, personality, and some other aspects we haven't even thought of yet. This depth is totally worth pursuing, because I think your future is **about creating possibilities** by synthesizing all the various aspects of this massive breadth, and learning to use as much of your identity as possible in your daily life. It's not about finding a few strengths to pitch at potential employers. That road leads to medicating the unfulfilled parts of your identity with materialism (or worse, pop music). Please help stop the madness.

So what of this deep space do you know of yourself? Were you able to list 20 things that are true about you in the last few pages? Or do you mostly know what you're not? Most people can recite screeds of rejections, comparisons, discouragements, and failed attempts at being themselves. And in this way, those memories continue to shape our view of what we can do both today and in the future. In a fascinating look at calling, James Hillman reminds us that we are "... less damaged by the traumas of childhood than by the traumatic way we remember childhood as a time of unnecessary and externally caused calamities that wrongly shaped us."[34] The focus on damage distracts us from recalling those powerful yet fleeting moments of inspiration, and the callings of our child-like soul. So in asking us to remember those passions, or who we really are, it's a struggle to list five things off the bat. Which is understandable given the lack of attention on identity, but it's still a tragedy because we're actually very deep. Growing up is hard. We remember

---

34 *The Soul's Code: In Search of Character and Calling,* Random House, 1st edition (1996), pg 4. By the way, if you're presently a practicing psychologist or want to become one, I suggest you have a read of this book.

negative experiences really clearly and start to define ourselves by overreacting to lost races in school, or poor grades, or a devastating youthful relationship. Man, I still remember the awkward dance I had with a girl in high school. She said yes, but really didn't want to, and I could see it in her eyes. I haven't asked anyone to dance since. Who knows, I could be this amazing Tango aficionado by now if not for that. Well, not really, but you get the point. We develop entire personalities by continually protecting our self-image from stuff like that ever happening again.

How have the experiences of the past affected what you think of yourself today? What have you become as a result? We need to workshop this because there's probably a real gap between the affected version and the real you. This is significant, because the present view of yourself may not be accurate and therefore really limiting what you think is possible. One of the issues I've had to work through is whether I could be a committed person or not. I liked flexibility and freedom, and the example (nurture) presented to me was one of broken commitment. My father, and his father, modeled divorce as an option for dealing with relational tension and this became part of how I saw myself: unmarried and super flexible. The reality is that I am a family man, and an amazing one at that, when I can overcome this identity lie about being 'flexible'.

The real you is capable of so much, but needs some encouragement to breathe again and come back to life. And while I think it's better to focus on true identity statements, sometimes we need to see what we've become in order to move past it.

Down to earth

with Kate Osterloh

Growing up, well-meaning parents and teachers were quick to point out my strengths and gifts—but all too often, they selectively praised those strengths that society had a use for and discarded the rest. Many people can probably relate to this process. While I was applauded for my motivation, my curiosity to learn, and my aptitude for reading and writing, no one ever stopped to applaud my penchant for turning everything around me into a story. The fact that I liked to connect dolls, dress-up clothes, gardening, performing, and art into complex mythologies in my head did not directly relate to success as a student or individual, and so it was ignored. It took me years to realize that these creative activities (sewing, cooking, writing, performing) quickly became frustrating to me when they did not connect to an overarching and meaningful story. The emphasis on success—which left little room for the creative trial and error that is a necessary part of growing up—taught me to base my value on achievement. Consequently, I was terrified of failure, and I became my own harshest critic in the midst of any disappointment, whether academic, moral, or professional. It's hard to relax and enjoy life when your own harshest critic is constantly at your elbow hounding you!

Beginning with a stint in a non-profit, and then re-entering the 'real' world, I began to see the destructiveness of this mindset. I couldn't tolerate my own presence anymore. How could I enjoy the richness of life when I had no room to explore, to create, to fail? My spirituality had to undergo a radical shift. I began to view my life in terms of a long, sometimes wearying, sometimes exhilarating, journey. Personally, I am a story-gatherer. I love to soak in the beauty of the world through travel, through adventure, or through conversations over a well-prepared meal. Not knowing the destination—or even where I stand at any given moment—can be frustrating, especially around people who expect me to define my life or beliefs concretely. But the freedom to explore and fail is gradually teaching me to embrace uncertainty and find beauty in it. Spiritually, I am a questioner. I am drawn to stories that hint at the divine, rather than dogma or ethics derived from those stories. I like to find the nuance and the possibility in spirituality. I connect reality to God through the meaning people place on experiences in their own lives. I find myself attracted not to well-defined personalities or belief systems, but to stories—nuanced, dynamic, full of struggle.

Socially, I am a motivator, an advocate, and an innovator. I tend to challenge existing beliefs or norms through my ideas and actions. This led me into the field of human rights law, where I recently obtained an M.A. I feel inspired by the possibilities inherent to the subject matter, but I am struggling to find a place for the artistic aspects of my personality. For the last two years I worked with refugees, and found myself concerned not with fitting their human rights abuses into organizational schemas, but with listening, understanding, and calling out the potential that lies ahead of them. This puts me at a disadvantage professionally, but also challenges me to confront the legal structures that dehumanize vulnerable people. I still feel at a disadvantage in the creative world because of the difficulty of turning integrated storytelling (storytelling that brings together art, music, performance, and the written word) into something commercially viable or socially significant. Sometimes I come up with kooky ideas, like "Massage therapy and herbal gardening retreat for Refugees" or "The Theatre of Academic Innovations Toward Social Justice," but entrepreneurship seems a tall order when I have a pile of school debt and zero assets. Wise people in my life have pointed out that this may be a question of timing, so perhaps after a few years in the professional world I will be in a better place to exercise risky creativity.

Praxis:

1. What are some trauma based identity statements that you think you've become, that aren't really you? *For me, this would be things like 'I am controlling' because I didn't want my family to fail like my parents. Or 'I am stupid' because I could never do well in school. Now I know better, school is stupid:-)*

....

....

....

....

....

....

2. Try to list as many things that are true about you as you can in three minutes. Use the term 'I am...' Just go for it without thinking too much about it. Your soul actually knows a lot when you don't slow it down with self-image filters.

....

....

....

....

....

....

3. Looking at the two lists above, what would you say has developed in your identity because of your nature, and which parts formed from nurture, or a result of your environment?

....

....

....

....

....

Part One

Checkpoint

I've suggested that you read through the entire book to get a feel for the flow, and maybe see where you're at in the identity scheme of things. If you've done that, and are now ready to work through the details, this checkpoint is designed to give you pause and ask **"is there anything at the foundational level I should work on?"** For instance:

Am I free to call out my own future and move towards it?
- if not, consider reading *Psychotic Inertia- a book about calling and confusion*
- or articulate the roadblock (from the **PRAXIS** at the end of Chapter One) and process it with some friends, or in counseling if needed

Have I already looked at identity through other means?
- was that a positive experience?
- if so, what did you learn: gather that information and add it to the mapping process we'll do later in this book
- was the previous identity / personality process not so helpful? If not, what happened and what was the problem? Maybe you could go over that with a friend or coach and see what you can learn

Do I have an idea of what I want, where my energy level and motivations are?
- if so, proceed to the next section and use everything you can to create a context for that energy
- if not, what needs to happen to re-energize you? Perhaps unfolding identity in the next section would encourage you, but you may also need to address, or at least understand what's happened to your energy and passion. In this way you can be aware of pitfalls, or traps where you may tend to give up your authority and lose motivation

So, if you need to work on anything that's come up during this time, or through the chapter praxis, please stop and take the time to do so. Get some runs on the board by building good foundations. You'll need that platform to make the next two sections really worthwhile. I'm not saying everything in your life should be perfect before proceeding (as I've mentioned before, sometimes it's the development of identity and caring for others that moves us out of the ruts we get into). But if there's something really big you know you need to address, please do so.

If it's a matter of some niggling concerns or past issues,
you probably just need to press ahead and let them die of attrition.

Like:

- *Sometimes the past has been mired by laziness or fear. In this case, it's simply a matter of acknowledging that and putting in the hard work to understand ourselves better, and then applying that knowledge in a loving way. You can't sit around having staring contests with fear hoping it'll blink and go away. Instead, you walk towards your identity and act on your potential, gaining some confidence along the way...*

- *You can't pay attention to the generational myth of financial security—there's no such thing. Your parents were right that if you don't work, you don't eat, but security can never be based on money. Security is founded on holistic living (spiritual, relational, and physical well being). Money follows the value you create, it's that simple. So don't worry about it, focus on creating value from your identity and you'll be fine, or at least, you'll be happy.*

- *If you're wondering if you'll ever be 'good enough' to do the things you really like, you'll have to give it a couple hundred hours to see. You cannot know the difference between an interest and a true ability without this kind of effort. The only thing you need to know now is whether the efforts you're about to spend on something is in line with your identity or not. So be bold and read on.*

THE HUMAN INDIVIDUAL LIVES USUALLY FAR WITHIN HIS LIMITS; HE POSSESSES POWERS OF VARIOUS SORTS WHICH HE HABITUALLY FAILS TO USE. HE ENERGIZES BELOW HIS MAXIMUM, AND HE BEHAVES BELOW HIS OPTIMUM. IN ELEMENTARY FACULTY, IN COORDINATION, IN POWER OF INHIBITION AND CONTROL, IN EVERY CONCEIVABLE WAY, HIS LIFE IS CONTRACTED LIKE THE FIELD OF VISION OF AN HYSTERIC SUBJECT BUT WITH LESS EXCUSE, FOR THE POOR HYSTERIC IS DISEASED, WHILE IN THE REST OF US IT IS ONLY AN INVETERATE HABIT—— THE HABIT OF INFERIORITY TO OUR FULL SELF...

The Energies of Men
William James
First published in Science (1907), N.S. 25 (No. 635), 321-332.

Part Two

The Raw Material

Stuff we'll look at in this section:

- *Celebrating the natural design of your identity*
- *Reckoning with it's busted reality*
- *Redeeming the mix*

In a perfect world...

- *your existence was heralded by words of encouragement being sung to you in your mother's womb*
- *your childhood was inspired by dreams made believable with games about those dreams, unfettered by poverty or abuse*
- *your "coming of age" ceremony was greeted by the community celebrating / validating*
- *your identity and the resulting hopes you expressed your teenage years were full of brave exploration, revealing more of your unique nature*
- *your dreams are now real, tangible expressions of what your soul was singing about all along*

In the real world...

We are things of dry hours and the involuntary plan,
Grayed in, and gray. "Dream" mate, a giddy sound, not strong
Like "rent", "feeding a wife", "satisfying a man".

But could a dream sent up through onion fumes
Its white and violet, fight with fried potatoes
And yesterday's garbage ripening in the hall,
Flutter, or sing an aria down these rooms,

Even if we were willing to let it in,
Had time to warm it, keep it very clean,
Anticipate a message, let it begin?

We wonder. But not well! not for a minute!
Since Number Five is out of the bathroom now,
We think of lukewarm water, hope to get in it.

Kitchenette Building
by Gwendolyn Brooks

How to reconcile these two worlds? On one hand, we dream because our souls know how. They know how because there **is** more, we come from more. Our hopes and longings come from a real place that leads us to expect there can be more. There's an expectation that our lives can be made better if all was put right... and that there's a right way to put it. There is a design and we know we can get back to it.

On the other hand, we live in families that are under pressure. Pressures handed down from previous generations—reincarnating financial fears and other ghosts made real, again and again. Our burdens are largely internal; nervous greed and overblown cautions hold us in place. Which is tragic, because the external world is dying to see the real us, to multiply and bless us. But we turn that potential world into our ghost's world, into the fallen image handed down to us. And so we break the design. How then to reconcile these two worlds?

I've always been a bit of an idealist. I grew up in the '60s when J.F. Kennedy was saying things like: "There are those that look at things the way they are, and ask why? I dream of things that never were, and ask why not?"[35] Rockets were being sent into space and people had huge Afros... nothing seemed impossible. The next two decades knocked a bit of that out of me (especially the early '80s! Disco?). But as time went on, I was blessed by being around people who helped me look at life's root structures (thank you Landa) so I could improve on whatever I was handed. I don't look at the sick world around me from a symptomatic point of view anymore, I want the histology. I want to look deeply at the core issues and compare that to a healthy system. All I really need then is to understand what a healthy system looks like.

I've spent the last 27 years looking at this, and in particular, the familial development of identity. I think there is a design, or at least a rough sketch of one, that can give us a handle on what we're looking for. We've been given a lot to work with in terms of knowing ourselves, but a sometimes lousy environment in which to express it. My hope is in the resilient nature of the raw materials we've been given, and that given a chance, our soul will come to life in a powerful way. My experience has been that, despite the environment, identity will find a way, even redeeming the detrimental spaces it finds itself in. My wish for you now, is that you'll be able to build on or redeem whatever life you've lived so far by extracting the precious from the worthless. By using all those positive and painful experiences to draw out the stories and context through which your identity has been trying to emerge.

---

35 Kennedy was quoting George Bernard Shaw from a paraphrased line delivered by the Serpent in Shaw's play *Back To Methuselah* : "You see things; and you say, 'Why?' But I dream things that never were; and I say, 'Why not?'".

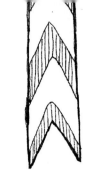

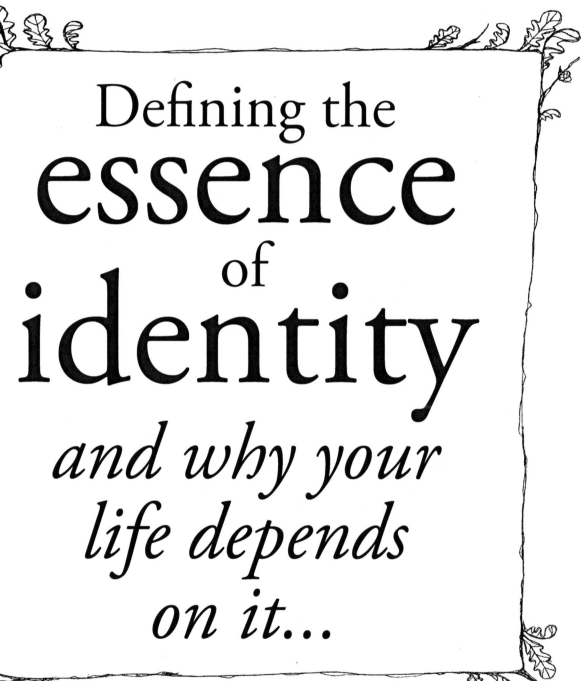

Chapter Five

Defining the **essence** of *identity*

and why your life depends on it...

Life presents us with some big questions, like 'which film is getting an Oscar?' and 'what should I wear today?'. Somewhere in the mix is 'where did I come from?', 'who am I?', and 'where am I going?'... which are kinda complicated, so it's usually back to 'does this color look good on me?'. All of us know identity is somehow central to our lives, but it's just been too dang hard to get a hold of, so we default to dealing with the day to day. The urgent things, like fixing our car, tyrannize the important things, like knowing where that car could be taking us... I think we need to come back to the scary (and scarily exciting) possibility that we can answer the bigger questions, and that actually our lives depend on it. Literally. The rest of your life depends on the detailed knowledge and practice of your identity.

Beating the tyranny of the urgent requires some

perspective on your identity. Your everyday choices need a larger context to make sense of them. Plus, the bigger questions of your future need an internal wisdom to chart a way forward. The capacity to meet all these needs resides within the wiring of your soul. And when that soul is empowered, has some purpose, and can master its calling, you will be the happiest person on the planet. Or, at least as Dan Pink implies with the following principles, you'll be happy enough.[36] My take on his theory is that:

- **Empowerment** happens when you can articulate your identity. Meaning that based on your strengths, you educate yourself to create your own job descriptions.
- **Purpose** happens when you point those abilities at something really important.
- **Mastery** happens when you spend 10,000 hours (5 to 10 years) refining your identity's expression so it has an impact, becomes truly beautiful...

This is a life well lived and we shouldn't settle for anything less. Because anything less is usually a life defined by others.

For Instance

My father-in-law, Raymond Windsor, is a great example of these three facets coming together. From an early age, he was empowered by educating his various gifts. He dedicated himself to the study and practice of his creative capacity as a pianist, singer, rugby player, and later on, surgeon. He pointed that multi-faceted identity at the needs of his community and of the world at large, which took him to India where he worked as a doctor. He developed his mastery at first in New Zealand where he was part of a pioneering heart surgery unit. He then went to India and Pakistan where he lived and worked for over 20 years, perfecting his medical practice which spanned out to the establishing of entire hospitals. In Ray's case, not only did his life thrive by knowing and practicing identity, the lives of others depended on it too.

We need a solid starting point to engage in this empowerment / purpose / mastery process for ourselves. So, in this chapter I'd like to outline the broader, kinda philosophical, aspects of identity. We'll start with some of the material from Chapter Four, and then in the coming chapters we'll use these frameworks to go really deep in an effort to unfold the essence of your identity. Here are the game rules:

1. *You are eternal and therefore cannot be completely defined.*

2. *There is no algorithm smart enough to unravel the complexity that's you. You're a living soul, expressed in light, captured in millions of memories. Those memories form your story up until today, but they also act as a platform for the story you're about to tell.*

3. *Everything is useful, including the algorithms I trashed just now, as long as it points towards something you really resonate with as an 'I am' statement.*

4. *You are soul, mind, and body, and therefore you have a lot going on. Be okay with complexity, it comes in handy later when you'll need that broad pallet to paint from.*

5. *You are primarily a relational being, which means you should walk through this with at least two or three of your most important relationships. No person is an island unless they really want to be.*

---

36 Check out Dan Pink's work on motivation. He sites many studies on empowerment, purpose, and mastery and adds a lot of his own great perspectives: www.danpink.com

I think the essence of our identity resides in three distinct, but well connected, dimensions. Our soul, our mind, and our body all play interconnected roles in this expression. There are libraries full of books discussing each of these dimensions, but for our purpose, I'd like to talk about how each embodies and expresses who you are. In a sense, it's a very simplistic approach. But I think if you start any inquiry into these three core areas with identity in mind, you can then branch out into their expansive nature with a better foundation.

A LOT HAS BEEN WRITTEN ABOUT WHERE THE SOUL RESIDES... WHETHER THE MIND IS JUST A MATTER OF NEURONS... AND IF YOUR BODY HAS AN AURA OR EXPRESSION OUTSIDE THE ITSELF...

So TO START THE DISCUSSION, WE WILL ASSUME THE FOLLOWING:

HERE ABOUTS ?

Your Mind
—INPUT
—PROCESSING
—PERSONALITY

SOMEWHERE IN HERE ?

Your Soul
—SPIRIT
—HEART
—WILL

Your Body
—DNA
—HOMEOSTASES
—STYLE

THE STUFF OUTSIDE ?

Identity and your soul

The first, and I think most important, part of this broad identity pallet is your **soul**. This is both the most amazing and the hardest place to start. It's that ethereal part of you which science can't pin down, and which poets are better at deciphering, but never completely. It's been described to me as the meeting place, or the interaction, of the Spirit of God and your body. It's therefore a relational space, and so always calls us deeper into relationships. And while I think your overall identity is a mix of all your intelligences, personality, and physical makeup, etc., I'm pretty convinced the core of your identity resides in your soul. Your soul houses the unique ID that inspires the rest of you (your mind and body). It's that distinct personhood that makes one twin super different from the other. It's nuclear in that it can inspire great architecture or a loving response to Trisomy 21.[37]

Your soul is also a universe within. To get a handle on identity and the soul, let's look at some of its functions:

1. Your soul is **spiritual**. It **connects** you to God, and therefore to other people. Its function is to commune with, yet still be able to transcend, all the physical stuff around you. It allows you to receive from outside of yourself and be known to others beyond your façade. All this means we therefore have a **spiritual identity** that can be known and expressed. Most people know this about each other but it's sometimes hard to describe for ourselves. For instance, my friend Ann is a passionate helper of those in need. Her spirit goes before her making people feel at ease and comfortable, but also challenged at the same time. She can easily motivate, inspire, and facilitate those she comes in contact with. Ann's spiritual identity is obvious to the people she works with, but it's taken a few years to see and articulate for herself.

2. Your soul has **heart**. It's where your passion and intuition live, along with all their evil siblings (greed, fear, and lust). Its main function is to love. Your emotional processing, or E.Q., churns away in neurological regions designed to structure these types of information, but the emotive results live in the soul. Your heart primarily relates at the social level, in which it gives and receives heart to heart input. You therefore have a **social identity,** or a familial name, in which you express yourself when you're with others. For instance, my friend Chris is a world class friend and networker. Concerned and capable, he makes people feel heard and loved, and then he makes things happen for them. His name is connector, helper, problem solver, change agent, entrepreneur. Chris' heart connects with others in such a way that he forms family over time with those blessed to know him. His social identity is that part of his soul which connects his life to theirs.

3. Your soul also has **will** or volition. Your intellect processes all the data, but it's the soul that makes choices based on your will's values. Your will is the source of your second, third, and fourth wind. It's what you call on when you habitually say no to something detrimental. It's the ability to do something brave, which has an energizing effect. Your will is strong because it's meant to protect the integrity

---

37 Down Syndrome

of your identity based on your unique qualities. These qualities form preferences that you intrinsically understand as likes, or dislikes. You therefore have a **personal identity** which reflects your will's distinctive values. For instance, my friend Emma-Kate is learning to listen to her distinctiveness as an artist. She's inspired by ideas and loves the challenge of visually / physically expressing them. By doing this, she's allowing her intuition to come through in the production of art, crafts, and then the rest of her life (relationships, interior design, business development...). The things she makes come from a connection to ideas, textures, colors, the needs of her friends, trees along the river... all of which speak to her from the inside-out. Emma-Kate's will allows her personal identity to freely flow into beautiful expressions, simply because she listens closely to her will.[38]

To understand the three identity levels of the soul, we will eventually unpack three simple questions, which I've already mentioned as:

1. *What is your spiritual identity?* Based on **what you've been called spiritually**.

2. *What is your social identity?* Based on the **names given in family** and community.

3. *What is your personal identity?* Based on **what you love, and what's natural** to you.

Sorry to repeat these, but I really think they're central to the process. We'll use them to try and draw out what's true about your soul—revealed through intuition, life stories, events, and motivations, etc. On the one hand this is a difficult process because the soul is so ethereal, but on the other hand it's easy because identity is so natural, or integral, to who you really are. Meaning, if you start looking, it pops up everywhere. The trick is to start talking about it, remembering, validating, celebrating... Which is exactly what we've forgotten to do with each other and why this book has become necessary. It's not all that complicated, but you will feel a little sluggish starting out.

We'll also look at the inter-connectedness of these three questions / dimensions. When all three are known and functioning you're doing well, but if one is dominant then your life could be out of whack. In fact, when I first started looking at identity, I only thought of the spiritual and personal angles. My brother-in-law John had to remind me of the social or familial side of identity because it wasn't a strong part of my life. The person who only knows their spiritual identity has a tendency to over spiritualize everything, and often ends up stuck waiting to hear something from above. The person who is out of balance with a social or familial identity can only move at the speed of the group, which is fine in balance, but not cool if you're of a culture where you're bound to your family in a negative way. And the person who's obsessed with personal identity (read: Californian Hedonist) only sees the world through that lens, which eventually kills off their spiritual and community involvement via an overblown attention to self.

---

38 To see what I mean, check out Emma-Kate's ETSY site at www.etsy.com/shop/snappystuffbyek

What about you? Is your spiritual, social, and personal identity in balance? It may be too early to comment, but have a go:

....

....

....

....

I think a living example of integrating these three dimensions is Mr. Dave Andrews. I (Blue) first met Dave in Brisbane, Australia about fifteen years ago and loved seeing the way he tied his spiritual, personal and social identity together in a unified life:

Spiritual: Dave has a deep spiritual understanding of the beatitudes (Matthew chapter 6 in the Bible) which he connects with internally. From this connection, he understands his place in the world of need around him, as the beatitudes call him to live that identity out by meeting those needs in his own way.

Social: As a networker, activist and innovator, Dave's social identity connects all kinds of people in his neighbourhood with each other to heal wounds, create better businesses, and train others along the lines of committed communities.

Personal: Dave has a huge love for life, people and community. He's a gifted communicator and a caring listener. Father, friend, and mentor are other identity statements that he combines with his spiritual life, allowing those personal aspects to shine through all the stronger.

In my opinion, Dave Andrews is a holistic being. The integration of these various identity pieces creates a freedom for him to walk out the strengths of all three in unison with each other. The core of this integration is based on his applications of the scriptures—or what he's called 'Be-Attitudes'. Not content to have an isolated aspect of his identity (i.e. being 'pseudo-spiritual'), he forces the integration of these attitudes into the real-time needs of his neighbourhood. Have a look for yourself at:

http://www.daveandrews.com.au/index.html

Identity and your mind

After the soul, the second major aspect of this identity pallet is your **intelligences**, or your **mind**. Your intellect and processing skills are both an expression of your soul, and a dimension of identity in their own right. Your intelligences are also the vehicle of expression for your musical passions or an architectural dream. But they're not just tools. The broad collection of your intellectual strengths and the workings of your mind are distinct identity properties in themselves. Overall, our identity is a set of complex interactions between soul, mind, and body. And your intellect is the processing center of these interactions. It's also wonderfully distinct from everyone else's in the world. As the processing center for your overall identity, the mind develops best within the context of facilitating relationships (starting out in the home, and then in good schools, or in challenging work situations later on). For this reason, I think appraisals like I.Q. testing have had a damaging effect on the understanding of intelligence (and standardized tests should only be issued to the people who make them!). But recent research has shown that while your brain possesses common processing centers (like math logical, or language...), you

have distinct and varied mental strengths which you uniquely combine to solve problems and make things.

Your intelligence and the workings of your mind seem as deep as your soul, but there are some great tools emerging which can reveal a good working knowledge of what you've been given. I've learned a lot about my intelligence through Howard Gardner's theory of multiple intelligences and the work of Edward DeBono in thinking styles. And while these theories are still developing, they're super valuable in that they dethrone the idea of a single intelligence (like everyone is or isn't math logical) as they highlight the diversity. Here's what I'm learning about this part of us:[39]

1. Input: We all take knowledge in differently. Some input distinctions have been defined as:

a. auditory - some process information best when it's something they hear
b. visual - others need to see something to truly understand it
c. kinesthetic - others still, prefer to handle the input to make sense of it

Knowing how you best receive information may only be a small part of your overall identity map, but it's crucial to validate each part of how you tick. And these are just general headings. For instance, I find that I get big picture information best by hearing something like an audio book, but in order to really grasp the details I need to see or read something. The more nuance I know about how I learn, the more I learn...

A simple learning style test can be found online here:
http://www.personal.psu.edu/bxb11/LSI/LSI.htm
but like all algorithms, they can't describe the nuances of how you receive inputs. I guess the main thing is to be sensitive to and validate your particular style as you pay attention to it. Wanna note anything about your input learning styles here?

....

....

....

....

....

....

....

---

39 I am using the term intelligences and mind interchangeably. I'm also using the terms loosely as the technical definition of intelligence would be more about the computational functions of the brain and not its sensory capacities like being a 'visual learner'... The reason I'm not going into depth on these distinctions is that firstly, I'm not qualified to do so and secondly, I'm using these terms in the vernacular so that we can focus on the identity elements of our minds.

2. Processing: Once stuff is in our heads, we process it with our own intellectual priorities / strengths using those multiple intelligences. According to current M.I. (multiple intelligences) theory, there's eight or nine of these intelligences, but most of us put three or four of our natural strengths together to play music (some with a sheet reading bent, others via improvisation) or build bridges (some via blue prints, others with a hammer)... Gardner and others have defined these intelligent strengths as:[40]

a. **math / logic** is the ability to think critically or in mathematical terms
b. **spatial** is the ability to think in pictures or process within three dimensions like an architect or sculptor
c. **musical** is the ability to process sounds and be sensitive to pitch and tone, etc.
d. **naturalist** is the ability to recognize and classify species and relationships in the natural world, and to interact with that world
e. **inter-personal** is the ability to empathize, see, and appreciate the other
f. **intra-personal** is the ability to be aware of and reflect within yourself
g. **linguistic** is the ability to think in words and sensitively communicate
h. **bodily-kinesthetic** is the ability to think and express in movement

Temple Grandin (an engineer with a PhD in animal husbandry), and others functioning within the autistic spectrum, have helped expand these superficial definitions in beautiful ways, such as the ability to empathetically think in pictures... which she uses in the development of cattle herding systems.[41] Other processing styles—including dyslexia or synesthesia—spotlight the various other ways our neural networks process input. As time goes on, we'll understand more and more of the universe that is our intelligence and processing styles. For now, I think it's worth knowing as much as we can while still being in wonder of all this depth. And also, to know and apply your strengths so you can stop wasting time polishing up on your weaknesses.

I've put a very basic multiple intelligence assessment in the appendix. So if you're interested, jump to the back of the book, answer the questions, then come back here and list what you think are your top three or four intelligences. I've found it helpful to not only know my intelligence strengths, but to combine them as well, which creates a unique approach to the projects I'm working on. Makes me come off as really smart... So what are yours?:

....

....

....

....

....

---

40 A good explanation of these intelligences can be found at: http://enhancinged.wgbh.org/research/multi/examples.html

41 Have a read of her brilliant story *Thinking in Pictures - My Life With Autism* or watch of the film with Claire Danes entitled *Temple Grandin*.

3. Output: Once we receive input and process it, we each have a unique way of expressing our mind's identity. I see this expression as the place where our personality and mental processing come together. Expressed, for instance, by how we design clothes in a certain way or how we function in teams. The beauty of discovering and articulating our personality is that we get to define our connections with people from the inside-out. Which means we stop looking for a certain kind of job or status in order to be acceptable. We are who we are—and it's more than enough. As we use various tools to discover out mind's output, we'll gain a sense of self that can be more at ease connecting our intelligence to the work of our hands.

For example, my brother-in-law John fought with his education until about the age of 16 when an internal interest in health, and in particular for surgery, was inspired. From that point he dedicated himself to gain the right input (a medical education), processing according to his strengths (spatial, interpersonal...), and then expressing himself as an academic surgeon. His mind's identity created a structure for his life which included on-going education, medical practice, teaching, and writing. He also expresses himself as a father and as an entrepreneur in the field of simulated medical procedures... which I think displays the typical diversity all of us possess. Having grasped some of the priority and capacity of his mind's identity, John has created a diverse lifestyle which naturally extends to, and blesses, the world around him.

Your mind on Myers-Briggs?

I think Myers-Briggs and StrengthsFinder are particularly good at helping you understand your mind's output, or what I'd call your identity's intelligence. As an example, Blue is going to summarize how this has worked for him in his life:

I'd like to combine our chapter four discussion about Myers-Briggs with this section on our mind's identity. I want to keep the integration of these various elements (Myers-Briggs / Mind , Soul, Body etc.) in front of you so we don't get stuck or too focused any single part of identity.

One of the things I do each year is help run a large youth camp. There's over 4,000 in attendance so you can imagine the massive logistical undertaking necessary to pull it off. I'm so lucky to serve as part of a great team with some very gifted people in the mix. For my part though, Myers-Briggs has helped me see that I'm a **P** (perceiving) which means I'm pretty open ended. I see the big picture, patterns, and most of the time feel pretty confident about pulling it all together. One of my main roles at camp is running the day to day programme. Let's use that as an example of how this tool (**MBTI**) reveals a part of my mind's identity.

Input: I am highly **kinesthetic**. How that works for me is that I need to experience what I learn. I need to touch it, feel it, and then apply the information. For example, when I'm involved in the programme I don't want to be too prescriptive and just fill in the run-sheet. I want to be in the audience and experience the same thing everyone else is experiencing. I want to laugh at the funny stuff, cry when I am moved, I want to feel the energy when things are going crazy. This is the best way I can 'intuit' what's really going on (the **P**erceiving part coming through).

Processing: As far as the processing goes, I depend on my '**linguistic**' intelligence. From what I feel / see, I naturally (and hopefully sensitively) put those thoughts into words. Usually it's on the spot in front of thousands of people.

Output: The results are what would appear to be unstructured (this is the difference between the **P**erceiving and the **J**udging). From a combination of being part of what's happening—hearing the speakers, feeling the energy, listening to the story unfold—I can then contribute to what I sense is developing. For me this can't be a formula or too structured. As long as the basics of the programme are in place, so it doesn't fall apart, I'm really happy to leave the rest open ended and pull it together as we go.

Note: In the coming chapters, we'll have some practical tools to add these bits to your overall identity map, so note down whatever comes to you now and we can combine it with all the other stuff later.

Identity and your body

The third aspect of this broad pallet is your **physical makeup** or your **body**. I like how the Bible describes this facet as your **strength**, the physical representation of self that reflects what's going on inside... I'm mentioning this dimension of our identity last not because it's unimportant, but because it's been made too important in a world where, sadly, identity has become about what your body looks like and what it can do. When you don't know who you are, your body becomes a front to cover up the loss. Marketers love this kind of insecurity and do their best to capitalize on it. But our body / strength is an expression of what's within, and shouldn't be a mere shell to exhibit popular makeup. Our countenance shines when it's an honest vehicle for the soul, which I'm sure you've seen from time to time in others, and maybe even in yourself. Our physical self is a collaborator with the soul and mind which adds a beautiful touch to the deep and wonderful world within.

Similar to your soul (core identity) and mind (intelligences and processing styles), you don't get to choose your body. You can foster all three of these identity expressions, but you don't choose the color of your eyes, or the content of your soul. You're blessed with them and have no say in what form that blessing comes. And therefore you cannot complain or worry about it. I would have loved to have a smooth Somalian or Norwegian complexion (I'm not picky, I'd have taken any color as long as it was smooth), but instead was handed down a WASP / American Indian blotch of ruddiness. But the more I've been freed up to be my whole self, I find it hasn't really mattered to anyone *but* me. The truth is, by celebrating the interactions between your soul and body, your physicality reaches its amazing potential.

In order to appreciate your physical identity, it's helpful to understand and nourish the body you've been given. Here are a few areas to consider:

Your history: Where have you come from? What did they eat? What values and physical traits have you inherited? Knowing this stuff is important for a few reasons. Your DNA includes dietary patterns that should be understood and developed (some negative that should be eliminated and some positive which should be nurtured). This physical heritage should be honored and celebrated, which also has a direct impact on your health. Your historical connection with a certain part of the world reveals the kind of place most suited to you. Knowing where you've come from also gives you a sense of place. Being grounded with a name, a people, and a land, reminds you that you belong, and can therefore extend that belonging to others. My mother has done a fantastic job of going back as far as possible to show her children that we came from somewhere, and that we have a diverse and wonderful story to carry on. This roots my identity in a broad group of people and helps move me past myopic self-centeredness.

Wanna ask your family about your roots? Note anything about your history that's worth pursuing:

....

....

....

....

Your health: Being aware of your inherited body's propensity for skin cancer or heart disease (I have to look out for both, thanks a lot!), or knowing how your metabolism functions best, has tons to do with how *you* function, and therefore feel, and therefore act. This can be as detailed as tracking thyroid function (a key indicator for health even amongst children) to simply staying fit. Health is related to identity in that you are your best self when you're healthy. Both your soul and your mind depend on a healthy body to express themselves. You already know this, but like me, may need to know your true value before you take health more seriously. This is where a healthy sense of identity comes in. Hopefully, during the journey of this book, you'll change your regime in order to facilitate a healthier personal expression?

Your health also shows an aspect of identity described as your countenance:
> (ORIGIN Middle English : from Old French *contenance* 'bearing, behavior,' from *contenir* (see **contain**). The early sense was [bearing, demeanor,] also [facial expression,] hence [the face.]).

This countenance also reflects your mental health which comes across in relationships (from job interviews to a musical performance) and reveals how you're doing / being. Taking care of your physical and mental health allows you to show others who you are at your best.

What are some things you already know you should be doing in terms of improving your health?

....

....

....

....

....

....

Your cells: Related to your health, another aspect of appreciating your physical identity comes from learning to listen to the mind / body connection. Our bodies are constantly communicating to us through obvious channels (like pain) and the more subtle mediums (like tension or stress). It's speaking about the physical and relational connections in our life and reflecting how we're doing in both fields. For instance, when my relationships are out of sorts, my body knows it! When I stop to rest, I sometimes get sick because my body finally has a chance to get out of overdrive and remind me that things aren't well. These mule kicks are my body forcing me to reckon with the relational / physical connection. But what if I could learn to listen to it's more subtle messages before getting kicked?

My physical self has a distinct personality which I need to understand. I've already mentioned metabolism above, but there's so much more I need to know about my inner workings to function better, heal, and flow as a person. For instance, homeostasis is the steady state our cells need to operate in to be healthy. So if I introduce too much sugar to my system and throw it out of balance, I can develop onset diabetes... My body is constantly communicating within its various systems to maintain this balance. And a huge part of this balance is affected by my identity / self-image, which if out of balance may be why I'm eating too much sugar in the first place, right? So if I could listen in on this communication, be sensitive to it and know what I'm listening for, the health of my identity can have a positive effect on my body (and therefore my life). My only tip here is to get into meditation.[42]

Your style: This is the fun part. If you're living out identity in an integral way, you get to craft a physical portrait that exposes the deeper aspects of your heart and mind. You get to celebrate your humanity with layers of color, texture, and smell; all of which combine for a unified expression. Once you lose the wannabe mentality, you regain the unique appearance that not only speaks of your diversity, it empowers others to be themselves alongside you. Again, I mention this last because too many people start at this level and try to reverse-engineer their identity, which becomes a status quo disaster.

Close the gap

Most of us take a very casual approach to our physical selves, but I think we have to take our bodies a lot more seriously, even right down to the cellular level. These neglected parts are killing us, and therefore killing our motivation to change. In fact, one of my great struggles in working with people and their identity is helping them take action. Most people simply aren't motivated to make real changes in their lives, which I think is largely based on our mental and physical health. Practically, I can't think of any one source to point you towards for understanding the mind / body connection. I guess being sensitive to it means your radar will be looking for this, listening better. Which is what I do. Knowing that the mind / body link is important draws me towards podcasts, news articles, certain books, and conversations, all of which further my understanding and practice with this connection. The results are things like learning to fast well, meditate (with deep breathing practices), or just being aware of my physical self throughout the day so

---

42 I've found a couple wonderful podcasts about meditation on Krstia Tippett's *On Being* which you can begin with: http://being.publicradio.org/programs/2011/healthy-minds/

that I'm breathing right, eating better... I haven't gone into the more hippie aspects of yoga, but I probably will one day soon. I mean, like a manly kind of yoga, that isn't even called yoga... but something like 'ManStretch' or 'BreatheTough'.

There's often a huge gap between the way we think of ourselves today and being fully aware of all the aspects we've covered in this chapter. When I started this process, I knew I had a soul, a mind, and a body but I didn't know much more. You may be just waking up to a lot of this, and if so, don't lose heart. Your identity is resilient. Even though it may be a mystery, repressed or forgotten, its spark cannot go out. As the Irish poet John O'Donohue puts it:

> *"Your identity is not equivalent to your biography. There is a place in you where you have never been wounded, where there's a seamlessness in you, and where there is a confidence and tranquility in you..."*[43]

Finding that space and giving it room to breath again will unleash the immutable gift you've been given. It's primarily creative and will make a way for itself. And when I say creative, I mean that its main role is to make something; it wants to get out and play. Once you give it an inch, it'll want a million miles. My hope is that as you unpack and remember all that you are, you'll be able to stand on the bow of that knowledge and look way out to sea. As I've said, your life and future depend on your ability to see what's inside. Because it's from that place that you get to project what YOU'll be doing next year, in 5 years, or in 15. But don't fret about that now, there's a process and we're starting to unfold it. At this point, it would be great if you could go out with a few friends and celebrate the fact that you're all fearfully and wonderfully made. Speak out what you know about each other, your distinct personalities, intelligences, and those glimpses of each others souls. Get used to giving encouragement at a deeper level, we all desperately need it.

---

43 From an interview with Krista Tippett entitled *The Inner Landscape of Beauty*. http://being.publicradio.org/ programs/john_odonahue/transcript.shtml

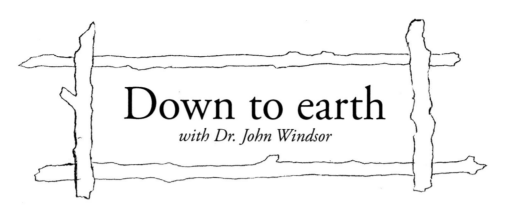

Down to earth
with Dr. John Windsor

That identity can be considered in terms of soul, mind, and body is helpful, for each dimension uniquely contributes. The appropriate development of all three contributes to a wholeness of identity, while the atrophy or hypertrophy of one dimension over the others may explain a problem with spiritual, personal, or social identity. For me, identity is not discovered and then stored for future use. Identity is an ongoing discovery, an unfolding or flowering. It is a present continuous process and not an achievement or a summative articulation. And it is certainly more then the sum of its parts, so tidily dissected in this chapter. For me there is sometimes a dissonance between modern psychological theory, which puts 'me' in the center, and my experience of God and the way He works in my life when I choose to surrender the center. I see identity but dimly, but what I see is taking shape, and it goes something like this.

Healthy identity is found in relationships. Relationships
with others and with God. I cannot think of myself outside of those I am part of. My regard for myself comes from how others regard me. And their regard is based on the way I present myself to them. And so others provide the mirror in which I see myself and shape my identity. The opinion of others is a major determinant of identity. While we cannot choose our parents, whose influence on how we regard ourselves is unmatched, we can choose those we spend time with and those to whom we give ourselves. In fact relationships, which I regard as the fabric of life, are initiated and established by the way we give ourselves. And the simple fact is that we cannot truly give ourselves if we do not have a health identity. Finding ourselves, understanding ourselves, and appreciating ourselves are necessary steps toward healthy identity. These are the struggles of adolescence and individuation, and sometimes the struggles of a lifetime.

Certain things have helped me develop a healthier identity. The first has come from my family and extended family within which I have been nurtured and encouraged. The second has been a growing appreciation of who I am as a son (beloved, redeemed and enabled) of my Father. And then there has been the deep seated motivation to make a meaningful contribution to those around me, which seems keener as I age. Dan Pink's work referred to in this chapter resonates with me. The sense of direction and purpose of my professional life was formed early. In the words of 'a student's doctors prayer' given to me by my father as I entered University, I wanted my work 'to be a sacrament', and I wanted a calling which 'spent me in His service'. The mastery of my skills as a surgeon and leader were just a matter of time, practice, and experience. The real challenge was Pink's first dimension, that of empowerment. Indeed the biggest impediment to a meaningful and durable contribution has so often been the way I have thought of myself. It can hinder. My sense of self and purpose is now tied to the realization that life becomes meaningful through the service of others and that a healthy identity is an essential enabler.

Chapter Six

The Flow

An Overview of the Flow

1. FAMILY DESIGN
2. RESTORING THE YEARS
3. MAPPING THE TRUTH
4. FINDING THEMES
5. STORYTELLING THE FUTURE
6. MAKING PLANS
7. GETTING HELP

Identity can act as a compass in your life-long pilgrimage. Your journey has already covered a lot of ground and will continue into uncharted directions. But there is an arc to your story that I'd like to plot out with you. I've found that by knowing even just a little of where my story started, where it is now, and what I may be able to expect, gives me a lot of grace for the road ahead.

This path includes working through the origins of identity, dealing with points of its departure, rebuilding it, and applying a holistic process to create a better future. Knowing the details of this path is a huge help in being able to walk it out, especially if we've been crippled in any way. So, I'd like to share how I've learned to see this roadmap from two very different perspectives. The first view came from my being the recipient of a typical outside-in approach to life; getting told what to learn, where to work, and how to live... with little or no reference to who I was. The second perspective I'd like to offer was formed by working with lots of people who were very clear about who they were, and also from raising my family with the intention of learning to live, and teaching my kids to live, from the inside-out. Which meant all of us focusing on identity, choosing an education that facilitated that identity, and creating a life based on that identity.

What I'd like to do in this chapter is to summarize these milestones in the path you're on. I'll cover what I think is the order of their importance, to give you a sense of their flow or chronology. In particular, I'd like to outline the basics in knowing who you are right through to mapping out a future based on that knowledge. We'll then look at these areas in detail in the coming chapters and workshop them for your unique situation. I hope you'll take the time to work these details, because in doing so you may be able to regain some lost ground. Consider this chapter then, as an opportunity to go back over the key junctions of your life and perhaps take another shot at them, only this time from the inside-out. Again, this is an overview, so process or note what you can at this point and we'll capture the details later.

By the way, this overview is not meant to come off as 'THE Way' to live or 'Patrick's Seven Secrets'. Instead, I see this as touching the key areas of life which need to be addressed, understood, and to a degree, re-written. They're macro puzzle pieces which I think are really important, but how you work on them will, of course, be your call. It's not about me prescribing solutions, even if I come off like that some times.[44]

1. The Familial Design

Where identity is formed, appreciated, and developed...

The principle: As mentioned in my previous book, I think our parents represent two distinct qualities which we observe and absorb as children. Our mothers start us off by fostering our sense of **security** through modeling unconditional love and provision. This overall security gives us a platform to learn about ourselves and the world around us through play, language, and breaking things. Her unconditional love allows our identity to unfold unhindered by expectations. Her provision gives us the basic physical and emotional nourishment to develop our inner and outer lives. Our fathers build on this by developing our sense of **significance**—by acknowledging our value and encouraging its destiny. This sense of significance becomes the precursor to confidence and creativity. The specific value statements he instills solidify our growing knowledge of self, while the dreams he facilitates give a sense of opportunity or destiny. The thousands of mini-messages we receive from our parents in these regards create a platform for living from the inside-out.

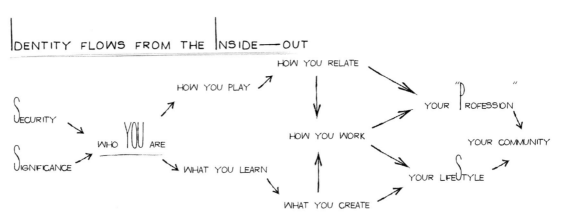

---

44 I'm actually a very nice person. But I do have a tendency to sound like 'this is the only way to do things...' It's just that I'm passionate and I've found some really helpful clues to life which I share in an intense way.

Growing up like this would be pretty sweet (and if this was your world, you need to call your parents and remind them how awesome they are). What tends to happen to most of us is quite different...

My upbringing: I can sum up my identity development through 18 years at home in the following way: My mother: "You could be President", and my father: "Get a job". My mother didn't tell me how I could be President and my father didn't tell me which job I could get or why, but there you have it. I remember a lot of useless classes at school and even more useless peer pressure, but aside from my mom's general encouragement, I didn't learn much about myself at all during those years. I knew I liked certain kinds of music and that I liked to draw and write, none of which was really appreciated in school or fostered at home. I hope your experiences were much more helpful, but the result for me was that I had to learn about identity the hard way once I left home.

Starting over: With some of my close friends, and then with my own family, I've learned four crucial things about identity. First, **identity is obvious if you pay attention**. My kids were naturally themselves and displayed identity in their play, language, and relationships. Second, **identity needs encouragement and facilitation**. We're all vulnerable and need people in authority (people we trust) to validate what's forming inside us. Third, **identity is massively diverse**. Instead of being frustrated that my kids wouldn't focus on book-work, I tried to appreciate and help them see that synthesizing their abilities was much more fulfilling than drilling down on one subject. Forth, **identity takes time**. Each of my kids (and friends) develop at a different pace. Acknowledging this is essential for the more nuanced aspects of identity to unfold.

The important thing is to recognize that family is THE starting place for identity. Get it right and a lot goes really well, and creatively so. Get it wrong and it takes years of untangling. But even in the worst case scenario, I've found that recovery was not only possible, but happened a lot faster than I'd imagined thanks to the resilience of our souls. Even better, I learned that I could have another go with my own family and help them get going even earlier in life—which they can do for their kids too...

2. Restoration

Where we go back and reckon with any loss in order to move forward.
I'm a big fan of how positive forward movement can heal and deal with issues from our past. But due to the nature of identity, I think we have to look back and acknowledge stunted growth in order to see a way ahead. For instance, if encouragement from people in authority is an essential part of validating identity (which I think it is), and our upbringing lacked this kind of affirmation (which I think most of us have), then we can't just press ahead without it. We'll just get blocked at some point or run into the past as it cycles back around. If negative words (anti-identity) have crushed things inside of us we've probably developed weird personas.[45] So taking some time to restore what was lost will help us from going in circles, or dating the wrong person...

---

45 The Latin term literally means a mask, character played by an actor.

I AM A BUILDING BLOCK

I AM INTIMATE

I AM A LEARNER

Here's what I suggest we focus on:

The places of authority: I think we should go back and review what happened to our identity in the key relationships of our lives. How did our families speak life or death into our identity? What messages did we receive from school that either confirmed or distracted us from who we were trying to be? What other places (church, clubs, work, etc.) had a key impact on us and what was the result? Articulating these experiences helps us see possible points of departure, or events that defined what we've now become. I think this is essential because we need to see where may have got shot down etc., and are therefore still afraid to take risks.

For me, people in authority were those who always had a different idea (than my own) of what was best for me. I always seemed in conflict with teachers etc., because my soul was trying to fight for itself. The problem is that I developed a general reaction against authority altogether, even towards those being helpful. I'm now trying to reverse that trend. *Does anything come to mind here? Things you want to process?*

Expectations: What were some of the pressures or expectations put on you from those places of authority? My father telling me to get a job is not bad advice, but that I should take any job just to create financial security is an unhelpful expectation. I think it's really unfair for anyone who had the opportunity to develop our identity but who did a poor job of it, to then turn around and expect us to be or do certain things we weren't properly equipped for. Part of this pressure comes from the broken dreams and lame expectations over their own lives, as in, "I had to walk six hours in the snow, **just to get to my shoes**". Learning to extract good advice from inherited expectations takes some skill and grace, but for now, what are the chains you carry that are placed on you by others? Especially parents, close friends, teachers, and spiritual types.[46]

---

46 By the way, I don't think God ever places unrealistic expectations on us. But we can feel these nonetheless as a result of the weird things people say in the name of God.

....

....

....

....

....

What I've tried to do with my kids is limit my expectations to their passions. I do slip from time to time, offering suggestions that aren't really where they want to go... Overall though, I try to develop expectations based on what they want to achieve, and then try to help them turn their objectives into milestones or goals they can set for themselves. We'll see how that goes.

Identity statements: What are some impressions of yourself that you came away with from your upbringing? We're looking for the positive and negative words that may still define you. We need to see what's true and build on it, and what's become you but is now holding you back. For instance, a positive word might be that you're a highly relational person, and so you've become just that... While a negative word might be that you were not smart enough to get into medicine, and so you place that same stigma against any new education options... Try and list a few of these impressions, or 'I am' statements, that got attached to you over the years and place them in true and untrue columns:

UNTRUE LABELS PLACED UPON ME   TRUE I AM STATEMENTS GAINED FROM THE PAST

Having an intra-personal intelligence as a teenager, I thought a lot about my self and most of it was negative. The positive stuff wasn't tethered to reality either because there was so little encouragement or validation to be had. What we've tried to do with our kids is speak out clear and substantial words of encouragement at key times (birthdays etc.), or when something happens that allows us to see a bit of their soul. We don't always get it right, and we have to be careful for those words not to become prescriptive (as in "wow honey, see how he cut that steak, he'd make a great doctor"), but overall, calling out what we see is setting some really good foundations for them.

Stripping back the layers: As a result of reviewing the last three areas, you may slowly be able to strip back the layers of a created persona or mask. You may see how certain points of departure or discouragements formed reactions, which eventually forged a survivors mask (fake persona). In the process, you should also be able to see the strengths that held you through that period, and identity truths that stayed in place regardless. Or where the encouragement and validation you received was so precious and powerful, it actually grew into something beautiful. The key here is to strip off the reactions but hold onto the strengths, the truths about you. Sometimes this is done by speaking it out, visualizing it, or just praying. But action needs to be taken to solidify the positive aspects.

Personally, this has taken me quite some time. The jumble of what's really me, and what I've developed as reactions, takes effort to untangle. Helping my friends and children to understand their own identity has also brought clarity to my own process. You could help your process along by making your identity renewal a group effort.

Re-parenting your identity: Although we're kinda grown up now, we still need to affirm the original design of identity development. This is done primarily through our relationships with people who've had a symbiotic connection with us, or an ability to see into our souls. This isn't restricted to our biological parents, although if we can we should either start or continue the conversation with them. We can also do this with others who are really committed to us—people who will help walk through the primary design by facilitating an unconditional love, provision, value, and destiny to reform our growth.

As odd as it may feel right now, this re-parenting starts by us reminding or asking people of authority in our lives to regain their place as encouragers. It may take years to get this ramped up and we'll need a tremendous amount of grace and patience to stick to the process. But if we can rebuild even a little on their past or recent encouragement, we may also regain that child-like ability to take risks again. This could lead to new experiments which may get us back in touch with the dreams of our youth. Because dreams of this nature come from the soul, the place where your identity was always trying to communicate from. Given another opportunity through authoritative encouragement, that inner voice may come out loud and clear.

What do you think about re-engaging with your parents, or whoever, in this way?

....

....

....

....

....

My process has involved many people, including my parents, parents-in-law, siblings, teachers, friends, and God. And again, part of the re-parenting in my life has happened as I've parented my own children, which was in itself taking a risk on my identity as a father. Parenting, as scary as it is when you're lacking in self-image, has given me a framework to understand my own identity issues and helped me see a way forward. For you, it may be a very different process with very different people, but it will probably include taking relational risks so be ready for that.

3. Mapping

Where we extract the details of your identity.

Our lives so far are being stored in millions of three second intervals (about the time span in which the brain captures events). All these events form a living narrative which we can draw from to see who we've been. My theory is that the brain remembers, among other things, what the soul knows is important. These mental highlights are stories we can use to unpack identity statements. Those statements, and I mean lots of them, can help create a visual map which will give us a fantastic overview of our complex selves.

Until around the age of 22, I could mostly recall a lot of rejection and only a little bit of encouragement. Like bad '80s hair, my identity map would have been a lopsided mess of confusion. But as I started asking deeper questions, in a new context, I started to see a long and diverse list of 'I am' statements which seemed to keep unfolding. As I sketched these statements out on scraps of paper, and then later on digital mind maps, I started to get a feel for the overview. Which is the same process I'd like to go through with you. Your version, that is.

Throughout this book / journal, we'll unpack events and the stories of your life in order to see your 'I am' statements. For instance, when I was around 14 I remembered staying up all night with a friend talking about a girl he liked. At the time, I was crap at forming my own relationships but I actually had a lot of humorous advice for him. In looking at that event, I can extract things like "I am satirical" or "I'm an advisor"... There's a lot more to it, but that's the basic process: look at the story and extract an identity statement from who you were being at the time. In order to see the breadth and inter-connectedness of all your 'I am' statements, we need a lot of material to work with. To get you warmed up for the rest of this book, please have a go with the following exercises.

A. Warmups: What do you already know that's true about your identity? What's obvious about you? *Like "I'm generous" or "I'm good at math".* If any of those 'I am' statements are generic ("I'm musical"), try unpacking them a bit (like, "I'm a performer", or "I'm a composer", or "I'm an improvisor")... See how many things you can come up with from the top of your head.

....

....

....

....

....

....

B. Family: What positive words came from your family while growing up or recently? At this point, we're only interested in the positive words. Can you convert these into 'I am' statements that you feel truly represent you?

....

....

....

....

....

C. Stakeholders: What have other key people said about you that you think is true, and represents something in your soul? Even if it was encouraging an action like an achievement at school, what was the identity piece motivating that achievement?

....

....

....

....

....

D. Environments: What places were you drawn to growing up and why? We're you hanging out at the beach, or the library, or the place where the cool kids were smoking? What motivated you towards 'third places'[47] and what did you want to do there? Try seeing those places as spaces for you to *be your self.* What were you being?

....

....

....

....

....

....

E. Big wins: Write a quick story of a single success in your life. Something you felt you did really well, regardless of what others thought. What were the things that motivated you? What were the particulars involved in the achievement? What were you BEING in this success?

....

....

....

....

....

....

....

....

F. Dreams: What are some memorable dreams (daydreams or otherwise) that you can still recall? What were some motives behind the dream? Be careful to not judge yourself, just try to see what the dream says about who you were being in the dream.

....

....

....

....

....

---

47 The third place refers to social surroundings separate from the two usual social environments of home and the workplace.

G. Soul questions: As mentioned before, we want to unfold your soul's **spiritual**, **social**, and **personal identity**. We will unpack these dimensions in the chapter on mapping, and you'll probably end up with a huge list of identity statements just from these three areas. We'll then add other **personality / intelligence** statements you've already received (via StrengthsFinder etc.), to get an even bigger map of your soul, mind, and body. From this overview, we'll move on to the next part.

4. Themes

Where we look at the inter-activity and possible synthesis of your identity statements.

Having a long list of personal attributes or a broad visual identity map will be wonderful, but also a bit daunting. After celebrating your expansive nature, you may get a little confused as to what to do with all that stuff. What may seem like a confusing list of words is actually the foundation for you to make a new thing in the world. The point is to capitalize on your diversity through synthesizing various 'I am' statements into creative possibilities. We want to make connections between things like your relational skills and your love for nature, to see what kind of projects / jobs you could create from that mix.

A good starting point is to look at natural **themes**. Themes are the main motivations which keep popping up in our lives, or the way we apply our identity throughout the day. For instance:
- *Relational* themes reveal the style and values with which you relate to others.
- *Environmental* themes show how you choose to live and create a space for others to share.
- *Creative* themes show how you make things, why you make them, and what you hope to do with them in the future.
- *Educational* themes show how you learn and apply knowledge, and what ways you'd like to share it with others.
- *Vocational* themes show what motivates you to interact with the market, or world around you, sometimes making money from that connection and other times not, but in all ways creating social value.

As you start to group your 'I am' statements into these major life themes, you start to see possibilities or outcomes. The idea is not to reduce the complexity or boil you down a short list, but rather to start brainstorming with all these cool lego-like pieces, putting them together in uncharted ways. You could also just take random statements on the list and ram them together to see what you could be or do with that. Overall though, themes help you recapture a sense of potential which spans to the development of a lifestyle covering all 168 hours of your week.
(Note: One of the core ideas of this book is to help you avoid pegging simple identity statements to possible job descriptions. We want you to see how the breadth of your identity can lead to the life-long stories you tell about how you'd like to relate, create, learn, or work...)

5. Stories

Where you develop a narrative of your future

Stories have had a powerful role in humanity throughout the ages because they're grounded in reality. They come from real lives, and they create real lives. Fantastical examples can lead us to think that stories are merely a form of amusement, something to medicate us through the drudgery of life. But the very reason they have any effect at all is because they show us what's possible. Science fiction is a good example in how it projects future scenarios from the basis of grounded values like exploration, creativity, and as always, love. In this case, life mimics art *and* art mimics life.

Stories are the sexier version of project planning. They move away from the sterile approaches of setting disconnected goals and objectives, towards bringing ideas to life by igniting our souls. For instance, getting a university degree for a job to survive is a just a project; studying Migration & Refugee Studies in Cairo to place a proper dent in the world is an adventure worth living. Stories draw out the details of identity and put them to work in a believable future. At their core, stories move past defining a possible job towards a life truly worth living.

At some point you'll need to form a narrative of your own life. When you to start placing your relational, creative, and vocational themes together, you'll see a larger story that could become a direction, a destiny... From there, you can break that overall direction into doable seasons. The tendency is to limit yourself to one aspect of your story, like which job you'd be doing, or what your wife should look like... So in the telling of your larger story, you'll need to encompass as much of your broad identity as possible. Spread over decades, your story is about the life you'll live, not just the way you'll pay for that life.

Since this is such a lost art, I want to get you thinking about storytelling your future now so you're ready for when we get to that part of the book. We'll start with simple brainstorming to tease out your dreams. This is done by looking at the identity map you'll create, and from it placing various pieces together in different ways. Looking closely at your 'I am' statements naturally informs these stories, so it's not hard to do. For instance, if I wrote down that **I loved cooking, training others, and helping develop relationships**, what could I do by combining all that? As you start to put these diverse ideas together, you can then write out a short story of what a week, or a month, of your life would look like in 15 years. It can include your relationships (will you have a family?), creativity, environment, education, and work. I want you to see what you could grow into over all those 15 years.

Your story may start out by describing the simple connection between your love for kids and teaching in a school, or how you like coffee so want to run a cafe. The more your identity unfolds, the more nuanced and creative your story will become... Even still, the idea of a longer term story freaks some people out as they just want a plan. But that won't do. You have to see that your life is not a done deal or fated to one thing. You're capable of so much, and need to see at least a glimpse of the eternity you carry around inside. From that vantage point, you can at least project a few very different scenarios before taking the next step.

My experience growing up was not about stories, but rather groundless daydreams. I had a lot of ideas of what I wanted to do, but no real reference points to build on. So, I just kept daydreaming and did very little at all. With my kids however, I've listened closely to those childish ideas. At the age of eight, Jasmine went from wanting to be a mechanic to a shepherdess within six months. Fine. What I was listening for was what her soul wanted to say. I didn't really see the artist inside during those early years, but it was there; her quirky nature, her love of the natural world, and her random processing skills were all coming together. Her ability to eventually get there was partly based on the freedom she had to bounce from idea to idea without getting checked or blocked along the way. Stories, and the way they move inside of us, are a natural planning tool. They need a lot of room to grow before they get acted out. As you move through these pages, give yourself that room for your story to re-emerge.

6. Seasons, projects and plans

Where, over time, you turn your story into commitments
Committing to something has become quite a problem for many of us. It's actually really natural to invest time and energy in the things we love, but for those of us who grew up out of touch with that passion, commitment meant a form of slavery to the things we hated. Thus, our present fear of commitment. As the rubber of your identity meets the road of your future, the demons of failure and fear will try and remind you that you cannot succeed, even as the rules are changing inside of you. When you look over your stories, and it comes to a point of choosing, committing, and acting on them, how will you proceed?

First: This time it's different. You are about to create relationships, work, and homes, etc. out of your identity, not despite it. Your actions will not be motivated from the expectations of others, but from the living truths and creative possibilities you've always had inside. It's still a risk, but this time it's YOUR risk.

Second: Having a sense of destiny or destination that's aligned with your soul allows you to deconstruct the story into reasonable steps or projects, all of which rebuild confidence because they're doable on a day to day basis.

Third: You'll take steps towards the larger story because you now have milestones. Milestones are built on the fact that in two years, you're going to have a level of maturity, skill, or whatever's needed to reach those goals. In this way, you don't have to achieve the whole thing at once, but can set reasonable expectations to reach the next challenge...

Taking your story and turning it into manageable steps gives you a sense of possibility. Each step is like a season which has its own life and process attached. Once you can get your head around that season, you're away. In this sense, you're not basing your choices on the **confidence** to make life happen, you're simply using your **authority** to be yourself. The confidence comes after you've had more experience. It's like drawing on your childlike strength to dream a way forward. Eleanor Roosevelt once said: "Because they have so little, children must rely on imagination rather than experience."[48]

I've found it really helpful to map out my larger story as doable seasons. Seeing the story develop over time is way easier than trying to make a huge change happen immediately. Here are the five seasons I use to make the larger story happen:

A. Experimentation: Once I have the overall story, I may want to test a few things before I invest that 10,000 hours required to be amazing at whatever. This season allows me to spend a few hundred hours (or a few months) to see the difference between identity and interest. *(time frame: 3 months to 2 years)*

B. Education: After the experiments, this season allows me to educate or re-educate myself along the lines of my strengths. It may not be formal at all, but rather a customized curriculum I put together based on my identity themes and the goals of my story. *(time frame: 2 to 6 years)*

C. Apprenticeship: This season is where I put that education to practice alongside people who are really good at what I want to do. *(time frame: 2 to 4 years)*

D. Production: This season is where I start to hit my pace and make / create / build what I've always wanted to. I should also be creating my environment, and establishing my relationships at home, and in the community, in conjunction with my work, so I'm bringing an entire lifestyle together. *(time frame: 5 to 8 years)*

E. Multiplication: This season is where I start mentoring others and help them move forward based on what I've learned. And having learned even more about myself, I can branch into whole new chapters of my story.

I think another important aspect in working out these seasons is the location you develop them in. Most of us have become disconnected from the land and replaced a sense of home with cities that offer the highest pay/entertainment ratio. We therefore fear creating our own future because it threatens the circus-like platform we've developed. But you don't have to design clothes in NYC to be happy, and you don't have to practice law in London to be fulfilled. So, when you think of your larger story, and where you'd like to live out the seasons of its creation, think of creating a home over 20 or 30 years. It'll have a radical affect on you, and the consistency of being in one place may make your plans a lot more doable.

The final benefit of creating seasons out of your larger narrative is that it helps make sense of today. Once you have a destination, you can break that down into bite-size steps to get there, including **the one you take right now**. Large projects are beasts to tackle, but if you know what needs to happen in the next six months, to reach your larger goal, then that baby step is a real relief.

---

48 *You Live by Learning*, Westminster John Knox Press, 1960, page 17

7. Help from above

Where I deepen my relationships and add wisdom to my journey

A massive blessing in my life has come from asking for God's help through this entire identity process. I needed help **remembering** who I am, **forgiving** the damage of the past, and **brainstorming** possibilities for the future. I know that at the end of the day, I'm responsible to create with what I've been given, and so I call out the story and make efforts to put it into action. Along the way though, I know there's wisdom beyond myself and the world I inhabit. I know there are foundational truths that many others have called on to build cities (and brew better beer... Monks did that!), treat illnesses, and create art with... I want to call down that kind of relationship and wisdom into my seasons, so that I'm not competing on sheer talent or determination in a world obsessed with both. I want to thrive in a creative way, and do to so, I need to get in touch with what I see as the source of creativity. To do this I ask five basic questions, then add the answers to my daily activities, and therefore the unfolding of my story. Thankfully, it's made a massive difference. Here's what I ask:

A. *What is the nature and character of God in the thing I'm doing / being?*
B. *What do the scriptures say about what I want to make happen?*
C. *What can the natural world around me reveal about how to live / create?*
D. *What, in my field, have those in history learned and what can I learn from them?*
E. *What can I draw from my own life lessons and experiences?*

By asking these questions, I've learned so much from fields ranging from ancient poetry to biomimicry. These create wonderful reflections which I can apply to my own strengths, often in a journey-changing way. I hope you'll also find distinct wisdom for your process. But for now, I just want to highlight that the process is not one of independence, but rather of inter-dependence, and that you can seek a wider audience to develop your story.

So that's the summary of the overall process. Having a

sense of framework has really helped me to know there's some signposts to follow. Not a precise blueprint, but areas to work through and address so that I can move step by step into my own future. As you move through the rest of these pages, I hope that this sense of perspective will inspire your own sense of hope and possibility

Down to earth

with Jacquie Thiessen

I've always wanted to know 'who am I', but life's influences kept subtly or (not so subtly) telling me that it didn't matter, and not to waste my time on such a question. Thankfully I have had some key people speak truth into my life and validate that natural search for a better understanding of self. For me, this involved moving back home, investing in my family, and calling them into my process. While at home, I gave time and energy into seeking out what my childhood, life experiences, character, and God had to say about my identity. Through this process I decided to pursue becoming a midwife and to do so internationally. So I took off to the Philippines and started the training. I also knew that I wanted to continue pursuing photography on the side and planned for the two to collide in the future.

Pursuing midwifery has been a wonderful and trying journey. There have been numerous times where I was ready to quit, pack up, and go home. However, the story-based foundation that my decisions were built on have been crucial in maintaining commitment. My family and my closest friends (so glad I took the time to invest in them) have become my main support group. Every step of my journey I seem to learn more about my maker, his heart, and who he made me to be. The original story that I mapped out (my goals and dreams) has been completely re-worked over and over again, and is becoming way cooler than I could have possibly dreamed! A story can't grow and rock on if it was never imagined in the first place. I'll now be adding counseling skills to my midwife work so I can offer more holistic care. My original photography idea has morphed into film making where I now plan on making documentaries. I want to give voice to the amazing people and cultures I get to be a part of through midwifery. I'm walking in a place of freedom and joy because I just get to be me, all the time. The response of the people in my life is super encouraging. In knowing and just being myself, I've come to like me, in fact I like me a lot. That may sound ridiculous, but for so long I thought I had to be something other than who I am and really didn't like myself at all.

Looking back I think I expected things to be a lot less complex than they are. Yet I'm seeing more beauty and better outcomes from the messy side of life. There have been many times when I've asked myself, "How hard is too hard? Cuz I don't think I can do this." In the past, I was all about the short-term but as I view my long-term future it's become way easier to deal with the hard stuff by breaking down the plan and taking one step at a time. I get to do all this because I am a care giver, communicator, listener, learner, teacher, counselor, creative, passionate, compassionate, discerning, diverse, understanding, adventurous, and hospitable.

Checkpoint:

So far, I think we've laid some groundwork for you to think about your past, to understand your present self, and create some ideas about your future. What I'd like to do now, is go deeper into each of the sections paraphrased in the last chapter so you can build a very broad, but super practical, identity map. I think it would be good, however, if you could do this with a family member, or a close friend, or five. Computerized personality tests, books (including this one), and even one on one life-coaching sessions, all need the help of someone who can hear your soul and add validation to your process. It should go both ways as well, meaning that you're adding to their identity and their future development at the same time. Can you get those people to sit with you over a coffee? I suggest asking for a Generra (Mocha coffee with an orange peel sitting on the bottom which I first met at Uptown Espresso on 4th in Seattle).

Let's start this deeper process by looking at how family shapes our identity...

REMEMBER: TWO ARE BETTER THAN ONE...

Chapter Seven

Family and the forming of your *identity*

"*The mainstream manufactures people as monoculture. It turns us out like cloned rows of apple trees on pesticide-manicured fields. The mainstream 'trains' people by pruning. It forces growth in standardized ways. The song that we sing from within the mainstream is thereby not our own song. It does not issue from the opened gates of the soul. And so our personal branches and cultural roots atrophy away. We yearn for connection with one another and with the soul. But we forget that, like the earthworm, we too are an organism of the soil. We too need grounding.*"

- Alastair McInstosh[49]

---

49 *Soil and Soul*, Aurum Press, 2004, page 1

Our search for identity suffers in a disconnected

world. We drift when the natural tether of maternal security and paternal significance gets dissolved by abuse, neglect, or just too much TV. Slowly at first, but over time we become like dandelion florets blown by any wind of influence, and off into the sky we go looking for a new place. And the farther we fly, the memory of our roots fade. Our gaze is always ahead, looking for it to be better where we're going. And when we land, that new place forms us like we had no DNA at all. And in a foreign place we usually end up buying our identity... Eventually we become tired of this, and like the prodigal have to wonder what our family, after all, may have to do with our future.

Family relationships are super complex and easily left to simmer on the back burner of our lives. They effect everything we do, and yet most of us spend so little time understanding or developing them. As I go into this part of our identity, you may be tempted to wanna just move past it and get onto the other chapters. Understandable. But the influence of our family—historically and presently—runs deep, and we either acknowledge it, or keep running into it the hard way. So, please consider using this chapter to address those things you'd rather not, because one day or another, you will repeat what you haven't understood, healed, and redeemed (that is, as far as it depends on you).

Family makeup is as diverse as the names in the phone book. Your experiences will be very, very different from mine in most ways. However, there are some similarities which I want to process with you. Things like our vulnerability as children to be heard and seen for who we are. Or recognizing the power of words spoken by people in authority. Navigating the social space around us so we learn to collaborate instead of isolate... If we can work on these kind of things, we can gain a sense of what maybe should've happened, and what we can do next. In essence, we need to regain our real name and know its significance.

To assist in that recovery, I'd like to share four key things I've learned about family and identity. And then, have you respond with your impressions or experiences. Have a read and write down your responses, process what you need to, and be as messy as you like. If you're doing this with someone else, take the time to ask each other the questions listed or whatever comes to mind. Just write stuff down, share what you've written, and then go on to the next section. Be observant though, you may want to act on some of the relational things that come up, so be sensitive and make some phone calls or visits if needed.

1. Early signs

Because identity is obvious, relational and crucial

Children will find ways to be themselves in either secure or harsh settings. Some kids joined football clubs with all the flash gear to play out their sporty dreams, while others wrapped a t-shirt with some string and anything else they could find in order to kick that dusty thing through a makeshift net. All the important stuff happens in the heart, so the externals (a store bought or home-made ball), as far as kids are concerned, are not essential to expressing identity. If you look past the environment you grew up in, and into the heart of your motivations as a child, you'll see some early signs of identity.

These signs will often be inspired by the language of the environment. For my kids, it was living near a forest which provided a rich landscape for their imaginations. They became woodsmen and built huts, which later became fodder for their story telling identities. Then they became buccaneers and took up fencing (Épée). As they grew, so did their dreams and expressions, which would attach themselves to real things they could practice on. When Josiah started playing computer games, he'd often try to hack or mod them which foretold of his game design skills. Jordan started taking pictures but soon needed other gear so he could turn that frame into a *Ciné;* to capture stories as they moved. Each of these actions reflected, or was **identical** to, something already in their souls. They were communicating—via their ideas and explorations—a sign. What we tried to do was watch and listen closely to what was fairly obvious. Not that a budding job description was coming online, but rather the multi-faceted identity inside of them was on display like a diamond being turned slowly against the light, revealing different aspects...

It's essential to catch these early glimpses, especially against the light of social norms or expectations. When Josiah started on the computer at nine it was kinda cute, but after a while it became a concern. Was this blocking him from the real world? Was it going to stunt his real growth in some ways? Aren't computer games kinda evil? Um, yes and no. But when we looked at the breadth of his expression, including the board games he was making, the game characters he would spend hours painting, and the lego worlds he was building... we started to see that he wasn't simply a gamer, he was a world-creating, storytelling, educating game designer.

Our kids didn't use words to describe their identity. We didn't walk around with a clip board noting various behaviors, mapping them into cross-referenced statements linked to job possibilities... The discovery came through stories; events played out in their imagination, action, and language. The re-telling of which, whether putting them to bed at night, or our own pondering at their odd behavior, naturally highlighted the important stuff. They would remember what was essential to them, and repeat or add to it in the next day's adventure. In terms of family, the important thing was to let the adventure play out unhindered by premature expectations or a boxed-in, blind curriculum.

When I was a child, I can remember befriending the oddest kids at school. I somehow found the seven-year-olds who had razor blades in their pockets... One such 'friend' went off at me during recess for some reason. I still have this stark memory of his face, thick glasses and crow black hair, yelling at me before he brandished his razor and took a swipe at my stomach. My ever present, cat-like reflexes saved me from being bled on that occasion, but I'm pretty sure it was that same crazy kid that stabbed me with a pencil, the led proof of which can still be seen on my torso. When I look back at my propensity for being around people with stray blades and pencils, and look even closer at why I was with them and what I was doing, I can see the early development of a potential counselor of artists and other crazies:-) I would often be the one they could trust or be accepted by. I'd be the one who they would ask for help with school questions, or to play with because nobody else would. My response then was much like it is today when I meet someone who's being marginalized. Looking back at these stories allows me to see the nuances or early formation of my empathetic, listening, coaching self. So it goes into the mix.

Questions:

What were some things you loved doing as a child? Try and remember a story or two and note as much detail as possible. See if your family has any pictures or home videos that may spark your memory. Ask your parents if you can't come up with anything yourself.

What were you being during that story? Can you break these motivations down to 'I am' statements?

....

....

....

....

....

....

2. Drawing you out

Because identity needs encouragement and facilitation

As various identity traits emerged from our kids, we started to see the connection between those 'I am' bits and their possible future. This made us rethink what they should be learning at school and how we could help them play / create along the lines of these budding strengths. But even more importantly, we could see that their identity was the counterpoint to bad behavior or the darker sides of who they could've developed into. I think we've saved ourselves a ton of pain by focusing on their strengths.

For instance, my son Jordan had tons of energy and friends would often recommend drugging him down a bit. Due to the loss of his two front teeth from a playground accident at one-and-a-half years old, Jordan looked like a clown for the next seven years. He wasn't particularly good at math or other school subjects, and appeared kinda dumb in general. On top of all this, his kinetic nature pushed him to test every boundary which often got him into trouble. So, for all general appearances, he came off as a troublemaker. But when we spent time with him listening to his forest hut ideas, or the stories he would tell us in the living room at night, we would see something different. In looking past the façade of hyperactivity to where that energy was coming from, and where it wanted to go, we caught a glimpse of an intelligence that was very diverse and complex. There were many times where drugs would have created some peace and quiet for us, but it would've dampened the amplification of his identity. His energy levels were in keeping with the kinds of projects he'd soon grow into (like directing film). An outsider's advice would have been to put him in a class and tell him to sit on his hands for 12 years, which I'm positive would have ended badly. But from a father's view, from the ability to see into his mind and soul, it started to make sense that he had this nuclear thing going on inside, a drive to capture real life and tell it's stories in a visceral way.

So instead of prescribing Ritalin, we put a camera in his hand
and set him loose. Instead of speaking about math scores and school behavior, I spent time telling him about the intelligence I saw, the gifts he had, and what he could be if he focused on his strengths. I snuck him into screen-writing workshops when he was 13 in order to develop his storytelling self. We drove hours to certain skateparks so he could make short films and teach the other kids how to do the same. We took daily long walks together, giving his mind and strength a chance to breathe and unpack the myriad ideas racing through. In essence, I encouraged and facilitated the little that I saw and gave him time to draw out what was forming inside. As we did this, the winning side of his identity had a chance to combat the darker potential of his nature. His energy was released by taking pictures and editing short films, instead of damaging property (for the most part anyway). Instead of finding people to hurt, his emotional intelligence had a better story to tell. His intellect found real problems to solve, instead of standardized tests to contend with...

To some degree, we're all balancing our true selves with negative reactions. The true self wants room to grow, but when pushed, the negative reaction or the dark expression of our nature quickly pops out to defend and survive. With Jordan, that tension was ever present and it inspired me to speak out and affirm the good stuff, which didn't always keep the hounds at bay, but over time, gave credence to the real him. When I told him how smart he was, he became his version of smart. When I encouraged the story-teller he was becoming, he became a better story-teller. Not because I created this inside of him, but that through the familial voice of authority, I acknowledged him, then got out of the way.

I AM JOYFUL

I AM TACTILE

I AM A COLLABORATOR

Questions:

Growing up, where were you possibly misunderstood? What statements were made over your life that became misleading?

....

....

....

....

....

....

What chances were you given to be yourself, take risks, and what were the results?

....

....

....

....

....

....

At your worst, what were you reacting to? What was the ying to that yang? Like if you took your bad behavior and called out its opposite, what would that be? For me, my drug filled teenage years were a reaction to a boring education. The ying to that would be "I'm a dynamic learner. I need a challenge and love useful knowledge..."

....

....

....

....

....

....

....

....

....

Who has encouraged you and facilitated your growth? What did they see in you or speak out about you?

....

....

....

....

....

Any other 'I am' statements you can extract from this section?

....

....

....

....

....

3. Acknowledging your range

Because identity is diverse and complex

An ongoing problem resulting from the industrial revolution (in my opinion) is that we're still trying to whittle people down to factory-like job descriptions. If you like machines and cars... you're a mechanic. If you like kids, you're a teacher; and if you can't figure it out, you're a waitress.[50] Educational norms narrow you into a marketable position and you end up introducing yourself with monotone identity statements, as in 'Hello, my name is _____ and I am a _____'.
But children would never do this. If you ask a child to introduce themselves, they'll probably give you their FULL NAME. If you ask what they do, you may be delightfully surprised to hear the litany of activities that has filled their day so far, each thing an expression of who they are. The child has not yet learned to dumb down their name, that is, the name of their soul. It'll take them years to develop that skill and then decades more to go through the painful revelation of what was lost, culminating sometime in the mid of their lives, when they wake up feeling utterly retarded and somewhat lost. (Stupid industrial revolution!)

When Jasmine started making stuff around the age of seven, something was unfolding. When I saw some of her first drawings and paintings, I thought, cool, maybe she's a painter. I know all parents have that reaction, but her creations had distinct perspectives which caught our eye. Then she went on to start crafting things like paper dolls and knitted scarfs, and at some point it looked like she may

---

50 Actually, the waitress may be the only person who doesn't see themselves as their job description. The waitress knows they're something else, someone in transition. They know they're unfolding... The plumber however, is not filling in time waiting to be discovered as an action hero.

be growing into a designer. Um, nope, 'cause then she started writing and playing music—and it went on and on, until I could no longer categorize what she was doing. Which is good, because these typical boxes limit the souls naturally expansive nature. As a dad, though, I wanted to help her find a way to pay for her future. And most of our examples of being able to do that, the typical ones anyway, are singular approaches like being A painter, or A musician, or A writer... I mean, where's the market for a person who's all these things, right? Well, it's everywhere.

What I learned as a dad was to just drink the tea and head down

that rabbit hole. I learned to see how diverse and complex identity was, and to not limit or categorize it within pre-existing norms, even norms like what an 'artist' was. In following Jasmine's lead, observing how she'd go from one project to another, I was seeing the power of creative synthesis. That our 'I am' pieces are not designed to press us into service on a single point, but that they're meant to spark off of each other and create something entirely different. It's a glimpse of the eternity we have going on inside. Her illustrations would become fairy journals, which would morph into children's books, which would contort into paintings sold in cafes, which would become songs... No single identity statement can support the whole of our lives. It's the combination that makes life amazing. By the way, this process is natural to everyone. Don't consider this the domain of the artist, as though only they have this ability to synthesize and re-create. I've read of computer chip designers who learned layering techniques from their love of nature and observing snow flakes falling on top of each other... We all have the capacity to synthesise once we validate our breadth and are willing to combine our various strengths.

The narrowcasting of our souls is limiting our imagination. The market is not really defined by its present categories or job descriptions. It's a morphing, wide-open space, looking for new ideas and expressions to solve big problems and meet upcoming needs. The tension we feel when choosing a school or vocational direction is the nervous knowledge that we're only picking one of many, many options our souls know we're capable of. But once you stop looking for a job, you might start creating one. The trick is to go back to that diversity and not see it as a confusing array of options, but rather a deep pool of ideas to draw on and mesh together in new ways.

Questions:
Try to describe widely different things you were doing when you grew up.

....

....

....

....

....

....

Jump to today. Try and describe the disparate fields you're interested in like music, sports, politics, etc., and be as specific as you can about what in those fields interests to you.

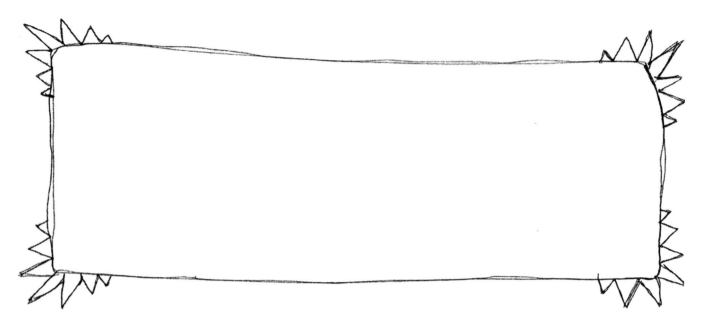

How did your family / school / church or whatever respond or react to your breadth as a person? Were you narrowed into a certain kind of school or class? Did the definition help you in any way, draw out other strengths? What got lost in the process?

....

....

....

....

....

....

What 'I am' statements can you extract from this section?

....

....

....

....

....

....

4. Giving yourself some room

Because identity takes time to unfold

A lot of people I talk to really want to get on with their lives. The pressure they feel is based on assumptions—or comparisons with their friends who seem to all be getting married, or have good jobs, and own homes, or whatever 'success' looks like in their part of town. They feel behind somehow, even though most people who went straight to college don't love what they're learning, while others don't necessarily like their jobs, and the married's with mortgages aren't necessarily living the dream either. In reality, no one is really behind at all. But the sense that we are often drives people to shortcut the identity process so they just, I dunno, get married or something, hoping the decision deals with the tension. By the way, it doesn't.

Being 26 or 36 and still not clear about who you are—which means you're usually not sure about what you want to do—is kinda normal. That we feel retarded is accurate in the sense that we haven't developed like we could've, but not in the sense that we're behind. We're all identity-stunted but we don't need to rush into a solution. I understand the frustration though, and felt it growing up, and am feeling it again with the slow unfolding of my son Levi.

As the forth child, Levi works the system (as I did at his age). He knows what he can get away with, and that he can't be compared to the other kids who seemed to have more clarity about direction at a younger age. He's taking his sweet time. He has the annoying confidence typical of his generation; the kind that's not built on inner ability, but on the idea that things 'will just work out'. Too much science fiction, not enough world history... So he spends his days cruising through the easiest of curriculum (bass guitar, classic literature, languages, and some writing) sipping his home-made rosewater mocha lattes. He's a decent Barista for being 17, and he's pretty good at picking up bass lines, and when he writes—it's pretty funny stuff. Levi could probably take any of these areas and make something of them, but when I press him on the question, he tells me to let him develop at his own pace and that he doesn't have to figure it out like the other kids did.

This really bugs me. Not just because he's right (which he is), but because I see all the things he could be doing... What I don't always see is what's slowly forming inside of him and what he could do with that over time. Things I can't even imagine because they're unique to *him*. Like, last night he told me that his life's call was to be an old, gnarly, bearded man with a spiritual connection to coffee, so that he could say to someone; "Come, let us partake of the ichor." What? I can't see the pace he really needs, or the space he needs to experiment at a level he's comfortable with. He's not just a set of vocational possibilities, he's a living soul with a unique emotional intelligence, and whole worlds of identity that need to come together at the right time, his time. If he's lagging, he'll feel that and have to deal with the consequences. If he's missing opportunities now, he can create other ones later. If he doesn't leave home at 20, I'll charge him rent as a preparation for the real world, but he can decide how he wants that to play out. My concern for his well being has to be worked through the grid of his personal ownership, style, and pace. In this way, he has the best possible chance to develop the full range of his identity instead of the expedient version.

Ultimately, the unfolding of who we are is the interplay of soul, mind, and body. Each person's unique combination of these layers calls out a completely different process than the person sitting next to them, even if that person is their 'identical' twin. Being able to celebrate this is a huge challenge for parents who are concerned about your financial well being. The truth is, your best shot at doing well financially depends on the intentional release of identity through all its various channels. Giving yourself time to let this unfold means you can put aside the distraction of comparison and premature choices, the very things that sink the process all together and leave you in a stink job. Ironically then, alleviating the rush to make decisions gives you the ability to make truly great plans, perhaps just a little later.

Questions:

What may have rushed you into your present situation? It could be a series of events and expectations, so take some time to untangle that. It's worth noting because you may see points of departure, and therefore places to revisit...

....

....

....

....

....

....

....

....

Is it reasonable to expect a person to nail their career choice after high school and come out of college running? Why? What's a reasonable pace for you to develop your identity, education, and community expression? How much time do you need? Seems to me the really cool cats are all a little older, right?

....

....

....

....

....

....

....

....

Where might you be lagging because someone else is paying the bills (or you are, but in a survival kinda way)? Are you taking longer than you need to? Are you spending your developmental years in a good way, or just spending them?

....

....

....

....

....

....

....

....

Who is understanding and supporting the right pace for you? If no one, who could coach you through this?

....

....

....

....

....

....

....

....

Your family today

I mentioned that our parents are wired to provide security and significance; both are breeding grounds for identity. The question is, how can that still happen in your present situation? I have two suggestions. Firstly, as much as possible, please consider bringing your extended family into the process of this book. Secondly, try to create a platform to process this in your existing community and your new family, the one you may now be forming. To highlight the awkward but powerful need to work with our family and our past, I've asked Blue to share a bit of his experience:

Years ago I was on a Greyhound bus from L.A. to Fresno.

My wife had given me a book to read while I was travelling. The book was old and beaten up and the title seemed a little corny, it was called *The Blessing*. The font cover had this to say: "No matter your age, the approval of your parents affects how you view yourself and your ability to pass that approval along to your children, spouse, and friends..."[51]

As I started to read through the book I found myself caught up in the stories thinking 'this is telling my story' and I couldn't put it down. The basic premise was that in order to know who you are and know what you can contribute to this world, you need the blessing of your family. This family blessing can be broken down into five elements:

- you need to have meaningful touch by your family
- they need to build you up with words of love and encouragement
- they need to see you as having a high value, you matter to them and that you know you matter
- they need to help you paint a bright future whatever that is
- they need to be committed to help you achieve that future.

In a nutshell, you need to have parents who love you unconditionally, and will walk with you through life to help you understand and apply who you are. That's what the blessing is, and if you've been given it, you can be more secure in yourself and more able to give that to others... Now, I didn't feel I had been given that blessing by my parents. I came from a rather dysfunctional family. I'm the youngest of eight kids and was surrounded by a lot of alcohol and violence. But this raggedy old book helped me understand why I'd been seeking a substitute for this blessing throughout my life, and in unhealthy ways. We all need to be believed in right? We all want love and acceptance. If we don't get that from our home base we strive for it in other ways from other people. I did this through my friends, girlfriends, or other father figures. I had a certain angst about me and was very confused. I needed love and to love others but found myself frustrated and angry more often than I cared to remember. When I realised I didn't get this kind of love from my parents I wept. Then I vowed to give this to my children.

The other way I found the book revolutionary was that it asked me this simple statement; 'if you feel you haven't been given this blessing by your parents, you need to ask yourself have they been given it by their parents.' How can they give me give this blessing if they've never received it themselves? This was one of those wow moments for me as I remembered my parent's upbringing. My dad lived in the Bogside area of Derry, just a couple of streets over from the Bloody Sunday massacre in a very hostile Northern Ireland. His dad left him and his mother when he was two years old. He was raised in an troubled environment full of poverty and hatred. No wonder he left as a young man and made New Zealand his home. My mother was raised in a small rural NZ town and worked hard from an early age. They didn't get into university or have access to higher education. They didn't know how to help us create 'a bright future'. My dad passed away when I was a teenager and I felt a lot of resentment for my turbulent upbringing. There was a lot left unsaid and unresolved. When I read this book on the bus I started to realise that my parents had no real way to give these foundations to their family. So I decided that I was going to take up the challenge of the book and give a blessing back to my mother. To love her the way she should've been loved from the beginning. This meant telling her I loved her, valued her and what she did, and that I believed in her. Over time, she became a wonderful nana to my children and a huge part of their formation. When she passed away there was nothing left unsaid or unresolved, she was loved and celebrated.

---

51 Pocket Books; 1990. Cover

138

A few months later a few of my brothers got together for a family function. One of them was holding a picture of my mother and grieving our loss. In a moment of anger he said some harsh things about our dad and the way we were brought up. I could see he still carried the years of resentment. I responded by telling him "I'm one hundred times a better dad to my kids that my father was to me." He couldn't agree more and talked about the ways he thought I was a great dad. But then I said "But I tell you what, my dad was one thousand times a better dad to me than his father was to him!" Everything went silent.

We can go through life never realising the generational effect on family, and thus identity. We can never be a blessing to our family unless we have a sense of gratitude for what we have been given, broken as it may be. If we don't grasp this we could be in danger of striving for acceptance or self worth in our workplaces, our sporting achievements, our sexual prowess, whatever. In my observation, if you don't work this stuff out it tends to stay with you and you end up blaming everyone for your upbringing, which ends up as a trap. Instead, look to what you're thankful for and build on that.

I talk to my kids about my past all the time, sometimes they laugh with me, sometimes they're sad for me. I tell them the stories of my life so they understand me, where I'm struggling and where I'm finding joy. I want them to be smarter, healthier, less driven, more aware than I was at their age. I want to give them a better start than I had so that they can find out who they are, live out that potential, and hopefully do the same for their kids. I want them to have this blessing as much as I understand it today. Which is exactly what my dad did for me in his own way.

Working with what you have

In terms of working with your present family, we still need to be giving and receiving **unconditional love, provision, value**, and a sense of **destiny** to each other. Going off to college or another city means we may have to work harder at it, especially if issues from the past make it difficult to even talk with your family. I would suggest you start by asking those you can to help you answer some of the questions in this chapter. It may rekindle opportunities you didn't think you had. I find that parents from the previous generation had lots of expectations while their kids were growing up but, once they left home the parents tended to back off from giving any further input. Your extended family needs to know they still have a vital role.

I've learned to listen closely when my mom talks about her upbringing or when we were growing up. I can often pick up clues about how I related, played, and what was important back then, some of which lead to real 'aha' moments that I can build on. Inviting your parents, grandparents, siblings, etc. into your process gives them the permission to continue the very important role they still have. Namely, to use their inside connection to your soul, to validate and encourage it. I know this may not work in certain situations, but as long as you do your best, they can respond as they like. Try not to assume they can't contribute, because that judgement may freeze them into a relational space that they'd rather be free of. At least have a go.

Becoming your true self within the extended family is a nuanced process. You were once in your parents orbit—where they were central—and now you're spinning out, creating your own system. A lot of people break the gravity between themselves and their extended family in order to find the freedom they think they need. I would suggest however, that as you create your own orbit, invite them to be part of it by better understanding you as you grow (which has a lot to do with your ability to explain yourself), and you them. This may develop into new opportunities like coming to your shows, or helping with a small business start-up, or like some friends of mine in San Francisco, buying a home together with their parents... **Any efforts you make to invite extended family into your new planetary system will come back to you later when you'd like your kids to do the same thing.**

The extended community around you also creates a really good opportunity to contextualize your identity process. We've made this process a central theme to our parenting and our place in the community, which has had a lot of cool outcomes. When I go deep into my own identity, I naturally start seeing a similar depth in others. I can translate this into artistic development, training, cooking classes, or whatever context my identity gets me into. Taking that into my family relationships becomes a natural extension, which then blesses the larger community and their efforts in identity. This takes time, but I've noticed that people who know who they are, are also great collaborators in the lives and marketplace around them. For instance, my friend Nigel, who runs the cafe I write in, builds on his family / community connections to create space for local artists, business meetings, craft groups, and cooking clubs for everyone else. His identity spans out to validate and facilitate the identity of 50 to 100 people per day. Community is a great place to foster and multiply who we are because our souls work best in concert.

Allow me to repeat: At the end of the day, families (and their communities) will always need to provide **unconditional love** for each other. This creates the freedom to be ourselves, without expectations of what we may look like in the future. Those closest to us will need to supply a kind of **provision**, which is care, listening, and the nurturing of fragile identity. Families will need to use their authority to **value** each other by speaking out, validating, and celebrating the early signs of who we all are. And finally, communities come together to develop our **destiny** by working with us in practical ways, turning the dream that is us into reality. Some families do this by developing the family farm together, others can fund new houses, or short films. Others still may just be able to handle a better conversation than at last Christmas... Whether you foster this in your existing family, or the one you're gonna make, these four basic areas are crucial to just about everything we do in life, so get on to it. Try to move past it and we're like Pinnocchio racing to the circus, only to find the circus (read: city) is playing us. Dive into the family process and you discover depths you didn't know you had. When you tap into that natural flow of authority, and fulfil the responsibility we have to develop our soul in family, you start on a better footing. It took me decades to see this, so I offer this little time saver hoping you're brave and caring enough to go back a few steps now in order to surge forward later.

Down to earth
with Kathryn Hewitt

As I reflect on the early years of my life—playing racket games
in the garden with my brothers and cycling laps round the house, then climbing
the chestnut tree and doing acrobatics between branches... or our summer holidays
on the North Coast of Ireland building sand castles down in the cove at Castlerock
and then on to burger and chips at Grahams' restaurant where our booth would
have a perfect view of the Tom and Jerry cartoons played on the huge TV, then off
to Barry's Amusements for some dodge'ems, merry-go-round, helter skelter, and
teacups time with candy-floss, then Pooh Bear ice cream at Mauds before a few more
visits to the arcades along the street, and finally the drive back to the caravan where
I'd rest my weary head—I can see some identity statements forming which are still
true today. Same for the early teen years playing football with my brothers and their
mates, and my late teens running a drop-in cafe which allowed me to be with the
'drop-outs'; I can see that all along I am an important part of a team. I am surprising
and impressive, I am worth indulging, I am not like anybody else, I am interested in
the person behind the bravado and the bull...

I grew up with a lot of love around me. My parents often showed and spoke of their
love and affirmation which created a stable and safe place. My two older brothers
fulfilled some stereotypical brotherly roles in that they taught me what I didn't yet
know or couldn't yet do. They teased me within an inch of my life (although I was
often the instigator) and they were a refuge when I needed some help from the
big bad world. Mum was crucial to everything but Dad was definitely the Boss.
Mum could meet every need and fulfilled all kids of roles, whether that be cook,
seamstress, mechanic, or secretary. Dad was around after work and at the weekend
but had enough extracurricular things to keep himself busy, so as we grew older he
would let us get on with what we were doing. By our teenage years, Dad was very
present in our social lives as we spent much time at the weekend with the youth
in and around our church and he had an active role in its leadership. I think this
reinforced a sense of trust in our relationship with Dad. He often knew where
we'd be, what we'd be up to, and who with. Even though I'd be hanging out with
teenagers who were up to no good, Dad's unspoken trust in me to do the right thing
was enough of a motivator for me to honour that.

Early on my budding maturity and capability was called upon; I was given various
roles of responsibility in class (photocopier or messenger at Primary level) and at
Grammar School, amongst other things, I became the Art room printer fixer (!) and
in my last year was voted in by my classmates as Deputy Head Girl. My parents
believed in me by financially assisting me with buying a flat at 20 years old and my
husband continues to affirm me in the skills that I have, which I sometimes don't
fully utilize.

So I'm still learning and forming those identity statements. The last year or so has been a particular time of self-reflection. As a youngster, I remember my frustration at being told to stop whining, which was often met with me shouting, "I'm not whining!" (in a whining voice). I needed to be heard in that place, not told to stop feeling. This has been an experience that has awakened my consciousness to my girls' feelings. When my daughter is upset or angry and I believe it to be irrational, I try to take a breath and ask her about how she's feeling rather than tell her how I think she ought to feel. I've been learning that I am not my daughters, and so I don't really know what they think and feel better than they know themselves. I've also wondered just how involved my parents have been in mine and my brothers' lives. I know they had the best of intentions and did the best with what they had, but I can't help but wonder what it would have been like to have had them take a backseat on some issues and to have let us work some stuff out on our own. I have a very clear memory of Dad saying, "Well it's really your decision". It was such a significant moment, but since I was already 17 years old I wonder what it would have been like to hear this earlier on.

As I look at the things I enjoyed doing in childhood and those that I enjoy today, I'm learning how to celebrate the me I'm growing into. I am a doer rather than a thinker. I am constantly dipping in and out of projects—very much in the experimental / exploratory stages of the things that make me tick. I am doing more for others these days compared to how much I used to do for myself (still working on a healthy balance of this). I'm enjoying doing things alongside others rather than just meeting up to chat. I want to create memories of journeying together. I am getting better at enjoying my family, my friends, my health, my possessions right here and now, and not wishing for a perfect day in the future that may not exist.

Where we're at now is a new adventure in itself. I'm putting all this identity to work by living in community with our best friends. These last two years have been the most challenging and yet most life-giving thing I've ever put my hand to. It's like getting married all over again… learning the ways of another tribe, acknowledging the otherness that is all around, while seeing how much can be done in collaboration, how much time, energy and money can be saved when resources and talents are pooled, and being able to give to others out of this place of overflowing.

I'm blessed to contribute to this extended family by being:
- *my own person—with thoughts and feelings that differ to from parents, my husband and my friends*
- *inspired by others' experimentation with hair / makeup / fashion / craft*
- *free to experiment, teaching myself the balance between creativity as an art and as a means to beautification*
- *a mature, determined and responsible person, a nurturer, a mother to many, and a gatherer of people.*

Chapter Eight

Restoring me years the locust have eaten

Anytime you revisit the past,

even in the forward movement of recovering identity, you have to reckon with some damage. The emotional, neurological, and physical effects of the last 20 years' impact remains attached to our self-perceptions, and thus to our day to day choices. Which is gonna be okay in the long-run if we can proceed from better foundations.

For now though, we need to:
- *stop trying to race past the past (which almost always means we're fronting an artificial version of self)*
- *understand the actual loss, in detail...*
- *see how a possible healing can make us stronger and more real*
- *use our identity as the catalyst for the whole process*

Working the damage has become a way of life for me. I

know that if I can allow negative aspects of the past to show me points of departure, I can turn that knowledge into a positive direction and redeem most of the pain. More importantly though, I need to remember what my child-like soul was trying to tell me during that same time. Because my soul and its callings are stronger than trauma. And over time, the past loses its dangerous edge.

For instance, I've mentioned my brush with evil English teachers and their evil grading systems. If I try to move past my messed up education and just try harder, or drop trying to learn all together, then my memories of a negative past win. But if I can revisit the situation with my soul / identity as the dominant voice, I can untangle the problem. I'll find that her grades were based on my typical behavior and that she wasn't looking at my deeper identity as a communicator. How could she? I gave her so little to work with (I cheated all the time) and she had so little time to see the real me. So in unpacking that, I have to acknowledge my laziness, a busted ed system, and the potential to be misunderstood. So far so good. But now, I need to do something with that knowledge. I need to somehow restore those years... to rebuild my potential as a communicator.

(Note: I realize that this is a fairly light issue to deal with. I've had harder, and others have had super hard... In some of these situations, counseling would be really helpful. The point here is that the soul and your identity is a great reference to work those issues through, because the tendency of modern counseling practice is to focus on the pain and not on the solution.)

Sometimes restoration means going back to a certain point and rebuilding from there. This could start by revisiting a passion you dropped long ago. Knowing that I am a communicator, I've been re-inspired to learn more about various ways to write, speak, and visualize. It's a bit late in life but why should that matter? For instance, I'm only now towards the end of *War and Peace*. I listen to podcasts on storytelling and I watch presentations on design... Now that I've left school (a toxic place for me, and me for the school) I've learned tons, only now I have context. My soul is leading the education, and slowly, the restoration.

In the previous chapter we outlined some basic areas to consider that may need restoring. Please review those and then look at the next section. This time in your life is about being honest about the past, and using it to regain your strength.

Outlining the process of renewal:

Restoration is a pretty huge deal. Sometimes, when things get too big, we defer them to another day (or year) and head back to watch more TV; the inebriator of our soul. Instead, I find it helpful to set reasonable goals so I don't get swamped by what needs doing. Here are the steps I've walked through—sometimes over weeks, sometimes years—to recover identity from the past. Restoration will happen as I stay engaged in relationships, family, and the original process of identity development we spoke of earlier.

Gratitude and forgiveness: These two world-changing principles are central to healthy living, or what the Hebrews called Shalom (generally: peace, completeness, and welfare). Practicing them creates a spiritual / emotional / physical platform for us to heal, and build on both negative and positive experiences. But you know all that, so what can you be thankful for so far and what do you need to forgive? Start by writing the obvious things down, or talk them through with someone close. Note any opportunities you had to freely express yourself growing up, for parents who saw you or friends who dreamed with you. Once you can recall the event, try to express what you were feeling at the time. Maybe you could write a few of these experiences or memories here? [52] Then start the thanking and/or forgiving.

....

....

....

....

....

....

....

....

....

I've found this works best on three levels. First, **start in the heart**, especially for the hard ones. I saw that if I could pray for or forgive someone internally, I could then move on to the next step (or just move on...). Secondly, **communicate practically** (phone, write, or in person), especially the grateful bits. Thirdly, do some small **act of kindness** in person, something that connects you with the people you need to work through things with or be grateful towards. What you're doing, as awkward as this sometimes is, is releasing yourself more than anything else. I've often heard it said that the inability to forgive is the poison we take hoping someone else will die. Forgiveness frees you to heal, and allows you to see what the self lost in the sometimes toxic past. Gratitude and forgiveness open the channels, at least in your own soul, if not in the relationships around you. It takes two to tango, so others may not be at the same place as you. Like, it took me 15 years to work through stuff with my dad... but all this can happen in parallel. As you're forgiving something over time, you can be grateful for other things, and keep moving. This is an ongoing process, so simply commit to it and stay sensitive. Which as all guys know, has the added benefit of attracting girls to your plight... Anyway, use the next page to write out some things that need to be processed from the heart, by communicating, or in acts of kindness.

---

52 A friend of mine, the amazing Hailey Bartholomew, has done a number of amazing projects on gratitude, have a look at her 365 Grateful projects at: http://365grateful.com/original-365-project

Hᴇᴀʀᴛ Iꜱꜱᴜᴇꜱ?   Pʀᴀᴄᴛɪᴄᴀʟ Cᴏᴍᴍ?   Kɪɴᴅ Aᴄᴛꜱ?

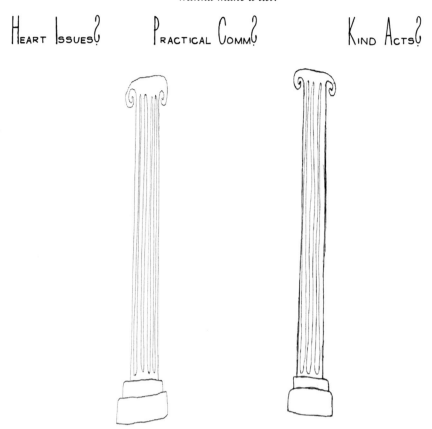

Remembering who I am: This will sound simplistic, but I think you should make every effort to remember who you are. Use sticky notes or whatever you can find to hold those few 'I am' statements in front of you, to give grace and hope to the process. Like, "because I am a **communicator**, someday I'll be really good at it..." Simple. As you start to build identity statements through this entire process, they need to find a way to get back to the front of the line. On top of the 365 Grateful ideas I mentioned in a previous footnote, you could also do a 365 day, or 52 week, or 12 month Identity project. Where you take snapshots of something each day, week, or month that represents your identity. Print it out, slap an 'I am' statement on it, and post it somewhere prominent.

Your soul has been trying to communicate to you, and the world around you, your whole life. The problem is that its messages are subtle and fleeting. A six year-old may blurt something out as a revelation to both herself and her parents. And then it passes. Why that fascination with words, or animals, or inanimate objects? If nobody captures and nurtures the thing, it can retreat as quickly as it emerged. As this restoration unfolds, and forgotten pieces of you get uncovered, find a way to give them some CPR. Especially your creative bits. They're usually the first to go. You may want to reconnect by picking up guitar lessons again, or anything to DO SOMETHING with that fledgling part of your soul. It's one thing to have a sticky note on your fridge reminding you that you're creative, but it's another thing all together to head to an open mic night and read your poetry, or join a Battleship competition at the local cafe. Putting that forgotten 'I am' statement into action defibrillates the thing. And remembering key identity statements will have a cumulative effect. They'll start to build up, slowly releasing a kind of spiritual cocktail in your system. This won't necessarily produce a sense of confidence, but something deeper. You will start to know your self again, and that self will become more obvious to others. Try and write at least one clear identity statement you want to focus on here:

I AM:

Ask those in authority (God included) to speak words of truth and encouragement to you. We're not only restoring your identity here, we're working on the foundational process whereby identity is developed. By asking your stakeholders to get back in the game, you're re-establishing the proper flow of encouragement. Both ways, hopefully. Redeeming these relational structures lays a better foundation when it's your turn to create family and community... Trust me, it's completely worth doing.

I know it's a little odd asking your dad or sister to tell you more about yourself. We have this strange relationship with identity, especially in the family and the Church. We both villainize it and desperately need it. Pride, we've been told, is talking too much about yourself... And while that's true for some people, most of us don't talk about ourselves at all—which, by the way, is actually a great environment to breed pride. So, when you approach people asking for feedback like this, it's awkward. Okay, but let's just get over that. Asking for feedback is fine. Asking for stories that help you remember who you are, so you can do something wonderful with it, is also fine. Reminding the key people in your life, that they have a place and you still want and need them in that way, is fine. In fact, the practice is good for both of you because while you're being encouraged and re-identified, you can be doing the same for them. And you have the authority to ask, because by doing so you're reinstating the value of encouragement in society in general, and then speaking it back into the lives of others.

What you're basically asking for here is stories. Things about your past that you may have forgotten or misinterpreted. You need their observations and impressions of you. Things they may have said before that have got lost in the mix. They may only be able to give you a few tips, which you can add to your overall identity map, but the real benefit will be the opening of the channel. Again, this is a longish-term process, so just keep trying. My mother was kind enough to put together a page of stories in a Creative Memories book she did for me and each of my siblings. I'd put it here but I'm embarrassed. Instead, I'm leaving room for your family to write some things they know of you, think of you, want you to remember:

From their vantage point, what can you extract about your identity?

....

....

....

....

....

....

....

....

....

Taking risks: Recapturing the power of your identity will require taking some risks. It's also recapturing the child-like nature you may have lost. Once you have a few things flowing in, you'll need to start practicing them. In the previous section on *Remembering*, I asked you to do something with what you were discovering. But in for this section, you'll need to establish or practice something long enough for it to reveal some depth. For instance, you may have written a song for a friend, but now you need to write 20 to really draw out the talent, and see what's really you and what's not. There's a difference between dabbling with song writing and telling your friends you're gonna try to write 20 songs. The risk is in the commitment to the thing. Your reputation (read: Identity) becomes vulnerable (which is a good thing) because it's out in the open again. So, you may have picked up a book on an old interest, but this time you could apply for night-school or some class to really dive into the subject. Doing some small business venture is always a good way to take risks... As long as you can tie the risk to your identity, it'll be worth the effort.

The hard part about risk is that you have no idea if you're heading in the right direction, or if you'll be good at something... Which is exactly the state you were in as a child. But at that point you didn't care if you were going to 'succeed', or if anyone was watching, or if you'd make any money. You were in the perfect state to develop your identity and its unfettered creative capacity. Taking risks puts you back into that vulnerable, free state. I suggest you pick a few identity statements and think about what you could do to practice them. Commit to something for at least a few months. It could be to develop a neighborhood accounting practice or volunteering in a local cooking school training homeless folks. Have a look and see what exists in your neighborhood that you could tie into. And don't wait around for confidence or a sign from above, just act like a child and you'll be fine. Try listing a few 'I am' statements on one side and then some risks you could take to put those to work:

Encourage others: This may be the most important part of the restoration. When you acknowledge the identity of others, it flows back to you in unexpected ways. I think the nature of identity is that it flows in all directions. If you only focus on your process, the thing has a way of drying up. But if you give as much as you're receiving, it keeps moving through you in a sustaining kind of way. And don't wait until your tank is full, either. Start by intentionally telling people the good things you notice about them. What you'll also notice is that as you encourage others, you start to develop a language for identity. It becomes natural in the sense that you now see the soul, yours and others. By giving heart (the root of en-*cour*-agement) to those around you, you restore a better way to communicate (like asking people who they are instead of what they do). You dismantle that industrial revolution view of humanity (that people are machines) and replace it with their soul at the center of the conversation. I love doing this in random conversations, where I'll just start asking questions about identity, dreams, etc. It often catches people off guard, but by the end of the conversation we're both just a little bit different.

Start with those closest (and sometimes the most difficult) to you.
Spend some time considering their soul, mind, or strength. Try to look past the façade—past **what** people do, to **why they do it**. Put language to that, or make something to represent what you see, and give it to them. This may freak 'em out just a little bit, because who does that these days? Fear not though, the awkwardness is soon replaced with a sense of gratitude, because you just broke through to soulful communication. Make that stuff common in your life and you'll be walking on

air. The more you do this, the more the language and process of identity becomes natural. Encouraging a persons identity also shifts their idea of what success looks like by slowly diminishing the values, norms, and oppressive expectations about 'financial security' or 'marriage completing you'.

Giving and receiving encouragement has become an awkward thing. Poor modelling in family, muddy social scenes (as in; 'Are you hitting on me?'), and confused self-image makes this simple and powerful principle a lost art. I know I am not alone when I say that in being encouraged, I have wanted the ground to open up and swallow me. Another way of dealing with this uncomfortable feeling is to fob it off, or make a joke about it.

Years ago I had a young friend whose life I was really investing into because I saw so much potential in him. He didn't have a dad and hung out at our place off and on for a few years. I remember we were out hunting once and he told me how much it had meant to him to have me in his life, he thanked me for being the dad he never had. What an amazing complement he had given me. I saw how hard it was for him to say something so meaningful and personal. But I was absolutely allergic to compliments, and made light of it by saying "Don't worry about it mate, It's all part of the job!" Wow, what a dick! I could see him immediately feel crushed and I felt like such a tool! I made it my mission in life not to ever let that happen again.

So, here's an encouragement tip: By going through this book and using the exercises with friends, you should be able to see **specifics** about your identity. When you can talk with specificity about these 'I am' statements, you'll find it easier to encourage because you'll be speaking to the person's core. Because you're being specific, the encouragement can be better understood and accepted more easily. Wouldn't it be great to be regularly encouraged along the way and being part of a community that notices when you kick it? When you can freely give and receive specific affirmation you can also create the environment you want to live in.

Who could you start encouraging and what do you want to say to them, or make for them ASAP?

Debrief: After a while (a few months from now), take stock of the process and see how you're doing. Celebrate the wins and recommit to those tougher areas that need more work / time. Since restoration takes time, you wanna track your progress and get a sense of the arc you're on. You may want to do this with a friend who's on a similar journey so you can hear each other's stories and get some perspective. I've found that the initial energy I have for something will pan out, and needs to be renewed so my commitment and energy levels stay in place. This can happen through making progress, but more often than not, you need to find encouragement during the long seasons of slow development. Regular walks with a friend, or collaborating with someone who's really good at what you're developing, can keep the process moving forward. Regular meals, at least once a month, with extended family can keep the relational side strong so that you continue to build on that platform too. I would suggest putting something in your calendar both weekly and monthly to remind you to stop and take stock. Find some people who you relate well with, and places you enjoy being at, to help you make this a part of your life. As the months roll on, you'll find that to the degree you've been intentional about restoration, it WILL happen. Within a reasonable amount of time, you'll be standing on a renewed foundation.

Three wishes

Finally, in order to add some hope (a positive expectation of something good) to the process, let's grant you three wishes. It's okay to ask for things that are really important, especially if you'll use them for loving your neighbor as your self. In kicking off the restoration, speak out what you want to happen and what you're looking for. I'm repeating myself here but I've found that when I pray, or verbalize what I really want to happen, I become more aware of the answers as they unfold around me. This receptivity becomes like a radar that's tuned into the frequency of my request. I notice people, ideas, and the answers I was seeking because I now know what I want. You may end up being the person who's responsible to make a lot of this happen, or you may be the answer to other people's prayers because you've just gotten a whole lot more proactive. So, for your restoration, what are you asking for?

Wish No. 1: What encouragement do you need to hear to move forward? *Be specific and state sources this could come from:*

....

....

....

....

....

....

....

....

Wish No. 2: What people do you need (your tribe) to move forward?
Describe the tribe who could help in the restoration and future collaboration:

....

....

....

Wish No. 3: What resources or tools do you need to move forward?
What do you have, what do you need (baby steps and big ticket items):

....

....

....

....

....

Meditation:

THE TIME WILL COME
WHEN, WITH ELATION,
YOU WILL GREET YOURSELF ARRIVING
AT YOUR OWN DOOR, IN YOUR OWN MIRROR,
AND EACH WILL SMILE AT THE OTHERS WELCOME,

AND SAY, SIT HERE. EAT.
YOU WILL LOVE AGAIN THE STRANGER WHO WAS YOUR SELF.
GIVE WINE. GIVE BREAD. GIVE BACK YOUR HEART
TO ITSELF, TO THE STRANGER WHO HAS LOVED YOU

ALL YOUR LIFE, WHOM YOU IGNORED
FOR ANOTHER, WHO KNOWS YOU BY HEART.
TAKE DOWN THE LOVE LETTERS FROM THE BOOKSHELF,

THE PHOTOGRAPHS, THE DESPERATE NOTES,
PEEL YOUR OWN IMAGE FROM THE MIRROR.
SIT. FEAST ON YOUR LIFE.

LOVE AFTER LOVE
BY DEREK WALCOTT

Part three
Mapping it out

This section is about:

- *Mapping and visualizing the broad range of your identity.*
- *Brainstorming stories, which can become plans, which can become your life...*
- *Facilitating the whole process with a little help from above, and maybe next door.*

So let's bring this whole thing together. Let's draw on all the stuff you've processed up to now. Let's draw the Myers-Briggs, Enneagram, and StrengthsFinder stuff together. Let's put all the encouragement, dreams, stories, and impressions into some cohesive visual so you can DO SOMETHING with it.

Processing styles:
Everyone processes differently. This next section takes a wide array of processing styles into consideration, so write words, sketch houses, share stories, etc. that help you see your <u>self</u> in your own way. If you're more of a verbal processor, talk out the questions with people and then note a few of the highlights in the book. If you're more kinesthetic, rip out a page, origami an identity statement (like, "I'm beautifully tactile"), and paste it back in the book... Whatever works, work something out, because if you just read through this without doing something, changing something, it can become like all those other efforts—where you found helpful bits and pieces about yourself, but you still end up doing the same old stuff. So be yourself in terms of processing, but take initiative, follow through, and work the details.

Teamwork:
If you're a real lone ranger, fine. Grab a horse and head out west with this in your saddle, and come back ready to change your world. Otherwise, please find a book buddy and go through this together. It makes a huge difference. If you can't find anyone immediately, look around, you may be surprised at who responds (you may end up married too, so be careful! Kidding!). If you have a crew of 6 to 10 people that you regularly spend time with, consider introducing this book to them and walk through the overall ideas, see who's keen to process the rest. Just a thought.

Time:

Once you get to the section on telling stories, you'll need to give those stories time to settle. You'll also want to get your energy levels up to the place where you're ready to take on a bigger project. But watch out here because you can take too much time and end up procrastinating. I suggest you give yourself a time-line that outlines the overall process. We'll give you the opportunity to sketch that out later in the book. Make sure you have the time you need to process the whole deal and then settle on commitments, but watch out that the cares of the world don't extinguish your fire.

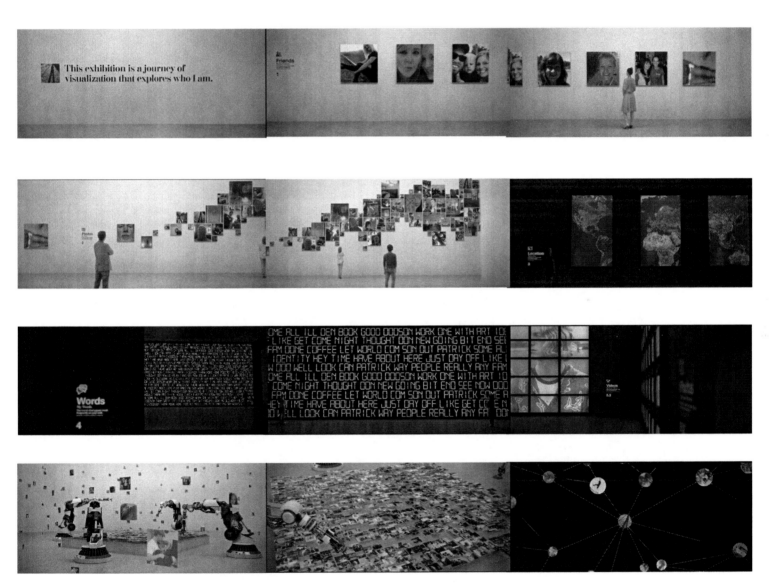

Here's an idea: Create your own virtual exhibit (go to: http://www.intel.com/museumofme/r/index.htm) and print out some screen shots, then paste it over my version here.

Chapter Nine

Identity

...self-focused.

God just flows

Love making delicious food.
(Cooking not baking)

Fall in Love easily.

Messy and unorganized!

Not wonderful at finishing.

Easily distracted but getting better.

Get recharged by having fun and being random.

I over think, it wears me out. So simple ideas and people explaining things simply are super helpful.

STRENGTHFINDERS
① Individualistic
② Strategic
③ Belief

Bold a...
secure...
who I am
in Christ

Son —

Brother - Incredibly loyal to my brother.

Old Friends Not sure what to do with me (friends in home town)

Love speaking in front of people

Comfortable on stage, equally comfortable sitting back.

Often steer direction of things. well when it needs steering.

Sa...
kn...
ar...
fe...

mapping

How do we capture and utilize the nebulous stuff of our soul?

How do we harness all those 'I am' statements and build on the possibilities they can create? How can we SEE our identity? Mankind has made massive breakthroughs in mapping our DNA and now visualizing our proteins (Proteomics). We can use quantitative neuroimaging to map out the fine detail behind our physical and intellectual behavior. And my doctor talks to me (A LOT) about the detailed markers in my blood revealing how my liver enzymes or cholesterol is doing... But what's out there to help us track the elusive substance of our identity?

In a healthy system, you would grow up free enough to express yourself,

get some encouragement, and practice it until your identity naturally wove itself throughout your thought-life and personality. You're ideas, choices, and the stuff you made would reveal identity, and everyone around you would get it because you would simply **be you**. You wouldn't need a DNA or StrengthsFinder read out, it would be **apparent**. To a degree, that's mostly true today. There is a lot about you that's obvious and wonderful. But we're also in conflict (read: retarded). The outside-in pressures of the world are contending with our inside-out potential and have muddled our self-image. So, in order to regain a clear image, we need some visualization tools to see what's become rather dim. This is where identity mapping comes in. Think of this as CT scanning your soul.

Just as a CT scan visualizes the internals of your physical self, identity mapping can put words, pictures, and form to your soul, mind, and strength. In the beginning it may seem a little clinical, which it kinda is. But once you have a decent visual of your identity, you can start practicing what you see and get back to that natural cognition / expression. The added bonus being that you now have a cool journal with meaningful 'I am' statements and pressed flowers... The idea is to articulate and share what's already true about you, but that's been hidden for all the reasons we've covered so far. And as mentioned before, instead of five strengths or a few personality tips, we're looking for the beautiful array of your complex self. If taken seriously, your identity map could be as extensive as your DNA (not really, but yeah, you're not five things).

To observe the diamond that is you we'll look at it from a variety of angles. In each approach, we'll explore different ways of seeing your complexity and slowly build up a compendium of memories, visuals, impressions, ideas, words, etc. The unfolding results will appear random at first, but don't worry, we'll unravel things as we go. Give yourself the time and space for this to develop. You may need to resist the temptation to look for quick answers so you can choose the right school, or girlfriend... Recapturing things that should have naturally unfolded requires patience, as well as a willingness to reform your life, so just take your time.

A. Living questions

You already know I'm not a fan of personality tests that use quantitative approaches. Pre-formatted questions rendering algorithmic results—regardless of how well researched they are—will never draw out the depth needed to make a good run at the future.[53] In order to see your nuanced identity, and the possibilities therein, we need to see where your soul is alive. This is where living questions come in. A living question is one which draws out the heartbeat of your interests, passions, and dreams. They tap into bedrock motivations which resonate within you and spark your imagination into action. They help you break through self-image barriers by allowing you to recall and articulate those powerful yet elusive details, the ones that I think hold the keys to your future.

---

53 This is not to discount the good stuff you've got from these tools. They're good tools. Again, just add them to the broader mix so you don't get hemmed in by them.

I AM A MOTHER

A DAUGHTER

A SISTER, A FRIEND

A living question is really a question about your story. Each scene holds all the dimensions and connections required to see **your self in action**. Stories contain the emotive responses (negative and positive) your soul recalls through its selective memory. Meaning, your soul remembers the important stuff, your stuff. For instance, if I ask what your social identity is, you may respond by trying to define a particular social intelligence or a Myers-Briggs result. So far, so clinical. But if I ask you to tell me the story of your involvement in the latest family gathering, you may reveal something like:

> *Our extended family got together for an engagement party.*
> *I didn't know half of the people there and was way out of*
> *my comfort zone. There were cupcakes and champagne.*
> *The cupcakes were all home made and really exquisite, so I*
> *tried just about all of them. Drawn out by those cupcakes,*
> *I eventually made my way around the large tree we were*
> *camped under and met everyone, trying to connect in some*
> *small way. I spent most of the time with people I knew except,*
> *for one girl who I discovered was finishing her nursing degree.*
> *We talked about her getting work, going to London and*
> *specializing... I find that when I can connect with someone*
> *who's processing their future, the facilitator in me comes out.*
> *Being in a social scene for the sake of being there puts me off.*
> *But if I have a reason or a purpose there, then I find a kind*
> *of flow and time disappears.*

As the stories emerge, you can see values, motives, repeating circumstances, etc., all of which starts to form a picture. You can also do this by using a photo of yourself from the event and writing a sentence on the pic (Polaroid's rule for this) like 'I am a one on one facilitator' or 'I am a good listener in intimate settings'. You can break the story down further to foundational truths about yourself such as 'I am a connoisseur' or 'people developer'... The story allows you to see the **natural angles** or facets of your diamond—usually obscured for lack of observation. Living questions look at living events (past or present) by asking:

*1. What's the **story** behind your spiritual, social, and personal identity as seen in the memorable events of your life?*
*2. What were the **motivations** involved in that story?*
*3. What were the **circumstances** you noted and why were they important to you?*
*4. What were the **key words** or statements that kept popping up?*
*5. Ultimately, what were you **being** in that story?*

The rest should unfold in conversation, or meditation, over time. Which as you can see, is not a canned process. Speaking out, listening to, and processing living questions needs to be relational and intentional. So again, get someone close to you and talk about these things. The benefit is that we learn about identity together, and in the context of real lives. Which is a really healthy process, especially because we need others (their support and encouragement) to help build on this raw material later, as we move from seeing identity to practicing identity.

Living question exercise:

Your turn. I'd like you to tell four different stories (building on your earlier shorter example) of your own successes. Events where you felt you did well, whether it was recognized or not. Try to describe the circumstances, feelings, environment, and what you were doing and thinking the whole time. After you've written all four, please go back (hopefully with a friend, or your mom) and ask the questions listed above. Take your time, and let memory and emotion blend back together. Don't look for answers, focus on the story and let 'I am' statements come to you. If you're an internal processor, you may be able to do this on your own so have a go, but I highly recommend sitting down with a good listener and unfolding these questions together.

*The next four pages provide some space to write out these stories and see what identity statements emerge. **Please start by using the space** on this page to write as many situations as you can remember where you felt you did well at something. Just jot down a few words for each situation, like "our high-school basketball championship" (actually, I sat on the bench during ours), or "helping my friends through relational crises"... Then pick the four stories you want to explore and carry on from there.*

My First Story

MOTIVATIONS? IMPORTANT CIRCUMSTANCES? I AM STATEMENTS?

My Second Story

Motivations? Important circumstances? I am statements?

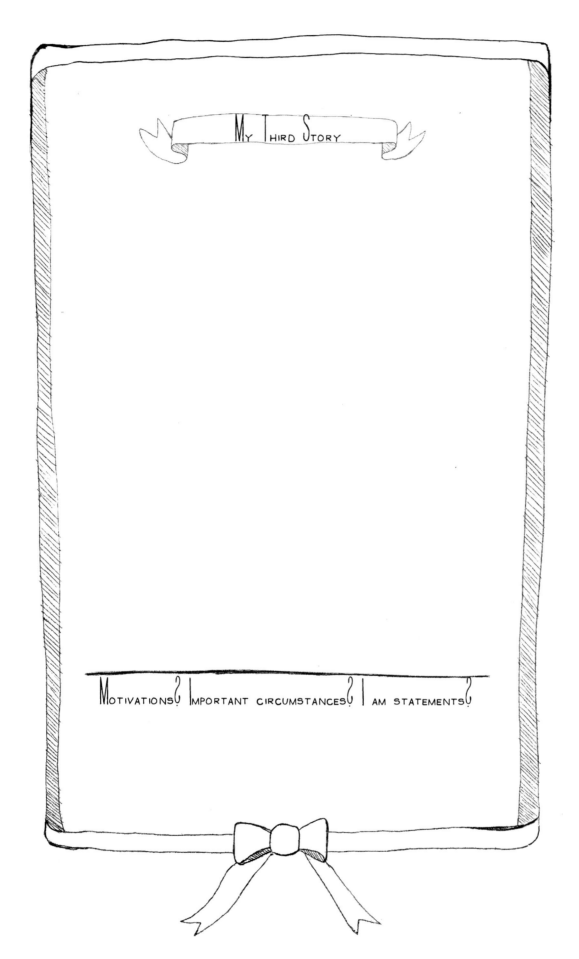

My Third Story

Motivations? Important circumstances? I am statements?

My Forth Story

Motivations? Important circumstances? I am statements?

Extra Points: Just kidding, there are no grades here. But if you want to push the living question angle further, try this: Write a short story about your life ten years from now. Describe what you would love to be doing, where you'd like to live, who you're with, what you're learning, and what you're creating... Write it as though resources and opportunities are not a problem. If you got to call the shots, what would your world (not just your job) be like? Then, ask the same five questions listed above to extract some more 'I am' statements.

....

....

....

....

....

....

....

....

....

....

....

....

....

....

....

....

....

....

....

What are the **motivations**, **circumstances**, key words, or **statements** that keep popping up?

....

....

....

....

....

....

....

....

....

....

....

....

....

....

....

....

B. Time-lining the obvious

Another way to capture the expressions of your soul is to look at the symmetry of those expressions. It's the consistency of your choices and behavior, which then reveal **echoes** or feedback from your soul. Because, one way or another, over time you will be yourself. Once you weed out the reactions and forced personas, you'll be left with what is obviously you. This symmetry can be visualized by using a time-line exercise my friend Stine showed me. It allows you to see the overview of key memories (things your soul chooses to remember) over many years. As you write and review them, you start to see your symmetry in these choices, actions, and therefore, identity statements.

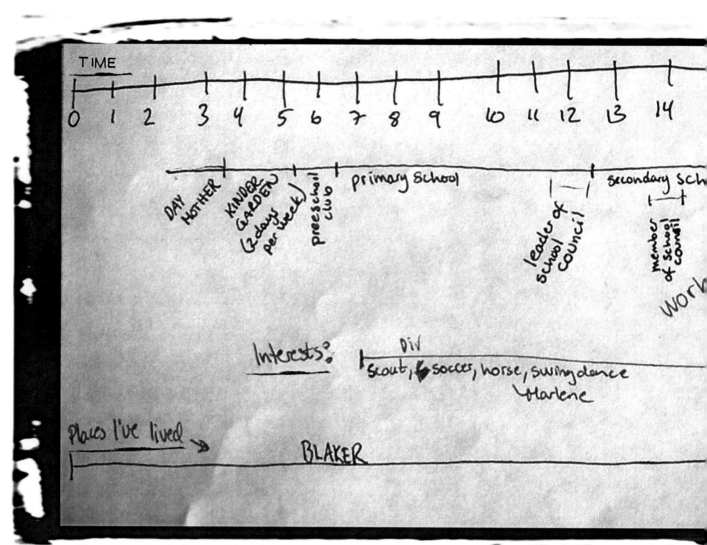

TIME

0 1 2 3 4 5 6 7 8 9 10 11 12 13 14

DAY MOTHER
KINDER GARDEN (2 days per week)
preeschool club
primary school
leader of school council
secondary sch
member of school council
work

Interests?
Div
Scout, soccer, horse, swing dance
Marlene

Places I've lived → BLAKER

This is an example from my friend Stine. She started by writing the activities she was involved with over the years. Then work she'd done. Then interests and places she's lived in... You can see various interests popping up. Things that were important in the early years and then stopped... New interests later on... The idea is to look at these events and extract 'I am' statements from it for your identity map.

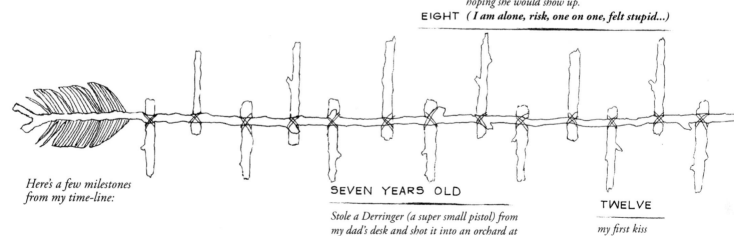

Here's a few milestones from my time-line:

SEVEN YEARS OLD

Stole a Derringer (a super small pistol) from my dad's desk and shot it into an orchard at the end of the street
(I am daring, risk taking, stupid, alone)

Went to the playground and saw Glenn Campbell. She and I were the only ones there. I went back regularly for the next month hoping she would show up.
EIGHT (I am alone, risk, one on one, felt stupid...)

TWELVE

my first kiss
(I am, um, ??)

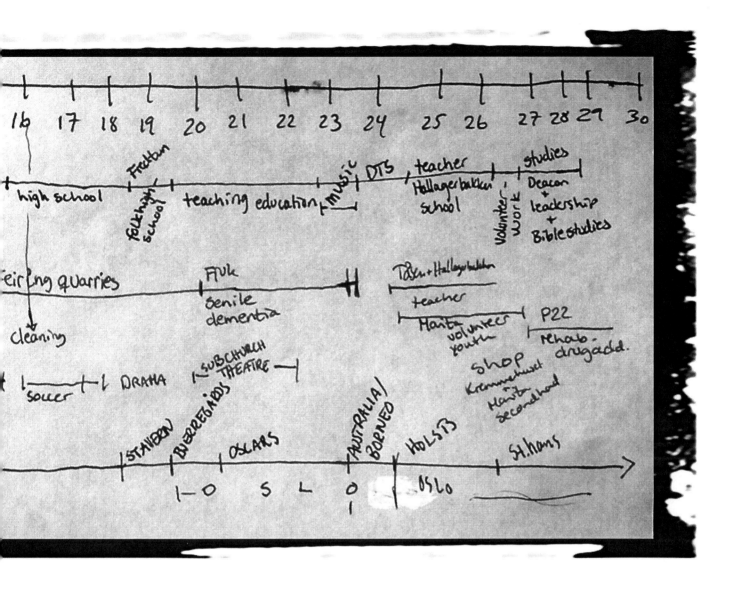

Started playing basketball, football, baseball and did track (high jump and 400m) A LOT.

FOURTEEN *(I am a team player, facilitator, friend)*

SIXTEEN

Got really good at cheating my way through high-school. Sold drugs, stole candy bars, sold them too. Bought my first car.
(I am entrepreneurial?)

'Alone' comes up a lot in my events. As does risk and doing a lot of dumb things. There's some change in here as well (like from being alone to liking teams). What I'm looking for is obvious identity statements, teased out through their repetition. Other obvious truths pop out by their sheer weight in the story. Like, you may feel strongly about something and realize that thing has always been really important to you as you see it repeat...

My Time—Line

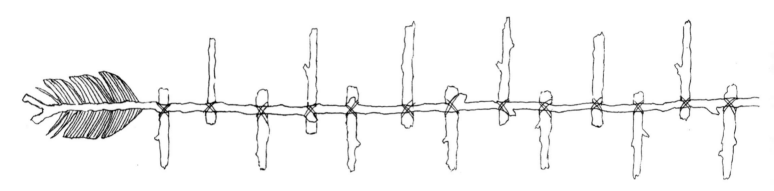

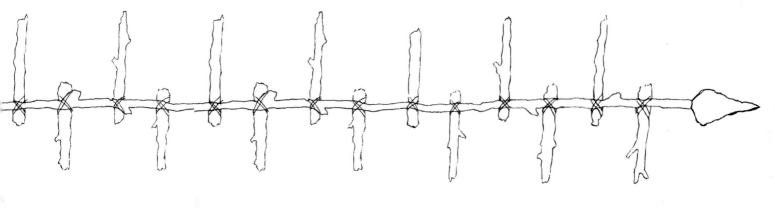

The time-line allows you to look at your overall development, as well as points of departure. You may notice key events put an end to certain behavior or dreams. Or that moving home changed relationships (friendships lost?) that you never recovered from, in terms of confidence or whatever. This is also really important because you may need to restore something that has dropped off the map.

C. Interests v. Identity

All this may start to look a little random, but remember we're intentionally not going for a linear approach, we're looking for as many facets of your diamond as possible. Once we have that, we can take these different approaches, and the details they reveal, and put together a larger visual / map of your identity.

So, another way to add identity statements to your overall map is to look at things you want to do and divide them between interests and identity. Interests are things you like, but **may not "be"**. Identity is what you are, or are restoring. For instance, I like music, but can barely think and chew gum at the same time, so I'm never gonna be good at playing the piano or guitar. I may, however, be able to write lyrics for a musician or help promote a local band. Knowing the difference between what I like and what I am helps me make much better choices.

Interests can often form from **identifying** with the successes of others, or people we admire. However, our admiration isn't always based on our similarities with them. It's mostly that we admire their ability to be themselves. And since we tend to be outside-in types, we sometimes think their job or talent was the key to their happiness... and maybe we could get some of that? I think the real reason we admire them is because they get to walk on their own water. So, when you look at your list of interests, you have to cross out the ones based on comparison or mere appreciation, and tunnel deeper on the ones that come from your soul.

Other interests develop by simply appreciating something. You don't have to read into it too deeply, you may just like something... It may be a shadow of what you'd like to create, and so using it as a starting point is totally okay. Just make sure you are pursuing a better understanding of self and not trying to emulate someone else's success. Here are some tools to do just that:

1. Start by listing 10 or 15 *things you're interested in in the first column. Don't read into anything too much or not write things down because you're embarrassed. Just go with your heart and make the list. Do this before you read the next point. No peeking!*

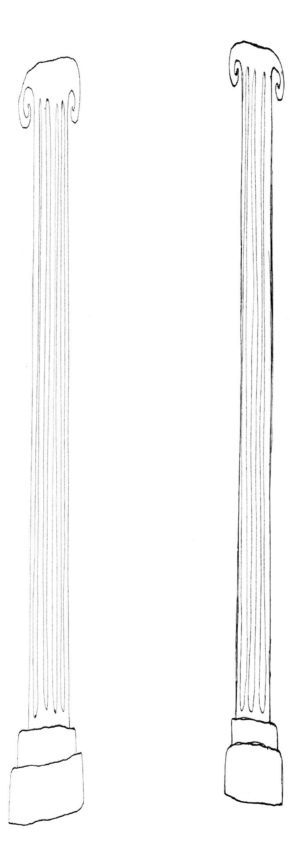

173

Are you peeking? Are ya? Okay then.

2. In the second column, *write down what you've actually done with the corresponding interest in the first column, and how much time you've spent doing that thing. If it's really you, you will have found a way to add it to your life.*

3. In the third column, *write down identity statements, or the talents, each thing on your list may require. So for instance, as an interest I would write down* **'being a chef'**. *So, in the third column I'd write* **'creative, a risk taker, artist, craftsman, hard working'** *(the last one aces me from that job, dangit).*

4. Now, go over the list again *and circle all the identity or talent statements you know to be you. The 'I am' statements that line up with your soul are the ones you're really passionate about, have invested time in, or that you know that you know that you know are you.*

The net result should be a few more 'I am' statements and a growing understanding of the difference between interest and identity. If you're both honest and brave these questions will give you some bearings. And remember, just because you haven't spent time developing something, doesn't mean you will never be that politician or horse whisperer. Some dreams never get realized because of a lack of encouragement, etc., so don't let go of something based on your answers above. Maybe this exercise reminds you of something you know you are and need to rekindle? One way to really know, is try something you're interested in for at least a year. That'll sort out the question.

Anything from the list you want to pursue, for a year?

....

....

....

....

....

....

D. Spiritual, social, and personal identity

Years ago, when I first started seeing the central role of identity, I tried to find the most natural, tangible process I could to let my identity speak to me. Instead of tests and outside-in measurements (like how well I did in school), I wanted my soul to reveal its obvious truths. Which I found wasn't that hard, as long as I took the time to listen with an inside-out perspective. To do this, I put myself on the *Coastal Steamer* which travels from Bergen to Tromsø, Norway. During five days of undistracted internal observation, amidst gorgeous scenery and buckets of herring, I meditated, remembered, and journaled what became the foundation for this whole book.

Here's what I did. I spent the first day writing down all the memorable events of my life. Ordered chronologically, I wrote down single sentence memories from childhood to the present day. Similar to the time-line idea mentioned above and based on the notion that our soul remembers the important identity bits, I was able to see threads and themes laced throughout the unfolding story of my life. I suggest you try this yourself, maybe adding to the time-line? On the second day, I looked at my relationships by drawing concentric circles placing me and God at the center, then my family, community, city, etc. Each circle described where I was at in relationship with the identities around me. It was like a bird's-eye view rising above all the connections that my identity had formed. This was a great 'relational snapshot' which gave me a sense of the now. On the third day, I wanted to project into my future and make some plans for the coming years. I'm embarrassed to say that my initial approach was to simply pray and ask God for direction. Which isn't a bad idea in times of desperation, or when a more intentional collaboration is needed to co-opt some wisdom... But as a knee-jerk request to find quick solutions, it's kinda lame. Wisely, God didn't play my game, and gladly, I was not psychotic enough to fill in for Him. And whether God did unfold the following structure as a better response to my question, or it was just the natural echo of the ethereal space our soul lives in, I did start to unpack a kind of framework.

As stories revealed priorities, and choices seen over time started to speak back to me, a kind of symmetry developed. The things I knew intuitively (like that I am a communicator) and the things revealed through living questions (like that I am a trainer / facilitator) started to fall into natural categories. In fact, it was so natural that I hesitate to use the word category or put any structure on it at all. But I found that there was organization to my 'I am' statements which later became the basis for my inside-out thinking / lifestyle. This natural structure for identity made more sense as I started to understand the nature of organic systems. I now think there may be a design and infrastructure even at the level of the soul, which if understood, can be articulated and built upon. I also saw that organic isn't random, but beautifully structured and full of purpose. This is one of the reasons I both believe in and love God.

My 'I am' statements started to fall into three main categories which I've mentioned before as our **spiritual, social,** and **personal identity**. And once I noticed these dimensions, I was able to tease out stories and questions that helped me tunnel deeper, always with the results falling into these three parts of me. Now, I'm not saying that all identity statements fall into these neat spaces, just that I've found them to be a clarifying way to view such an abstract subject. As mentioned before, our intelligences, personality, and the things we're still learning about, all contribute to our overall identity, but I've found that delving into these three dimensions has been a great foundation piece.

1. Spiritual identity: Let's start with what may be the hardest one. While the spiritual nature of mankind is a huge topic, and outside of the scope of this book, I'm going to proceed on the common knowledge that we are all, in part, spiritual beings. Therefore, our identity is partially spiritual and worth articulating as such. I would even go so far as to say our spirituality is actually our ontological identity and the very core of our lives. I also think a key aspect of spirituality that's becoming more apparent as mankind matures, is that our spirits are always connected in relationship. That they're tied to (and responsible to) their source. I think this relationship is the touchstone for identity. Our 'I am' statements need to connect with others to both make sense of them, and to fulfill them. So when I look at my spiritual identity, I also look at my spiritual connections and relationships to determine who I am. Here are some questions I ask to see my spiritual self.

(*Note: This level of perception takes some time to develop, especially the sensitivity needed to answer these questions. After 30 years, I'm still working on it, so give this some real consideration or come back to it later. It is important, but it may not be important for you right now. If it is, have a go.*)

a. How do you naturally relate to your spiritual connections?
Not, how are you *supposed* to relate in religious institutions, but rather, what are the natural ways your soul connects. Mine plugs in by taking longish walks, processing events in my life, observing the world around me and commenting in my heart. Listening, thinking—and largely being grateful that I get to consider and be part of the world. This shows me that *I am conversational, observant or a visual worshiper...* What about you?

....

....

....

....

....

....

b. What have you heard from your spiritual relationships?
Relationships thrive in conversation, so look at what you've heard and how you've responded. I know that *I am a son, a trusted communicator, and a challenger* all based on scriptures that have stood out to me or things I've intuited / heard spiritually. Which I realize can be suspect (as in, 'I hear voices'), but when cross-referenced with other observations, and things spoken about me (including all the questions listed above), I can get confirmations as to their validity. Also, over time, I learn to trust my spiritual intuition because it's based on the broad mix of experiences, hunches, and the mechanics of the soul. What I'm listening for are:
i. scriptures, poems, and other writing that stands out and why:

....

....

....

....

....

....

ii. things I've heard in prayer or meditation

....

....

....

....

....

iii. words of encouragement by others who are speaking into my spiritual identity

....

....

....

....

....

iv. conviction of something wrong in myself or my actions, which I can reverse engineer to extract an identity statement.

For instance, if I sense I'm operating from the wrong motives, or have been hurtful to someone, I can look at the surrogate motive and ask for clarity as to its angelic twin sister. I look for the gold trying to come through the calcified, self-protecting motives I developed in a harsh world. If I'm being inconsiderate, I listen for its opposite truth in me and allow that way of being considerate to come through. If I've communicated wrongly, usually due to insecurity, I allow the mistake to inform me as to why I did that, and what that's blocking. In doing so, I usually find a purer form of communication waiting to emerge. I've discovered that instead of being harsh or overly critical, part of my spiritual identity is actually to be a *challenger* or an *exhorter.* Both of which can be loving forms of communication, and being loving is the indicator as to whether something is truly me, or not. Conviction for you?

....

....

....

....

v. Intuitive knowledge.

All of us are gifted with an internal sense of where we've come from and who we are. Our faith that God exists also forms a faith that we can connect to God with our selves and our abilities. Sometimes this faith expresses itself by us succeeding against all odds. This intuitive strength encourages us to make radical choices, despite the lack of evidence that it'll go well. This intuition needs time to speak to us (in the quiet) and we need to listen to it (intentional introspection). If you were to pause and listen to what your soul knows about your spiritual identity, you may be surprised at what you hear. Didactic questions have no real place here either, you just kinda need to go somewhere reflective and listen, remember...

....

....

....

....

c. How do I express my spiritual identity?

Or, in which ways do I naturally share that identity in the world around me? It can be something as intra-personal as worship in nature or as inter-personal as yoga with a group of 50 people. I like exploring the connection between spiritual wisdom (which for me is personified in Jesus) and the most practical applications of that wisdom in engineering or health care. That exploration is me being a *researcher, or problem solver...* I love taking the spiritual relationship I have and the wisdom that comes from it, and applying it to specific daily expressions of media, business, the arts, etc. As I do this, a lot of my motivations and identity emerges, and becomes even more clear in the application of that identity. How do you **express** your spiritual identity?

....

....

....

....

....

As you'll discover, spiritual identity is a nuanced conversation. Do your best to practice listening at this level, as it really is an essential area within your spectrum. Also, if you want a holistic life, you'll need to engage with your spirit in a proactive way. What I find is that when people don't intentionally do this, their spirit ends up vulnerable to all kinds of outside-in religious / social weirdnesses. It may take a while to develop, but it's worth the time.

2. Social Identity:
Your creation was a bit of a team sport. You were formed in family and born into community. Your body needs physical interaction to survive and your identity needs relational connections to see itself, and express itself, to be healthy. Your well being is based on the way you interact with and care for your tribe, and therefore, you're naturally wired to relate. I call this part of your internal wiring a social identity. It's a combination of unique qualities that form the way you relate when you're with "us", or are "us". In any group situation, this form of identity is obvious, usually more so to those around you than to yourself. And despite the fact that we sometimes would rather be an island, it's impossible to not have a social identity. This isn't to say we're all extroverts, but rather that we all have a natural way of relating in society. (One of the reasons we like being alone, perhaps, is because in many settings many of us aren't being our true selves, and we feel awkward?) Knowing your social identity helps you to avoid both trying to be someone else, or being uncomfortable with who you are.

a. Family Crest:
Any one of your various relational networks can become a lens by which to see social identity. How you relate at home, school, work, etc. all draw out different aspects of your more collaborative 'I am' statements. But the one I'd like to start on is **your name in the family**. Your familial name is encoded with a wide range of identity statements. The myriad ways you relate to your family are often summarized in what you're called. I'm not talking about the name on your birth certificate, although some parents carefully consider and choose that based on an intuition about you. I'm speaking here of what you're called by those who see you being yourself day in and day out. A problem with this though, is we often have two family or social names. One name is what we get called when siblings want to be mean, and the other is who we truly are. Often, these two names are related so it's difficult to extract the proper meaning. So here are some questions to unpack social identity as seen through the lens of your family:

i. Obvious observations:
What names do your family call you? Write them all down (including the slightly negative ones). Look for the truth behind any given name and see if it resonates with you. If so, add the statement to your overall map later. For instance, my sister tells me I have an answer for everything. It comes out as a criticism because I can act all-knowing at times, but the name behind the critique is pretty accurate. *I am knowledge-able,* or able to absorb and synthesize knowledge. If used properly, *I am wise, I am a researcher* and if given the chance, *a teacher or trainer*—which is probably the aspect that bugs her because she never asked me to unleash my knowledge about a better way for her to cook :-)

....

....

....

....

....

ii. What kind of son / daughter / sister / brother / aunt / uncle / cousin are you? How would you describe the way you relate in these various roles. I just got back from taking my nephew to his first Barista interview at a cafe. I've worked with him on his identity map and then his writing, photography, and now CV / work opportunities. As an uncle, I can further describe this part of me as being a *coach, champion, provider...* How, and why, do you relate the way you do with all the people in your life? I would suggest drawing out a family tree, and under each relationship try and describe how you relate as 'I am' statements.

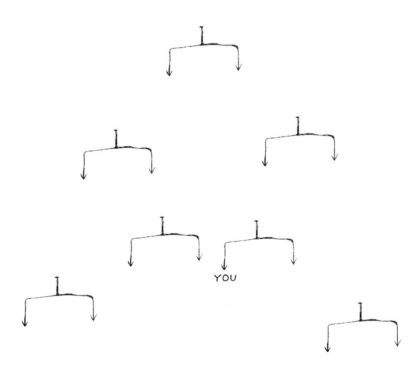

180

b. Social highlights:

Sometimes it's hard to look back at your family experiences and remember what you've been told or called. Another way to see your social self is to look at family / social highlights such as parties, conflicts, crises, or any other event that stuck in your mind. For instance, when Christmas or birthday parties rolled around, what were you doing / being. Some people are making sure the food is good and plenty, while others are sitting with grandpa making sure he's comfortable. Others may be organizing the whole thing, or performing a song, or getting many to sing...

Behind each of these responses to the event (if we're being our selves) are motivations which reveal social 'I am' statements. The one with the grandparents may be *caring, considerate, relational,* while the person icing the cake may be *creative, hospitable, provider...* There are nuances of each of these traits that you could take even further by asking how you're creative, or in which way you like to care. If you find it difficult to remember these highlights, grab an old family photo album and have a look at yourself. My mom was generous enough to create an album of each of us kids growing up. She also wrote a one page summary of how she saw us which has been tremendously helpful. Your social highlights were probably captured in some form (video, someone's journal...), so ask around and see what you can extract.

Please list as many memorable events or highlights as you can, including crises and conflicts. You can use any social highlight (from school or work...) to see yourself through the lens of that event. After each one, try to remember your role, choices, and any other memories that event evoked. Then, try and list your motivations for those choices.

c. *Social reflections:*

More often than not, the people around us have a better view of our social identity than ourselves. A self-image clouded by expectations distorts our own inner sense, so we need to enlist some healthy reflections from our family and friends to clear it up. I suggest asking for these insights in two ways. The first is a casual request to key people asking them how they would describe your social identity. You can help them understand the question better by asking for memorable stories and what they thought of you at the time. You could ask your long-term friends to give you feedback about what they saw you **being** in those situations, or over the time they've known you.

The second approach would be an intentional event, like an **identity party**. You may not be comfortable organizing this for yourself, so consider having a good friend do this, maybe around a birthday? The idea is to ask people to come prepared to tell you **what they see in you** (over dinner, at a park or wherever). It's a good kind of 'intervention' that may prevent the other kind of intervention. This idea draws on the strengths of rite of passage ceremonies; where your tribe speaks into your identity via community affirmation or encouraging challenges. It's a little awkward that you have to ask, because yes, it would be way better to have this naturally come from others over the course of your life. But we have to do something to get encouragement flowing in the right direction. Plus, identity parties can be a way we can restore rites of passages to an otherwise shallow western cultural approach to growing up. Think about this and please take it seriously. People know a lot about you and while it's lame that we have to ask, it's essential that we know.

Also, listen closely to the feedback you've already received. In many cases, we have been encouraged and spoken to, but encouragement can often bounce off due to the hardening effect of a broken self-image. Try to remember the things like a good report at school, or just a fellow worker praising you for a job well done. What do those words mean and what do they say about who you really are?

....

....

....

....

....

....

d. *Social circles:*

Fanning out now, I would like you to use some of the questions above to look at how you relate in the broader social circles you're involved in. You may reveal some identity statements in the writers group you're a part of and totally different ones when you are networking in your community to tackle a poverty issue. So what kind of neighbor are you, or what do you do in your neighborhood and why? I write and do some life coaching at the local cafe, and I manage some properties behind my house, and I have around 30 plus people a year staying in our home learning how to do life well together... Each of these things says something different about who I am. What about you?

....

....

....

....

....

....

Going further then, what do you do in your city / region? What are your relationships like, or what are you like at work, church, or in other groups you're part of? Then, what does your nationality mean to you, or embody about you? I suggest you use the concentric circles on the next page to represent your geographic connections. Starting with your roles, tasks, or relationships in your neighborhood at the center, list the ways you relate and work, and pull out some 'I am' statements from each one. Remember, we're looking for who you are naturally in these places, not what you have to do. Then, in the next circle out talk about your identity (or your connections) in the larger community or city. This could be where and why you work, where and how you learn, or something as simple as where you shop and why? Then, use the biggest circle to note your connection to your nation...

Another way to look at this (since this is such fun, right?), is to plot your movements over a week by showing where you went and who you were in those places. Like, on Monday I went to a house warming party because I'm an encourager... Where is your life being lived and why? What you may end up with is a lot of very different identity statements and some reflections as to how your daily choices are stacking up. When I do this, I often change some of those choices to bring my social movements more in line with who I really am.

My Social Circles:

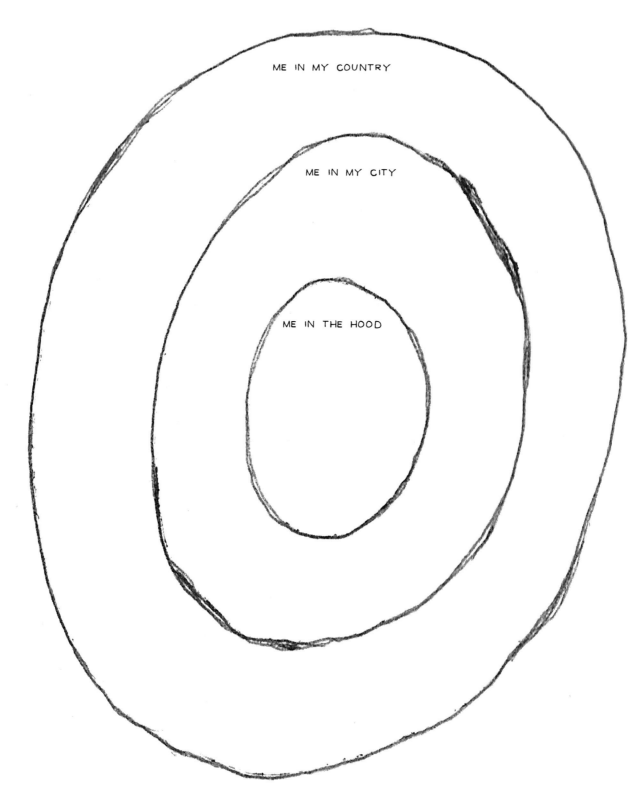

ME IN MY COUNTRY

ME IN MY CITY

ME IN THE HOOD

My Week:

PLOT OUT YOUR MOVEMENT THIS WEEK TO SHOW WHERE YOU WENT
AND WHO YOU WERE IN THOSE PLACES...

Sunday...

Monday...

Tuesday...

Wednesday...

Thursday...

Friday...

Saturday...

Social identity is often more about nurture (us being a result of our environment) than a reflection of our nature (our environment encouraging / facilitating who we really are). Taking the time to articulate yourself at this level shifts the balance back to a more natural way for you to know and be yourself in your community. It also gives you another way to see and relate to the other, to **see them differently** because you are different.

3. *Personal Identity:* A lot of my identity statements have come from asking the simple questions; **what do I love, and what's really natural to me**? This raw approach reveals a very personal angle, which is different from my spiritual or social identity. And in a sense, our spiritual and social expressions both reflect and interact with this core part of us. It's the unique stamp on our soul which I believe we were born with. Some of the questions we've already looked at (like your four stories and other exercises) tap into this personal identity, but I'd like to take this even further. What we're looking for here are pure forms of identity, or expressions of identity as seen through the grid of what you really love and what's most natural to you. I know the question isn't super brainy, and that's the point. The things that rise to the top of our heart, and the things that are really natural, are often the most pure and powerful revelations of self. Following are some questions to draw those out.

I've mentioned earlier that we seem to live out the 168 hours of our week in five domains. These five spheres of your life reveal identity based on what you think is important hour by hour. Take some time with these questions to observe both your past and present choices in the five domains listed below.[54] We'll also use these five areas of your life to explore your future options in the next two chapters. And, you can use some of the answers you've already written from previous exercises, but I'd also like you to stretch out your inner knowledge a bit here. Your imagination is well connected to your soul and will reveal a lot, given the chance. Sometimes our imagination is fueled by our insecurities, so be careful (like imagining a life of escape or comparison to others)... Otherwise, give yourself room to dream here, especially about what you love and what's natural to you in:

a. *Your creativity:*
Some people are artistic, but everyone is creative. How do you express your creativity? Like, if you got to make anything you wanted and had all the resources, people, and time needed, what would you make and why? Or, what have you made in the past that you really liked and what can you see in yourself through that project or process? Don't judge your outcomes or compare what you've made to others— we're all growing up—just look at your motivations and the natural expressions behind those projects. In the future you'll be able to develop your creativity based on these 'I am' statements. For instance, a friend of mine brews his own beer. It's pretty good as it is now, but as he takes this part of himself more seriously, the beer will get better and he'll be happier (because those two things are related, right?). Eventually,

---

54 I realize that all these questions could be stacking up on you. Please pace yourself, set weekly meetings with a friend or whatever you need to do so that you don't get swamped by all the questions. This book could reasonably take a year to go through so just move at a reasonable pace.

he can be the toast of his own parties (or of the nation).[55] In the hours of your day, how do you like to express your creative identity and what 'I am' statements can you extract from that?

b. Your learning:

A lot of us left our education behind when we left school. Which is a shame, because our minds are like muscles that function best when they're continually being used. One of the reasons a lot of people disliked some, if not all of their education, is that they weren't in touch with their intelligences / learning styles, or their school didn't facilitate those styles. As we mentioned in the earlier section on restoration, you may need to look at ongoing education from a fresh perspective. Your way of learning needs to be acknowledged and restored in order to fully develop all this raw identity stuff into something amazing. As you do, consider this question: if you could learn about anything you wanted, and in the way you wanted to learn about it, what would that be and why?

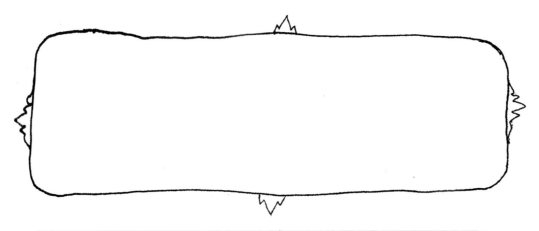

---

55 Like for instance, Ian Williams who spent many years working in the brewing industry, becoming the first person in New Zealand and the youngest person in the world to achieve Master Brewer status. He then came back to NZ to create what's probably the best home brewing technology in the world, called the WilliamsWarn.

c. Your environment:

Many of us have grown up in more than five homes. This often translates into a transient view of our environment (the space we live in, the land around it, and the community around that...). Which makes it difficult to see your self in these spaces since they've become a moving target. So one of the ways I've managed to imagine and then practice identity is to design my own environment, and see what that says about **my sense of self in place**.[56] Once I have a sense of my identity working itself into my home, I can then set about re-creating the space I want to live in.

Your sense of home encapsulates a lot of different aspects of identity, in particular, the lifestyle most natural to you. This includes how you'd like to live from day to day, who you would relate to, and how you would work (I work from home most of the time). **Try this then:** take the next two pages and make a simple floor-plan of the home you'd love to live in. Write in each room notes about what would be there or cut out clippings from magazines showing the furniture that matches you, the art on the walls, the music playing. Where would the kitchen be and how big is it in relation to the other spaces? What other rooms are in that home and is there a place for kids to play / create in? Visualize this as you like and journal what this place says about who you are. As in, are you a parent, furniture restorer, mechanic, house church pastor...

After you've drawn your house, go back over the drawing and write down what's going on in those spaces. If you take identity statements like, 'I am a writer', and look at your home design, you may write a little note in the home office of your drawing like "Here's where I blog about raising kids in the city". Stuff like that. Try to write about things you're being and doing in those spaces 15 years from now. See what happens.

---

56 Tom Sine, an old friend of mine, taught my marketing school students this exercise. I mention him because he continues to be a pioneering futurist and an exceptional community player, especially in the field where sustainable lifestyle meets a living spirituality. Check out Tom and Christine Sine's work at www.msainfo.org

Your Home

d. Your relationships:

When you're with people in general, what do you love about being with them and why? I'm not asking what you'd love them to be like with you or what you're looking for in a relationship, but rather what you deeply care about and are totally committed to. And not who, but what. For instance, I love listening closely to people, hearing their story, and seeing if I can help in any way. What's natural for me is to **facilitate and build** on their own story. When we're secure, and know our own significance, we're free to give that part of us in relationship to others. So how are you when you're at your best? Perhaps you could write a list of all the key relationships in your life, and note next to each one what you love about being with them and how you're your most natural self around them.

KEY RELATIONSHIPS   WHO I AM WITH THEM

e. Your vocation or work:

Tapping into your imagination again, if you could do or create any job you wanted to, what would that job be and why would you love it? The 'what' shows what you would love to do when it comes to work. The 'why' reveals motivations and values. Both of which can easily reveal 'I am' statements. For instance, I would love to find cures to unsolved diseases. And while most of my other identity statements and my intelligences show that I do not have the capacity to do this in the traditional manner (medical research, etc.), it does show that I'd like to be a healer, a champion of those in need... Using your imagination gives you a no-holds-barred approach to the kinds of vocations (callings) which your education or social status may exclude. Dreaming about how you'd love to work gives your soul a chance to tie a lot of your diversity together into a focused effort. An effort that could pay off in an extraordinary way by achieving the same goals traditional paths may have blocked.

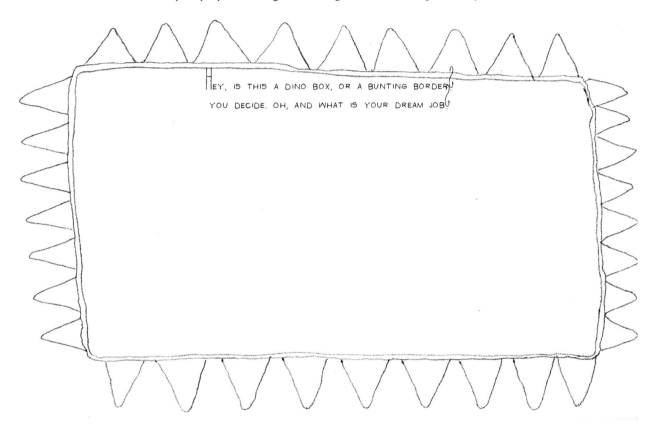

HEY, IS THIS A DINO BOX, OR A BUNTING BORDER?
YOU DECIDE. OH, AND WHAT IS YOUR DREAM JOB?

Identity drafts

Over time, you can come back to the stuff you've written, drawn, or pasted into this part of the book. What you've done so far may be really messy, sparse, or super well structured, according to your style or where you're at right now. Don't read into the results just yet. You can use this as a journal and keep adding to it until you're happy to go to the next phase (the story telling and planning part). But in order to get the broadest platform possible, I'd like you to add anything else you've discovered by using other means like StrengthsFinder or IDAK, etc. Maybe there's something we've not listed here that you've found really helpful and need to add to this journal? The next chapter will give you some space and questions that may help contextualize / meld the other inputs in your life into the broader direction we're taking. At any rate, well done for getting this far!

A word about building your 'I am' statements into true strengths

Before reading this book you probably had some idea about who you are or what you like. You may have summed up simple statements like loving to walk in nature, or that you're a night owl, or (like me) need to be caught up in the Christmas rush. As you've dug deeper, you may have seen your ability to solve technical problems or relational ones. Maybe you can talk an Eskimo into buying ice or lose yourself in a canvas?

These gifts can lie dormant, or become abusive, depending on how we understand and develop them. When we know who we are—and in a sense can shape our personal world from that knowledge—we can use that understanding to live in a way that empowers others. But we can also use that understanding to take advantage of others by what I would call a distorted use of identity. So I'd like to touch on the aspects of character, skills, and knowledge again to round out this whole thing.

For instance, my upbringing was pretty violent and I lacked good conflict resolution skills, so fighting was a natural way for me to cope. I had many fights at school, and although my opponents often got the compulsory spanking, I always talked my way out of it. I could talk myself out of anything. I was so good at it my teachers once commented to my parents that if talking my way out of trouble was an actual subject, I'd be an A+ student.

As I grew up, my faith in God started to have an effect on these identity strengths. I can win all the arguments if I want to because I think fast and talk faster. The problem is, I might win every battle but in the end, I will lose the relational war. If I really wanted to learn about someone's perspective, I really needed to shut up and listen. This is what I did:

1. I added **skills** to my raw identity by listening to great story tellers who created amazing word pictures, theme structures, and showed me the difference between sharing information and compelling people to act. I volunteered to speak at youth events, and whenever I was at birthdays or weddings, I always tried to move from saying nice things about people to talking about the real things that really mattered.

2. Next, I sought out **knowledge** to understand the motives behind why I wanted to talk and what I really wanted to talk about. I took a communal approach, with peer evaluations giving me feedback which broadened my perspective on when I was using my gift and when I was abusing it. This is where tools like the Johari window are super helpful.

3. Finally, when I was being true to myself, I found that I wanted to communicate in a way that was real, and beneficial to others. This is where **character** comes into it for me. In order for my character to continue to develop, I need to constantly choose to do good when it's hard and use what I naturally have to influence others for the good. The tendency to be a scraper and fight constantly needs my character, knowledge, and skills to keep it in check so that even that part of me can come out in a beneficial way.

Down to earth

with my 17 year-old nephew Aaron Astle

I thought identity mapping was a cool idea so I dove in. Early on, the process seemed odd—conversing with my past so it could tell me who I was—because who in the world does that? The first time I drew the map, I did what perhaps any normal person would and listed what I do, my interests, things that are outside me... After some evaluation I had another go and I went looking for spiritual, family / community stuff. As a quiet person who processes internally, I found being in the spotlight gave the internal statements a chance to skyrocket out of me. I'm also divergent and I found myself jumping from one branch of my identity map to another at an alarming rate. The environment I was in (a school Patrick taught at) helped me focus as people around me were mapping out their identities. Other than that time though, I didn't have a lot of friends that would do this with me, so it took a little self-discipline to finish it off when the school was over.

The map came out too large for my liking, so I condensed it three times to create different versions. The week long process I spent writing it out gave me a kind of identity filter—it helped me see the identity behind the things I did—but more importantly, I could start to see this in others. It gave the loving side of me an ability to relate on a level usually unknown to people my age. Identity themes combined into small things like "being loving" and "being literary". I started writing pieces for people's birthday (since I didn't have much money to buy them presents), and began encouraging / challenging my friends by being a teacher / trick guru when at the skatepark. Then onto long-term ideas, I integrated "leader" and "kinesthetic" and "artistic" to come up with a plan to start a local filming community for skaters... Another idea was to improve my musical abilities and create soundtracks to put alongside written pieces, maybe connecting with people from open mic nights and making short videos of their performances, poetic or musical...

All of those ideas utilized parts of my identity I'd never really acknowledged before, because while it's easy for me to map who I am, engaging in it was a huge challenge. Looking deeper at who I am though eventually encouraged me to think: "You're all these things, so relax and act natural." Now I'm seeing what else I can come up with, using that sort of childlike excitement and pushing the boundaries of what I'm truly capable of. Because for today at least, I know that I am:

- *a warrior*
- *a leader*
- *multi-talented*
- *innovative*
- *a peacemaker*

Chapter Ten

← Prior discoveries

In asking my friends about their experiences with personality tests and other identity tools, I often hear that they were helpful in certain ways, BUT... The 'but' is usually followed with how 'tools can't define you', or how limited they were in seeing diversity, or that they limited you to a static position and not what you could build them into, etc. The same applies to this book—no single source can define the eternal part of you. These tools, and this book, functions, best when you're driving a broad process of discovery and application within community. True discovery happens when you explore the various angles of your diamond—using all the tools possible—and the application is where you put that knowledge to work in a meaningful way (via relationships, life direction, your creativity).

So this section is dedicated to pulling the strengths out of your StrengthsFinder results. It's to build on your Myers-Briggs / Enneagram / IDAK / SIMA findings by learning to assess them in a life changing way, meaning you change your life for the better because of what you now know. This part is about assimilating, and then intentionally combining, these attributes / strengths / 'I am' statements together in such a way that you can create something new. Not a new you, but restored expressions of what you were born with.

Most of my friends gained a better appreciation of themselves knowing that they were 'ENFP's'... but that didn't necessarily translate into a clearer sense of direction. Also, the all or nothing language of some systems doesn't make room for a dynamic synthesis of other inputs out of which you could build a creative future. What they gained was just better day to day maintenance without all the self judgement. But that's not enough. My hope is that you can get all kinds of inputs together and dream from the overview.

In chapter five we made a bunch of recommendations about the most popular tools out there. If you haven't done StrengthsFinder or looked at the Enneagram and really want to, refer back to that section and have a go with what interests you. Otherwise, just add whatever you've already processed to this section, but have a look at the questions we're adding.

Your StrengthsFinder strengths:

As a well trained and effective StengthsFinder coach, Blue highly recommends you find someone to coach you on your results, what they mean, and how to add character / better life choice elements to the mix. To add your results to our overall process though, Blue suggests you please:

1. Write down your top 5 strengths. Have you read the results and do you agree?

....

....

....

....

2. Can you articulate the general themes from your top 5 without using the terms? (*E.g. can you tell someone about your strengths without using the jargon?*)

....

....

....

....

....

....

3. Can you think of past or current stories where you have seen these strengths at work in your life? And do those stories unlock any other 'I am' statements?

....

....

....

....

....

....

4. From your understanding of your top 5, have you put a plan in place where you can use these more in your day to day situations? If not, got any ideas?

....

....

....

....

....

....

5. What steps can you take to add skills and knowledge to two of your strengths so that you can sharpen or hone them? (E.g. For my communication strength I did a communication class that helped me with my public speaking. What I took for granted was strengthened by understanding the pitch, pause, and pace of communication. I used to speak to crowds of 50, now I speak to crowds of over 4,000.)

....

....

....

....

....

....

Articulating your strengths can have day to day implications, and effect life choices as well. As an example of this, I've asked Blue to share a story here about using your strengths with work choices:

When I first moved into the city, I went to work for a good friend of mine who ran a high rise window cleaning business. I began what was supposed to be my six week training before we went 'on rope' for real. On the third day I was cleaning windows 14 stories up and loving it. The sun was shining, the views were amazing, and the work was really interesting. But on the fourth day something felt terribly wrong. The only way I can try to describe it was that it felt like I was going to a funeral. I thought it might just be a mental block that I had to push. Maybe I was just scared of the height I was working at. So later that morning, as I was hanging off the side of the building about ten stories up, I asked myself a great question, 'What of my top five Strengths am I using'? As I went through my five I realized something, four of my top five are what is called influencing themes. This means I use these themes to influence others around me. I'm a pioneer, I have to start new things with people. I instantly understood what was happening— while I was dangling off the side of a building all day (fun as it was) I didn't have the chance to interact with lots of people. The by-product for me was that I felt disconnected which made me feel kinda numb. As soon as I realized this I went to my friend and explained why although the work was fun, it wasn't a right fit, and I could not see myself doing this in the future.

I left that day and explored other working opportunities that had opportunities to interact and influence people everyday. I'm amazed how many people I come across who 'work for the man', so to speak, and hate what they do for a job. They started off excited like I did, but it soon grew stale because they didn't have an opportunity to work in their areas of passion or Strengths. Find a fit you'll be passionate about or keep looking, keep aligning your strengths to your choices.

Your Myers-Briggs types:

More good questions from Blue:

1. What are some of the things you've validated in yourself having done the MBTI?

....

....

....

....

2. What do you now understand about others through this process?

....

....

....

....

....

....

3. Now that you understand the difference between the Introvert and the Extrovert, how could you be recharging your batteries by using other identity strengths? *For instance, if you need to recharge by being creative and alone, you may need to tie your song-writing capacity into your introversion...*

....

....

....

....

....

....

....

4. Do you know anyone else who's done the MBTI test and has a different result from you? *I.e. the T vs F dichotomy or the P vs J dichotomy.* Try talking through your various life / work scenarios together and see what can be learnt. Not to argue about who's type is better, but to articulate who you are and how you might live / work better together. Seeing differences is as valuable as seeing your uniqueness (especially when it comes to marriage:-).

What you may have drawn from the Enneagram:

1. If you've been able to identify a **home base** for yourself on the Enneagram, think about three or four stories in your past and note the 'health and unhealth' aspects of that home base in the story. Where do you go on the Enneagram in conflict, opportunity, etc.

....

....

....

....

....

....

....

....

2. Have you become more self-aware of your home base since you did the test, kind of ah-ha moments? What were those moments and what do they say about who you are:

....

....

....

....

....

....

I AM POETIC

I AM FAMILIAL

I AM JOY

3. List two things you'd like to commit to practically as a result of what you've learned from the Enneagram. *Like, let those closest to you know where you **disintegrate** or communicate to your work-mates what your home base is so they can collaborate with you better...*

....

....

....

....

....

....

....

....

E.Q.

Daniel Goldman wrote a helpful little book called Emotional Intelligence. It's not so much about having distinct emotional traits different from others, but rather an outline of what a healthy emotional range looks like. Having read it, I couldn't help but see certain emotional intelligences that I was better at than others. I'm not sure if all seven traits are meant to be strong in every person, or that not having a certain emotional intelligence means I'm lacking... But I think it's worth having a look at to see how you tick in this regard, what the healthy range looks like, and if you need help / counseling to improve areas you know you're weak in.

I would suggest reading the book[57], or finding a good online assessment and then noting here what you've learned about your own emotional intelligence: *Maybe you could start by rating yourself (1-5) on the basic list Mr. Goldman describes?*

.... **Knowing your own emotions**

.... **Managing your own emotions**

.... **Motivating yourself**

.... **Recognizing and understanding other people's emotions**

.... **Managing emotional relationships**

---

57 *Emotional Intelligence: Why It Can Matter More Than IQ*, Bantam, 1st edition (1997), 368 pages

M.I.

We've included a **multiple intelligences** assessment in the appendix. Take a moment to do this helpful assessment and list what you've discovered. Then add what you know of your learning styles, etc.:

....

....

....

....

....

....

Anything else?

You may have done another assessment like SIMA, IDAK or SOI (Structure of Intelligence)? Take a few minutes to drag them out and have a read. After a bit of consideration, list the important stuff that you've gleaned from the assessments, or perhaps add to them with other insights you've gained over the time since doing the test:

1. What was the assessment and what were the results of the assessment (what feedback or answers were you given)?

....

....

....

....

....

....

2. What were the insights gained, or what did you think of the results?

....

....

....

....

....

....

3. What did you do with those insights, or what could you do now having learned all this new stuff?

....

....

....

....

....

....

I know we've given you stacks of homework in these last two sections. The more you can articulate the broadest possible picture of your identity, the more you can create with that knowledge. Which is what we want to do in the next few chapters. So pace yourself, hang in there, and get ready to do something extraordinary.

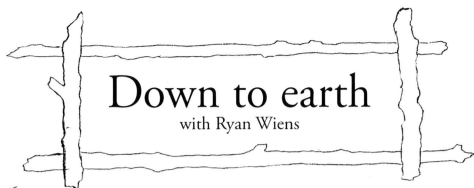

Down to earth

with Ryan Wiens

6 years ago, I gathered the results of my StrengthsFinder and Myers-Briggs tests and sat down with Patrick to incorporate these results with his own method of identity analysis. After paring down a page full of words we tried to zero in on actionable themes. Words like Learner, Analytical, Creator, Teacher, Context, and Guide rose to the surface. These are "thinking" words. I had known that I was a "thinker" more than a "relator", but I really needed to act on this identity piece for greater personal fulfillment. Teaching is a world full of ideas and I seemed to have a knack for explaining complex things in simple ways. My wife and I were in Switzerland working in a support role in an international non-profit. This satisfied our personal faith and desire to help others (another part of our identity), but didn't fit with this potentially new direction of teaching. Let's face it, Europeans aren't really interested in learning too much from young Americans.

So according to our identities and strengths (my wife's being quite similar to mine) we moved to China. China actively recruits teachers for all sorts of practical subjects. At first we began teaching seminars on subjects like world-view, marriage, doing honest business, and communication. As we raised our children (another big part of our identity), my wife started teaching breast-feeding classes and I started teaching parenting classes. All of these classes are greatly appreciated. I love the opportunity to learn and analyze new cultural ideas and provide easy to comprehend presentations that address practical needs in society.

Over these years I've also learned that there's a tricky line between knowing some details about yourself and effectively using your strengths. If I had gone the highly theoretical teaching route of normal universities, I would've gone crazy. I would also go crazy teaching young children the ABC's. I am a realist, practical, and want to add meaning and purpose to peoples' lives. Helping young couples improve their marriage or helping people of faith understand profound truths is rewarding to me. The more practical and useful the topic is for improving peoples' lives, the more I enjoy it. It's so good to know that not all forms of teaching suit me. It's also good to know where to put my identity to work. For instance, working in a country like China is vastly different than working in Saudi Arabia. Saudi's (to their credit) require months or years of relationship building... I could do this, but it's not my strength at all. Knowing my identity helped me distinguish what would work for me and what would not.

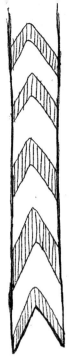

Chapter Eleven

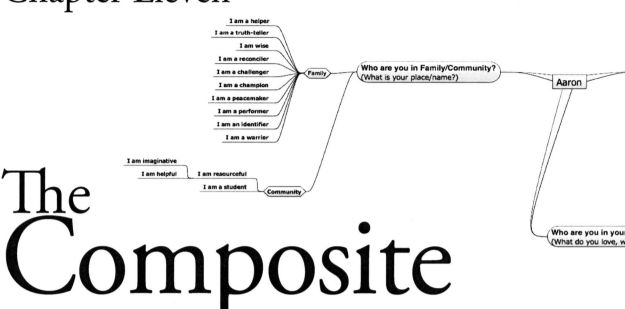

I am a helper
I am a truth-teller
I am wise
I am a reconciler
I am a challenger
I am a champion
I am a peacemaker
I am a performer
I am an identifier
I am a warrior

Family

Who are you in Family/Community?
(What is your place/name?)

Aaron

I am imaginative
I am helpful
I am resourceful
I am a student

Community

Who are you in your
(What do you love, w

What have you forgot

The Composite

So far, we've taken you through tons of questions in order to draw out a wide variety of truths about your self. It's been kinda random because we wanted you to be able to look at various angles without jumping to job descriptions or simple views of yourself. What we'd like to do now is bring it all together into a kind of **identity composite**. This map / overview will be really helpful in working through the next chapters on themes, stories, and plans. It's a bit of re-writing but I think it'll be worth the groundwork it lays for future action, or at least getting a raise. Honestly, a friend of mine took her identity statements to her boss in order to better align her workload with her true abilities and ended up getting a raise, and a fantastic performance review.

I'll include a few examples of how others have done this, and then add some headers to the pages as a suggestion, but if you're a visual processor, feel free to ignore the examples and map out the composite in your own way. The idea is to visually capture identity across the range of your soul, mind, and strength. To take all the stories, tests, and conversations we've covered so far and try to come up with a series of one word identity statements. You can use sentences of course, just try to get to the core of the attribute. You can add illustrations if that's how you see things, or whatever suits you (paste in some pictures...). But the goal is to see the overview so that you can also see:

- *how diverse and complex you are (go you!)*

- *that you can't be pegged to one job or career*

- *that you have relational, creative, environmental, educational, and vocational aspects of identity and that all these bits of you can be used in all of your life*

- *that if you started to see these as raw creative materials, and combined them to inspire new ideas, you would not be lacking for work, money, and happiness*

Scriptures — Numbers 16:47-48

"So Aaron took it as Moses said and ran into the midst of the assembly.
And behold, the plague had already begun among the people.
And he put on the incense and made atonement for the people.
And so he stood between the dead and the living and the plague was stopped

I am a peacemaker

m I in God?
has he been saying?

Encouragement
- **I am a speaker for my people**
- **I am a light for my people**
- **I am multi-talented**

Prophecy
- **I am a comforter**
- **I am a traveller**

- **I am spontaneous**
- **I am entrepreneurial**

Conviction
- **I am a leader**
- **I am a provider**
- **I am a lover**
- **I am a carer**
- **I am wise**
- **I am a troubleshooter**
- **I am a story teller**
- **I am an artist**
- **I am a creator**
- **I am a designer**
- **I am a freer**

Themes over the years
- **I am a leader**
- **I am authoritive**
- **I am caring**

Here's a few examples of what some friends have done:

to you?)

Creativity
- **I am an innovator**
- **I am an inventor**
- **I am imaginative**

Practically
- Making lego worlds
- Immersing easily into virtual worlds — Articulating that into writing, music, everything from the inside out
- **I am a writer**
- **I am a musician** — Melodist
- **I am gymnastic** — Skating / Balancing on things
- **I am an editor** — Film / Photography / Music (Remember editing Kelly's song on garageband instinctively)

Learning — If I could learn anything (what does that say about you?)

- How to make cameras — I love making things unique to me — **I am innovative**
- How to write
  - Poetry — I love my language — **I am poetic** / **I am linguistic**
  - Stories — I love creating new worlds — **I am imaginitive** / **I am visionary**
  - Books — I love archiving and organization — **I am resourceful** / **I am an organizer**

m a comforter
m a teacher

ent/Bold/Brave — Going on stage competitions / Speaker

- How to make films
  - Directing — I love managing — **I am a facilitator** / **I am a manager**
    - I love story telling — **I am a leader**
  - Editing — I love reconfiguring — **I am a designer**
    - I love tinkering — **I am an artistic engineer**
  - Cinematography — I love visual expression — **I am an artist**
    - I love using a camera — **I am an archiver** / **I am a curator**
- How to photograph — Integrating story with technique — I love reminiscence — **I am reminiscent**
  - I love instant story telling — **I am a story teller**
- How to speak to a group of people — I love sharing ideas — **I am a communicator**
  - I love companionship — **I am a friend** / **I am loving**
  - I love intimate learning — **I am a teacher** / **I am a mentor**
- How to skateboard
  - I love instantaneous design — **I am imaginative/designer**
  - I love connecting with skaters — **I am a friend** / **I am a networker**

- To influence teenagers at a young age
  - Change morale in school
  - Change schooling systems
  - Strip teenagers of their long-term apathy — **Transform internet time mindset** — **I am loving** / **I am wise** / **I am encouraging**
  - Encourage identity and self worth
  - Convince them of things beyond turning 20 and getting job — New-Branch
  - Deal with teachers who stigmatize mistakes
  - Start 10,000 hours
  - Give reasons to put themselves out there to start doing what they love (I.e. Get them to stop scratching the surface of their passions with "media studies")

MY IDENTITY

mostly more
physical stuff.

SIMPLE
THRIFTY
LAID-BACK
CALM
MATTER-OF-FACT
SENSITIVE

maverick, nonconformist,
free spirit, player,
badass.

TROUBLEMAKER
REBEL
INITIATOR
ACTIVIST
INSTIGATOR
COMPETITOR
STUBBORN
DETERMINED
ADVENTUROUS
FUN

VISUAL COMMUNICATOR
CREATIVE
OBSERVER
ARTIST
STORY TELLER

film maker,
creative communicator.

things i am in God.

STRONG & COURAGEOUS
SIGNIFICANT
BLESSED
EXCELLENT
A LIGHT

relational.

RESPONSIBLE
COMMITTED
HONEST
CAUTIOUS
TEACHABLE

reliable,
i don't know.

WISE
THOUGHTFUL
DEEP
SENSIBLE
INSIGHTFUL
PROBLEM SOLVER
LEARNER

logical thinker.

FRIEND
COUNSELOR/MENTOR
SUPPORTER
ENCOURAGER
FAITHFUL
LOYAL
RELATABLE
LOVER

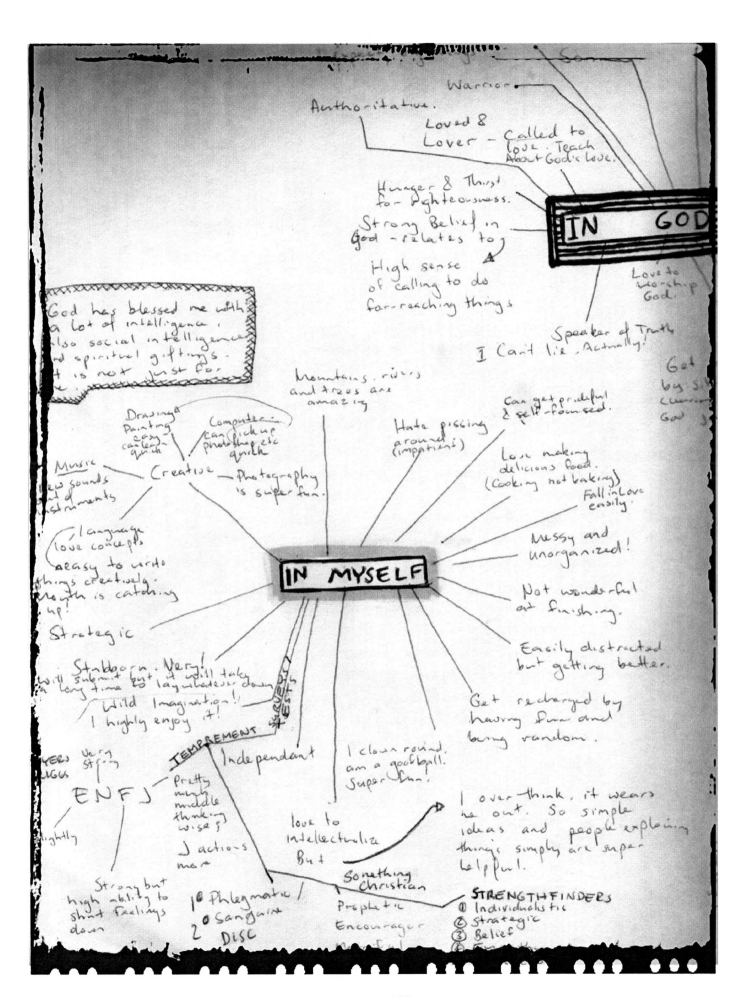

Warrior

Authoritative.

Loved &
Lover – Called to
love. Teach
About God's Love.

Hunger & Thirst
for righteousness.

Strong Belief in
God – relates to

High sense
of calling to do
far-reaching things

IN GOD

Love to
worship
God.

I Can't lie. Actually!

Speaker of Truth

God has blessed me with
a lot of intelligence.
Also social intelligence
and spiritual giftings.
It is not just for

mountains, rivers
and trees are
amazing

Hate pissing
around
(impatient)

Can get prideful
& self-focused.

Love making
delicious food.
(cooking not baking)

Drawing &
Painting
easy
can learn
quick

Computer –
can pick up
photoshop, etc
quick

Creative

Photography
is super fun.

Fall in love
easily.

Music
New sounds
and
instruments

Language
love concepts.
easy to write
things creatively.
Math is catching
up!

IN MYSELF

Messy and
unorganized!

Not wonderful
at finishing.

Strategic

Easily distracted
but getting better.

Stubborn. Very!
Will submit but it will take
a long time to lay whatever down
Wild Imagination!
I highly enjoy it!

Get recharged by
having fun and
being random.

Very
Strong

I clown around.
am a goofball.
Super Fun!

Independant

TEMPERMENT

ENFJ

Pretty
much
middle
thinking
wise?

love to
intellectualize
But

I over-think, it wears
me out. So simple
ideas and people explaining
things simply are super
helpful.

J actions
man

Something
Christian

STRENGTHFINDERS
① Individualistic
② Strategic
③ Belief

Strong but
high ability to
shut feelings
down

Slightly

1° Phlegmatic /
2° Sanguine

DISC

Prophetic

Encourager

So have a go, create your identity map here and then have a look at the next chapter. By the way, if this is not going to fit in these pages, please consider:

- *getting an A1 sheet of paper and pinning it to your wall at home*
- *painting a wall in your house with blackboard paint, getting some chalk and making your identity map a feature wall in your home*
- *getting some mind mapping software and typing away on your favorite screen*
- *breaking out the art supplies and a big sketchbook (at least A3 or A2) and visualizing your identity spectrum*

Tips:
- *You may want to scan through everything you've written in the book so far so you can bring it all back together as summary 'I am' statements here.*

- *Also, this not a test, so it doesn't really matter whether a particular 'I am' statement goes in the 'personal' or 'social' identity section, or if you double up. The sections (spirit, mind, body) are there to help draw out the 'I am' statements but you're an integrated person, just use them if they're helpful and white them out if they're not.*

- *Finally, try to **tunnel down** on the generic identity statements. Instead of writing 'creative', try and see **how you're creative** and write a more descriptive statement like 'composer' or 'crafter'. This last point is really important because we tend to oversimplify ourselves. But when you start using this map to brainstorm and plan out some future projects, you're gonna want some solid identity details which spark the imagination. For example, I first wrote 'teacher' in my social identity, but as I really thought about it, I'm much better being on the field with people making something happen, like a sports trainer. So I 'tunneled down' to trainer and coach, etc. which I then applied to my life choices. Imagine putting a guy like me in a class of 30 high-school students because I thought I was a teacher. Disaster! So spend some time and tunnel down on each important statement. Go until you hit some kind of identity bedrock.*

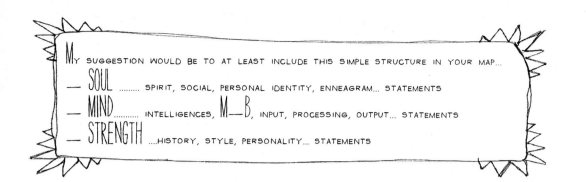

My suggestion would be to at least include this simple structure in your map...

— SOUL .... SPIRIT, SOCIAL, PERSONAL IDENTITY, ENNEAGRAM... STATEMENTS

— MIND .... INTELLIGENCES, M—B, INPUT, PROCESSING, OUTPUT... STATEMENTS

— STRENGTH ....HISTORY, STYLE, PERSONALITY... STATEMENTS

Checkpoint

It's time for your 'I am' statements to enter the season of trial and glorious error.

I was talking with a friend recently about his experiments in cheese making, or his intention to do so... As we talked, I had the idea that I'd love to grab someone in this phase of the process (or where they would be at this point in the book) and spend three months experimenting with the various projects they'd come up with from their map. Literally, to take every idea that matched their potential and just go do it together. I would encourage and inspire, and they would act and learn. Then we could assess each night over some food (or in the hospital) and see what happened, or rather, **who they are!** How cool would that be?

Maybe you should do this. As you look at the different expressions of your soul, start to put a few 'I am' statements together and brainstorm creative ideas you'd be willing to test. Before going to the next section, maybe you should set aside a period of time and grab someone brave, and go do what comes to mind having assessed and brainstormed ideas that arise from your identity map. DO ANYTHING you can and assess your **self** in that situation. Then go onto the next section.

Just a thought.

Chapter Twelve

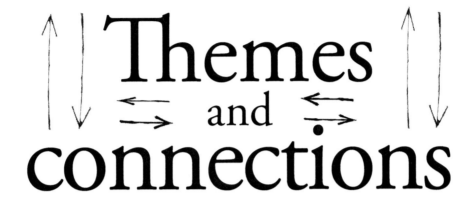

Themes and connections

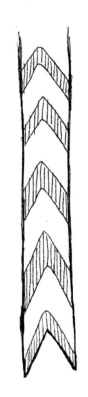

If you've done your homework,

you will now have a journal (or a wall, sketchbook...) full of 'I am' statements. So far, so good. At this point you may want to take some time to celebrate it all. Like taking some highlighted identity statements that have been dormant and re-engaging them by doing a cooking class, or buying some old furniture to restore... All this helps you massage those unused muscles back into health. Make sure to take a look through your developing map, pick a few things that stand out to you, and make some intentional choices to DO SOMETHING with them.

The idea is to start letting your identity call the shots. As you make intentional choices to act on who you are, you slowly reverse the pull of outside-in living. This, by the way, is the main reason I'm taking identity mapping to this extreme: to help you build a future with it. A future that may sprawl out and effect your children's children! Along with the essential question of 'who am I?', I think the follow on question is 'and what do I do with my life?' This, of course, is an issue of calling. Our calling, or the latin *vocatio* (the root of 'vocation'), is a sacred thing, which I would define as **being who we are in a loving way and meeting the needs of the world around us**. We're called to be ourselves, and to create value with that self in a way that blesses those around us. But how? Which of the 50 things that I am would be my best shot at helping the world in a meaningful way?

In order to work out the 'what's the best path?' question,

I've used my identity map as a foundation to plan a life that allows for the fullest possible expression of my soul. My only condition in this very freeing process is that my plans must be an expression of love for my neighbor, meaning, I must love them as my self. So I started by extending my identity map as far as I could. I wanted the broadest possible platform to create from because I didn't want to short sell myself by only working within a narrow identity spectrum. In a sense, knowing our full identity is a process that continues to unfold year after year, but you have to pause at some point, take stock, and use all you can know today in order to do something valuable with it. I take stock every ten years or so, add to my map, and build the next season on top of what I've learned over the last decade. Here's the last map I've done:

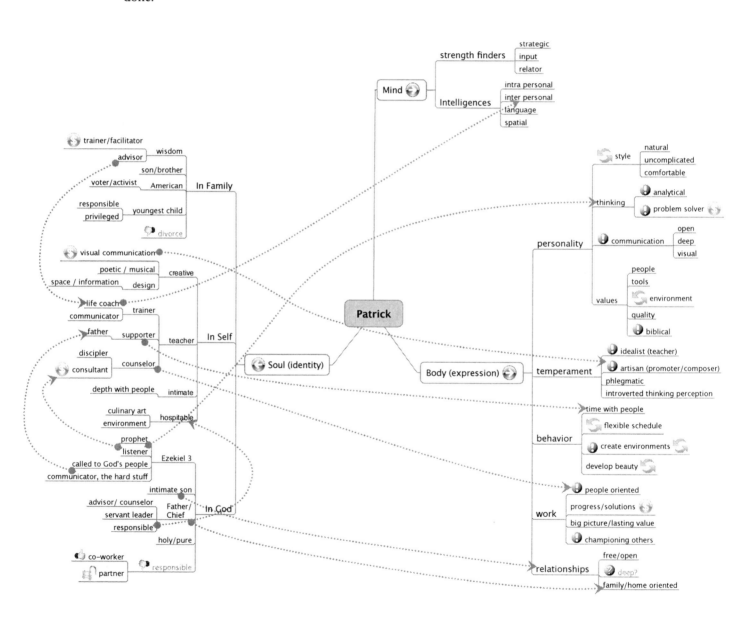

I look at this map as a way to **inform my sense of the future.**
It's crucial to approach your identity from the point of view of its creative
potential—or what you could make with it—and not for possible job descriptions,
or what it wants to make of you. This is ultimately a self-image question; am I only
worth what job I can fit into, or am I designed to create something new in the
world? Our sometimes nervous, outside-in orientation would use this identity map
as something to cram into a job application or google algorithm. But if you've slowly
unfolded and celebrated the diverse truths of your soul, you should also be revealing
the creative potential of that soul. Creative in the sense that you can look at that
map and invent ways of living that are distinctly your own. Creative by combining
and synthesizing diverse 'I am' statements into relational and vocational expressions
that only you can be. When you look at that map as a platform for brainstorming
possibilities instead of job types, worlds start to emerge. The world that you want
to create and live in starts to unfold, one connection at a time, until you can build
them up into cohesive themes and stories... These stories can easily be turned into
plans—plans you can actually break down into choices that can be made today—
choices that when stacked together, end up affecting your children's children.

Once I could appreciate the diversity of my map **as a creative platform,**
I started to celebrate particular identity statements by taking my cooking more
seriously, or spending more time with my neighbors and serving their creative
development. This was cool as far as today was concerned, but I wanted to build
something significant with the time I'd been given and affect that part of the future I
was in control of (which happened to be a lot). But trying to build a future from this
seemingly random list of 'I am' statements was like putting 100 monkeys in a room
with a typewriter and expecting them to write a better self-help book.

So, to turn that random list into something helpful, I stand in front of my identity
map and look for connections and themes. **Connections** are the natural (to me
anyway) associations that start to link various 'I am' statements on my map. For
instance, ways that I relate to people or things I want to learn and why... or how
I communicate. As I see the associations, I draw circles around them and link
them together, color coding them according to the life domains mentioned earlier:
relational, educational, vocational, environmental, and creative. But this is my
approach. You may look at your map and see other associations, the trick is to look
for natural connections as YOU see them. I use the life domains as a way to start,
but it can go in any direction you find helpful. Or, if you're doing this with a friend,
you may find they see connections you don't, which is cool as it leads to even better
brainstorming later.

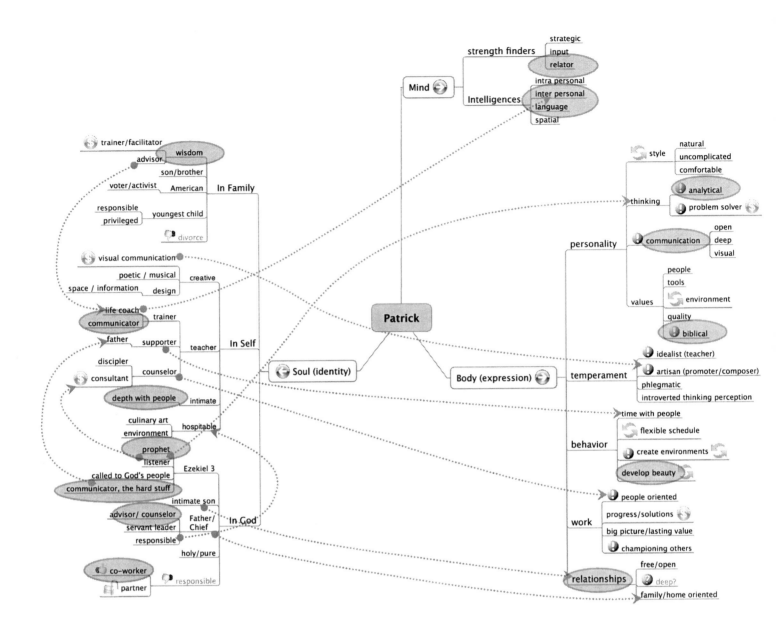

Once I start seeing associations and connecting 'I am' statements that relate to each other, I step back again and look for themes. **Themes are a way to summarize a group of connections**. For instance, if I look at all the ways I communicate, I start to get a feel for my theme in communication, which is to *'challenge and facilitate'*. Or if I look at my love for design, food, and hospitality, a theme emerges around *'food based love'* in the home and neighborhood, which also shows me that I wouldn't thrive in a restaurant kitchen... Themes help us see the potential of all our connections without limiting us. Themes are not meant to diminish or narrow us back down to a few things, but rather to help point out symmetrical yet distinct expressions from a very large list of words. The symmetry comes in handy when it comes to thinking of new projects, like where I use my communication themes in conjunction with my hospitality themes to teach a cooking class, or one day, a cooking show.

father
coach
chef
trainer
designer
international
counselor
partner
...

Once I have a decent list of themes,

I can start brainstorming even more possibilities. This moves me past cloned job descriptions, and banal ways to pay the bills, into more dynamic expressions of identity. If I put one theme's brainstorming possibilities (like running an illegal restaurant from my home) with another one (doing property management in my neighborhood), and another one (shooting photojournalistic weddings), I start to move into a narrative. These ideas all start to come together and form a story. Not a job, or the kind of wife I want, but a life lived with as much of my identity in play as possible. We'll explore the idea of forming stories more in the next chapter, but I've found these identity narratives a great way to help me move past a narrow view of my self and my possibilities.

Let's try this on your map. Looking back on the composite you've just done:

1. Connections: Grab a few friends to look over your composite identity map. Remember, the map doesn't need to be listed in order or categories as processed previously in the book. Sometimes, I have people write out a new list of 'I am' statements on a large board or sheet of paper, and have their friends start drawing connections. Just use what's most natural for you. You can use the life domains as a reference (like connecting a few of your relational statements, or your creative ones), or just let people make their own associations.

2. Themes: Look at a few of the connected identity statements and call that group something. For instance, your love for travel, people, outdoors, and taking risks could be a theme called *'I am adventurous'*... Name the theme for each group of connections you make. Use really descriptive words or short sentences that encapsulate the essential thing you guys see in the map. For instance, a lot of people assume their love of kids and books equals a 'teacher' kinda theme. When really, they may be a *'children's writer'* or an *'art coach to autistic children'*. Go down your own rabbit hole and don't use generic terms. This is kind of a nuanced process, so take your time and let your intuition draw out meaningful themes. The idea is to let those various 'I am' statements speak back to you and help you see your larger potential. A lot of this will be intuitive and you'll probably know these things about yourself already. It's just that now you're naming them, validating them, and hopefully later, acting on them.

3. Mini stories: In another section of your paper, create a mini story about what you could do with each of your themes (or a combination of themes) over the next two years. For instance, you could take your *'adventurous'* theme and add it to your *'hospitality'* theme to create a mini story about running a hostel in Kabul... From stories like this you can start to plan, choose, invest time, and collaborate with others. Identity statements and the themes they reveal can start to show us the potential pieces of our future. So, brainstorm those themes into short-term stories, and if you get inspired, start experimenting with the ideas you come up with.

Experimentation

As you start living out your identity (from the inside-out) you may come to a crossroad. Some people are ready to tell the story of their next ten years and to get moving on it. Other's, however, need some time to strengthen their identity and plans before they can commit to a larger story. If you've been living from the outside-in for most of your life, you'll probably need a good year or two to experiment with what you're now seeing as future possibilities.

Experiments help us regain the spirit of being 13 again. When puberty hit, we needed to be able to break out of the safety of childhood and into the risky side of developing our adulthood (based on our sense of value and destiny). The timing for this transition is perfect, because at 13 you don't care who's watching, or if you're gonna make money, or be successful at all. You just need to try a zillion things to see what sticks, what's truly you. If this didn't happen when you were young, you probably need to go through a similar journey, even at 19 or 29 or 39... Which will seem really hard, because now you think EVERYONE is watching, and EVERYTHING needs to make MONEY, and you MUST BE SUCCESSFUL. Capturing that 13 year-old spirit requires a fearless attitude towards your long-term future. If you wanna make great choices that actually redeem the time, you need to give yourself the space to do so. Here's what I suggest:

1. Create three mini stories of what you'd love to do based on your 'I am' connections and themes. Think like a 13 year-old; be adventurous and let your imagination be expansive. Don't let the calcification of the past ten years add fear to this process. Each story could be a simple paragraph about you combining various identity statements and coming up with a scenario, like starting up a local rugby club and your role in it...

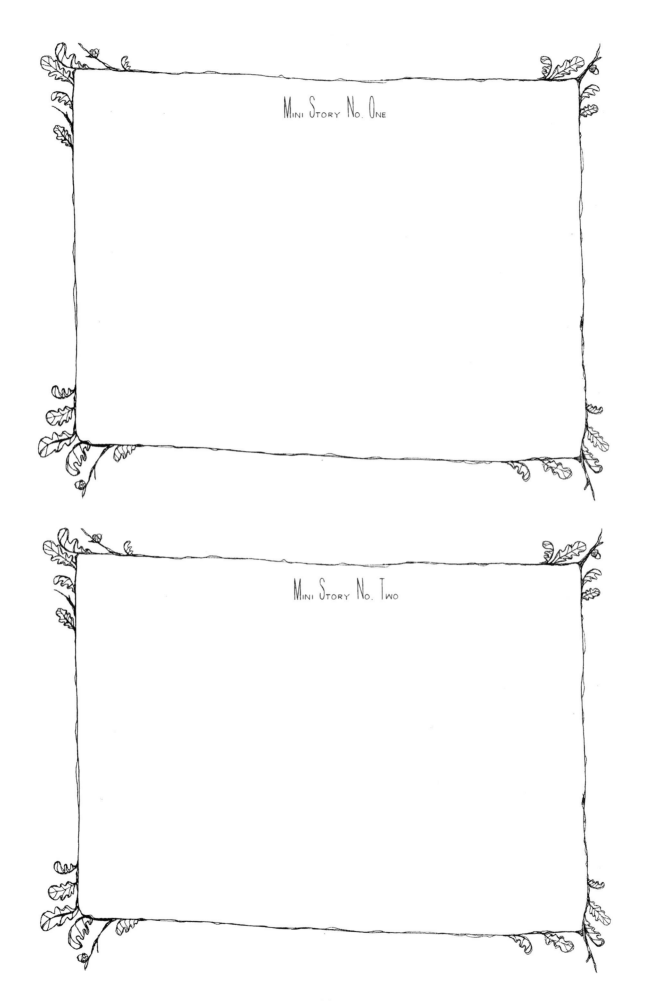

Mini Story No. One

Mini Story No. Two

MINI STORY No. THREE

2. *Pick one of these stories and create a **two year experiment plan**,* whereby you map out a way to test the story to see if it's something you want to commit to. It could include stuff you'd like to learn in that area, or an internship you want to do, or a job you want to test, a place you want to live in... Be as detailed as possible as you fill each three month phase of the mini story experiment. In the story, try to imagine how you would live, not just work...

MY TWO—YEAR EXPERIMENT PLAN

FIRST THREE MONTHS   ...

SECOND YEAR   ...

3. List the objectives or outcomes you'd want to see from this experiment. Things you'd need to know in order to make longer term choices later. What would help you know if this is worth your time after the experimentation? At some point, even the 13 year-old intuitively knows (usually when they're 15) whether they should pursue something or not. I saw this in my son Jordan, who started with photography at 12 or 13, but by the age of 15 knew that he wanted to tell stories as a film director. What do you need to see, feel, or experience to know if the story you're trying out is really yours or not? If you know what you're looking for, you'll know when the experiment is over. If you can't describe it now, at least journal your progress so you'll see when the due date hits.

So what are the outcomes, or results, you're looking for in order to make a commitment?

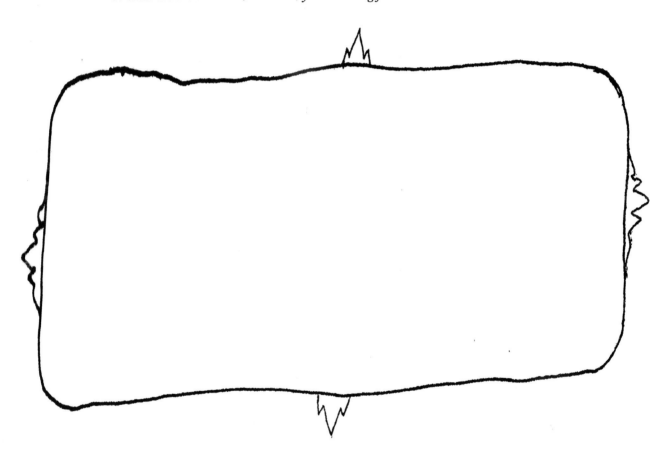

4. Set a time frame for closure on the experiment. At some point, you'll have to commit to a larger story or set of choices to move forward with your life. As a general rule, I would give the experimental phase at least a year but no more than two. At the end of this season, you can debrief and see what you've learned about living from the inside-out via these mini stories. You can journal / discuss with friends what you've learned and may then be ready to look a little further down the road. This may ease you into our next section about telling the story of your next 15 years!

Down to earth

with Louise White

One of the first challenges I faced in developing these connections and themes was articulating the parts of my identity that are less obvious or that have been suppressed. At 27 I thought I knew myself reasonably well. But getting beyond the first half a dozen things I enjoyed or things that were true about me, proved challenging. There are probably many reasons for this, both conscious and subconscious. I mean, once upon a time ago I was musical, but what was the point in pursuing my musical side if I was never going to make money from it or make it onto the music team at church?

I've spent quite a few months seeking a language to describe the complexities of me. I talked to close friends, I read, I did a little research into personality profiling, I've reflected on my journey as a primary school teacher (what I hate and love about that role and what that says about me), and lots of weighing it all up. Some personality profiling tests say that I'm very intra-personal and inter-personal. If I agree with them (which in this case I do) it probably explains why I have both really enjoyed all this talking, reflecting, and musing about ME, and really struggled to move past this navel-gazing stage.

Now I'm at the stage of being better able to articulate what makes me me. I'm trying to figure out how I can connect up different themes to create something that feels right, but I need other people to help make sense of this crazy and complex thing. Because once I have the connections, making plans, putting legs on ideas, etc.— that's the part I know I'm not good at. What I know about my identity has given me permission to value and enjoy my own particular expression of life, guilt-free. And for me that's been where I've had to allow myself time. A lifetime of confusing messages and ill-fitting expectations from church, family, and society unfortunately does not fall away over night. In order to derive some sustainable solutions for my future, I'm taking time to rebuild. For me, this looks like taking some time to live in a different country to help this process. Which is exactly what I'm doing right now!

Checkpoint

How ya doing so far?

What are some of the things you feel are going well and gaining momentum?

....

....

....

....

....

....

....

....

Or are there some concerns you feel growing inside as you proceed? Some of these things may need to be acted on, or need more time to address...

....

....

....

....

....

....

Pacing yourself through this whole exercise is really important. To get the most out of it, you need to work at a speed that continues to tackle the right things at the right time. The tendency would be to find 'the secret', or something more exciting, to help avoid having to deal with something you'd rather not. But the stakes of your life are so high that you really need to take the time to listen to your heart and your intuition. This may mean working to restore a relationship or to improve your health *while* unfolding your identity. We're designed to function holistically, so you need to process all these things in parallel (family, identity, creativity...) in order for them to fold back together into a solid foundation.

If you have concerns about anything **outside of yourself**, list them here. Like, expectations other people are holding over you. Some things are out of your control, and can be prayed for or committed to another time. Other issues, like money concerns or broken relationships, need to get attention because they've been niggling at you for a while. Journaling and acting on the really important stuff removes the chronic stress of inactivity and replaces it with the clear sense that action is being taken, even if that action is prayer or committing to work on it at the appropriate time.

What are things outside of yourself (expectations, pressures, circumstances...) and what can you do about that?

....

....

....

....

....

....

If there are concerns about things **inside yourself** relating to your identity, or whatever, write those down as well. Things like feelings of inadequacy, or plain vanilla laziness, or a niggling fear that you're too old to start such a daring plan... When you bring these back burner concerns to the front of your mind, you can start working them and looking for solutions. Ignoring these internal concerns leaves us plowing through choices and relationships only to hit a wall and have to listen later, the hard way... Take a moment and list what you're concerned about in this entire process that relates to self-image, acceptance, confidence, etc.

....

....

....

....

....

....

Finally, check yourself for **patterns that defeat you.** Repeating fears or other internal demons that try to tell you that you won't get to be yourself. Have they been raising their annoying little voices as you've progressed through this book? They come in all shapes and sizes and need to be exposed. Write down, draw, or verbalize the things you feel would try to stop you from projecting your true self into the landscape of your future. The next section is about storytelling your future, and if these gremlins are still hanging about, you won't get past next month. I suggest giving names to these fears or lazy attitudes. Call out the expectations others have bound you with, and maybe illustrate the fight going on between you and these things in comic strip form. The first panel could show something like Laziness tying you to the TV while you sleep. The second panel could show you awaking and calling on your super **identity powers**, and the third, you forcing Laziness into the TV to star in its own sitcom... That's my idea anyway, I suggest you create your own strip based on your situation. Even if you can't draw, get that internal stuff onto paper in some way. You need to know there's a real struggle going on for your soul. It's truly possible to be yourself, but you'll have to fight the forces to break out. You are not inept, you are fighting laziness. You are not incapable, you are working against self-image issues. You are not a common worker, you are standing against expectations built up over generations. Instead of giving in to what you think you're doomed to be, you need to spend your energy fighting. So write that stuff down, visualize the struggle, and get people to fight for and with you.

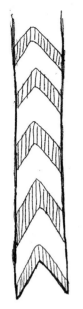

Chapter Thirteen

Story telling your future

When I first started listing identity statements on my five day trip around Norway, I was faced with a problem: what was I to do with this growing sense of self? On one hand, I started to see possibilities based on using those 'I am' statements in a creative way, but on the other, I had to face a kind of personal fatalism. I think most of us struggle with a variation of this foible. For some, it's the thought that fate is in control of their lives and they don't get to choose. For others, it's a sense that everyone else but them gets to determine their future. I had to face this problem before I could proceed, so I started by calling my sense of inertia what it really was; an internal spiritual force that was wreaking havoc with my soul. Any sense that makes me feel I don't have a large degree of choice about creating my future is unnatural. Everything within us is wired to imagine, process, and choose the kind of life we'd like to live. We may not have the power to fulfill every dream, but we sure as hell are designed to have a go.

So, I made a conscious decision to shift gears. I shifted from seeing the future as something I tripped over—or a series of things that happened to me—to choosing to look at the future as something I was actually able to create. The surprising thing was how natural this perspective became. Once I let my imagination connect to my identity, ideas started flying into my mind. Not vain things I'd never be able to accomplish, but tangible scenarios that given some effort and time, were completely doable. I think many of us give up on dreaming because we have no real reference for those dreams. But when you're connecting the realities of your soul (your 'I am' statements) to an imagination wired to connect the dots, you can't help but create a plausible story. So I suggest you make a similar commitment. Start this section by committing to look at the future as something you're mostly in control of so your imagination can do its job.

From the previous chapter on connections, themes, and experiments, you can see that I'm heading towards using your identity to make long-term life choices. At the easy end of this whole idea, you could use your identity to make everyday decisions, like comparing your 'I am' statements to job listings to look for a good fit. But the real potential in knowing who you are lies in the renewed ability to use that knowledge to create your future via storytelling. Linking identity to storytelling your future has tons of potential. For instance, when you have a story, you have a destination. This is huge, because if you know where you're going, you can easily see the steps you need to take to get there. Most of us live our lives in six-month segments. We look for the best possible way to survive the next 180 days based on outside-in values like where the money or fun is. We've become like the elevator operator in Huxley's *Brave New World* who has the same excited reaction every time he gets to the top floor. We get excited about the next idea or choice, but eventually we get to the end of the six months and have to start the scary decision making process all over again.

To beat the cyclical process of endless short-term choices, you need a larger narrative to follow. You need a story that embraces your entire identity, and from that identity defines the people you want to relate to, the place you want to live in, and the values you want to live by. Your story needs to inform the important developments of your life, like what kind of education will mature your 'I am's' into their full potential, or who's the tribe that will collaborate and grow with you, etc. This overarching story frees you from the stress of repeatedly re-cycling the short term by creating a long-term sense of direction, one that helps pace yourself. I realize though, that some people don't want to define their future too narrowly in case they 'miss out' on something. This concern, however, usually means people don't define a story at all, which means they miss all kinds of opportunities. I've found that stories don't actually limit your choices, they give you a larger context for movement. And once you're moving, you can interactively change the story as you go. All you have to do is keep your story integral with your identity.

Why use stories to plan your future?

Stories have always played a central role in human development, especially in helping us recount our past and speak out our possible future. And while tons has been written on this theme, from the journals of anthropologists to the many books on screen-writing theory, I want to focus on something corporations call **scenario planning**. Not that I think present day corporations are the ideal model of wisdom, but they've tapped into a kind of story that moves whole groups of people together by speaking out what that group can achieve, instead of just calling forth what the individual wants. Scenarios do this by creating the kind of world the story tellers want to live in. It's not just sales projections or production output, a scenario speaks of the **environment that will be**, and how people will respond to or create in that environment. These kinds of stories project likely outcomes, following the red line of history, and then allow the tellers to implement ideas that will manipulate that line according to their will. The bummer is, this is used by corporations like BP instead of you and your crew. In 2001, BP changed their name from British Petroleum to Beyond Petroleum and are now investing $1 billion per year on developing renewable energy sources. They use scenario planning to determine the kind of world they want to sell energy into and then they make it so. So guess who's gonna be selling you energy in 2025? In a very real sense, companies like this are controlling the fuel industry simply because they choose to. Which means you can choose other ways of getting around too, it's just that they believe and act on their story while the rest of us react to theirs. Pisses me off.

Scenario planning is based on a set of values the group wants to develop. They take into account the world they're working in, but they're not controlled by that world. The correct world-view they're operating from is that they were given a garden they get to develop. Their world is not a pre-determined one, but a place they get to shape. The results are often disastrous, as demonstrated by a greedy oil industry and its effect on the world, an effect the rest of us have to live with. Because sometimes, when larger groups use the power of scenario planning they end up planning everyone else's lives along the way. But whose fault is that? And what can we learn from this world-view and its process?

Here's what I get out of it.

Firstly, that the world around us is malleable. I get to
shape it, and am in fact responsible to interact with it in a holistic way. Because if I don't—if all of us don't—then the bullies take over the sandbox because they fully get how things work.

Secondly, my story has to be based on my values, my
identity, and my love for my neighbor as myself.

Thirdly, I need to work with the world as it is, but move towards how
I want it to be, which will take time. The longer time-frame I can stretch my plans out to, the more effective I'll be. By the way, this kind of thinking is typical for most people who aren't enamored with 'internet time'. For instance, a doctor will move from Karachi to London and take a job as a janitor if he has to, because he knows his son will get a good education and his grandson will end up in parliament... story achieved.

Fourthly, my story needs to involve a group. My family,
my tribe, and my larger community need to be part of this growing narrative because I'm not an island, and I can only truly grow and progress as a team player.

Mini checkpoint:

Are you ready to tell stories about your life?

1. Do you believe that you get to speak out your future and fulfill that story? If not, who does - who's in control of your life? *(you may want to ask for it back)*

....

....

....

....

2. What are the **core values** you want to express, via your identity, in this longer-term story? *For instance: I **value the underdog** and therefore want to help them move past where I've gotten to. I **believe family is the center** of the universe and therefore want to raise a family that will change the world in all different directions...*

....

....

....

....

....

....

3. What are some limiting factors you feel the world is imposing upon you and what can you do to change that over time? Where is the world calling the tunes that you're dancing to? *For instance, on the personal side - I've always been stressed over finding enough money to keep the family afloat, let alone pursue my dreams. So I choose to subject those concerns to my family and community, making myself vulnerable and open to input or support. In doing so, solutions start to emerge, including the way we've crowdsourced the production of this book. On the bigger issue front - I don't like the price of fuel, but I've been driving around town for 35 years, so I have to change my ways and walk more... In the long-term, I 'localize' my life as much as possible, which is only a small part of the big picture, but it helps shift the control meter from victim to activist. What about you?*

....

....

....

....

....

4. Review your time perspective as mentioned earlier. What's long-term planning for you so far, why? What can you do today to start stretching that view?

....

....

....

....

....

....

5. In terms of group scenarios, are you willing to move forward as an extended family? And outside of this, who's your tribe (local musicians, entrepreneurs, handicap care givers, film makers...) and how can you engage them to move forward with you, especially on new projects?

....

....

....

....

....

....

....

....

The power of story

What I'm always looking for is the magic of story. That special thing that happens when you see or hear a story which moves you to action. What is it that taps into the depths of our soul? And why do we resonate with or get inspired by stories? If we can understand what stories do to us and for us, then maybe we can learn to use that power. For instance, a **story connects our imagination with our soul**. It ignites a kind of hope which says 'if my soul can imagine it, maybe my identity could achieve it'. This hope inspires the 'I am' in us to commitment or action. An obvious example of this principle is how science fiction and inspired numerous ideas which became discoveries which became products.[58] For instance, how the fictional Star

---

58 Dr. Martin Cooper, inventor of the modern mobile phone, credits the Star Trek communicator he saw on TV after tripping over a phone cord as being his inspiration for the technology. The 2.5 pound Motorola Dyna Tec he designed was a far cry from the supercool subspace brooches Lieutenant Uhura wore, but most flip-phones today still get their looks from Gene Roddenberry's 1964 vision of the future.

Trek communicator eventually became the real iPhone. The imaginative mechanisms of story are a primal force, woven into how we tick and exist, which inspire identity into action.

Another powerful aspect of story is **the echo effect.** We really resonate with stories that we know to be true in life or in us. This resonance gives validity to our ideas / selves so we can then proceed, knowing our part in that story. So, for instance, when you see a relational story where the guy who screwed up sits, waits, and sleeps on the porch for days, in the rain, until the girl can let him back into her home and life, you naturally relate to how humility and forgiveness forge an even better relationship. This is an echo—something inside you resonates with that and reminds you what you really want to be like... In vocational stories, you read of how the woman with the beauty product shop decided to buck conventional wisdom and pioneer fair trade instead of milking poorer nations, and how she ended up making bank and multiplying The Body Shop all over the world...[59] You're inspired by how being different can be a profitable life worth living. These echoes are essential because they give us permission to break out of our boundaries, and rise to our own story. They allow us to move past the **confidence trap** ('I must be good at this now') to **exercise our identity's authority** ('I get to be me now and become amazing over time').

Finally, I think stories are super important because they **project what we get to be like when we're all grown up**. If I tell a story based on who I am today, my stories are kinda wimpy. But if I think about 15 years of learning, relational development, and creative growth, I can tell stories about what **my maturity** can create over time. Instead of being a school teacher, I might see myself as a curriculum developer, or instead of being a graphic designer, I might see myself as a graphic novelist. Stories allow me to look at life over time, and how that time will effect me, and how I'll affect the world. This is so freeing because instead of focusing on today's limitations, you can project into tomorrow's possibilities. This is especially important for those wanting to develop their entrepreneurial ideas. Having the goal in mind, taking baby-steps, learning and changing along the way, but always moving towards your story over time, is what usually separates the 5% of small business successes and the 95% of failures.

Stories and your time perspective

You will have tried a few mini stories in the previous chapter, but what I'd like to move you towards is a longer-term story. One that combines the mini ideas with the rest of your identity to see what your life could look like over the next 15 to 20 years. And stay with me here, even if your 'time perspective' is freaking out just a bit, because the further you can see, the more clear today's path becomes. We'll get there gently too, so take a risk with me here and let's see if we can turn that identity map into a story of your life. After all, it's only 15 years, so you can do this a few times in your life, right?

---

59 Dame Anita Roddick (23 October 1942 – 10 September 2007) was a pioneer in many areas including fair trade, HR management, and of course, really nice products.

I've found a good way to start a long-term storytelling process is to look at what changes when you're 40? That number may freak my younger readers out just a tad, but if you're only viewing the future from a 20-something lens, you're not seeing far enough. We need to see **what we're becoming** in order to imagine past our present limitations. For instance, when you're 40:

• *What experiences (education, practice, life skills) will you have had by that time and how will that effect your confidence? Especially based on using the strength of your identity for the next couple of decades?*

....

....

....

....

....

....

....

....

• *What kind of wisdom will you have developed over the coming years? You need to project how you'll grow as a person to give yourself an accurate assessment. For instance, I knew that if I grew in my communication skills over the years, I could predict the ability to write or teach in the way I am now... This is especially important given that we're inundated with 'the now' - with its short-term priorities killing our long-term development. So try and predict some of the things you'll learn in the coming years that would allow you to achieve a bigger story.*

....

....

....

....

....

....

....

....

• *What will your extended family dynamic be like? How will it be different from now? You'll have a growing network of family and community (if you care to) to work with and support each other in these adventures. What could that family look like when you're 40?*

....

....

....

....

....

....

....

....

• *What will your financial situation be like? It'll be different from now for sure. And don't assume it'll be worse, instead, base your projections on the healthy use of your identity strengths.*

....

....

....

....

....

....

• *What will the world around you be like when you're 40. Access to knowledge, markets, opportunities... all change, some for the worse, but I see the world slowly growing into a kind of caring maturity. If it does get worse, it's our fault anyway, so imagine and work towards the world you want to exist. You can start with infrastructure (like energy, water, food) and move towards technology, and then maybe towards your city...*

....

....

....

....

• Imagine you've put in 10,000 hours of craft development by the age of 40. Imagine being more fluid, capable of acting on identity in solid ways that are not only very fulfilling, but very bill paying too. What would your life be like practicing all that skill in a particular area?

....

....

....

....

....

....

Your ability to look down the road may be a little rusty, but we're totally capable of this. Spend a little time and look over your answers above carefully before you start telling your long-term stories. This is a world-view shift—or rather you're shifting your view from participant to creator—so do what you need to make this solid.

Mini checkpoint

Working with other people, how to process together...

A few people I've come across are internal processors who do really well creating their stories by themselves. Most people I've worked with though, do much better when they have a close friend or family member to dream with. Most of us need people who can listen to our identity statements and project scenarios together. And since we're talking about looking at your medium term future, the stakes are kinda high, so I suggest committing to a team that can help you make it happen. Over the past ten years, I've taken the opportunity to spend a week with various friends going over all the stuff we've talked about so far. We'd spend a few hours a day just walking through their 'I am' statements—revealed in the scenes of their lives so far—and then project some possible stories together... We'd process issues as they came up, and then look to the future with large sheets of paper, whiteboards, or long conversations by the river... I make the investment because this is important stuff. I mean, who does this kind of thing anymore, right? It's not typical to spend this kind of time on issues of identity and processing the future. We spend way more time in counseling. Maybe there's a connection eh? We need to call on our friends to regain this lost ground. If you don't take yourself and your future super seriously, no one else will. Engage those close to you in a deeper process because it'll be good for both of you. Here are some tips for storytelling together with others.

1. *Make sure you clear the decks. Pick a time, or rather, create some space for a few days together where you can focus.*

2. *Pick a good location. Your home is the best place to start but a lot of people don't really have a home, so where would you be able to process in peace and have room to spread out a bunch of paper, with some decent food. Make the environment match the value of the event (which is recapturing your future).*

I AM STRATEGIC

I AM TRUTHFUL

I AM GENEROUS

3. *When you start, design your day around your natural seasons, like when you're best with people, or which part of the day you internally process... when should you get out and walk or exercise... Create a basic schedule and don't get distracted.*

4. *Have your identity map ready for the day(s) but be ready to expand it as you tell the stories mentioned below. You may want to review the chapter where I asked you what you wanted. Start by taking a quick scan of that section, and jot down anything else you want to add to the 'what you want' part. Then take a few minutes and look at your identity map. Not looking for anything in particular, just let it soak in.*

5. *Take your time as you walk through the ideas below. Let your intuition speak up a bit. It's not about nailing the questions, but rather letting them draw out a natural process. Get used to giving time for your intuition to speak, it'll make all the difference.*

As I've walked through this process with many people, I'm always impressed with how each person takes it in a new direction. The framework in this book often moves from a few simple ideas to living stories as my friends unpack their own details and apply them in different ways. They then customize and stretch my ideas into their own wise way of seeing the world. It's been a joy to observe and to be a small part of their transition. See if you can evoke the same movement in yourself and in those working with you.

Warm-ups:

Your community: To get started, lets create some basic parts of this story. As I've mentioned before, we live our lives in relationships, in our homes, at work, etc. I've found that a natural way to get my future-telling skills warmed up is to draw these places. Since you drew your home in a previous chapter, I'd like you to expand that map by drawing your community. What exists around your home and why is that important to you...? Your environment includes how you spend time in this broader community. The places you celebrate and relax in, or the places you compete and develop in... What are you doing / being in these spaces? Have a go at designing what your larger community would look like in your best case scenario. You may need to do this on a larger sheet of paper. Try to note all the 'I am' statements you can from this extended environment, too. In the space below, or in your own journal / computer / blackboard wall, draw the community you'd love to live in. Again, when you're all grow'd up.

Welcome to My Neighborhood...

Your work: Odds are you won't have a typical career in a decade or two. You'll probably work through a series of projects which use your various strengths. Try and describe five different projects you'd be working on, large and small, and what you'd be doing specifically in those projects. Again, have your identity map handy to help inspire some of these work scenarios. Try to avoid the typical job description stuff unless it's totally you. And remember, you'd be 15 years older, smarter, handsomer...

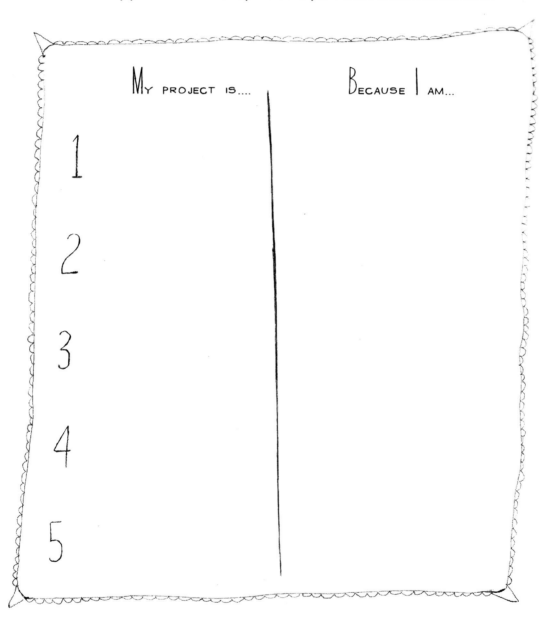

My project is....   Because I am...

1

2

3

4

5

Your relationships: Try and describe a family vacation 15 years from now. Are you a father or mother? And who else is in this vacation like, extended family, life-long friends? Where are you at and what are you doing during the vacation? After telling the general story (or your back story) try and describe your particular connection and effect on each relationship during the vacation. If you're not the vacationing type, try and describe your various relationships spread over a week's time living in a city like Portland or wherever. (for relationship / lifestyle tips, check out Portlandia:-)

These questions help draw out your relational values. Don't try and paint the perfect relational world, but the kind of family / tribe you want to develop in the coming decades.

....

....

....

....

....

....

....

....

....

....

Your education: You may have really liked or hated school, but if you could design your own education, what would it look like? Try and describe a class, or any environment that would perfectly fit your learning style, including the layout, what you're learning, and who's there with you. Or you could outline a university degree program that would train you in the exact way needed to draw out and polish your 'I am' statements. Or you could start with a learning objective like, 'I want to become a world-class choreographer with a huge international range of dance styles in my palette'. Once you have the goal, describe the kind of education you'd need to get there.

What you're looking for in these questions is your soul's natural learning preferences. Or even better, the language of your own education. Each of us has natural ways of developing, as the proverb says, "according to their own way".[60] Tapping into this natural flow is essential if we're to maximize and mature our identity. My sense is that we have to overcome the abuse of previous ed systems by inventing, or collaborating, to create a personalized curriculum.

---

60 Proverbs 22:6

Your learning environment?

....

....

....

....

....

....

....

Your degree program?

....

....

....

....

....

....

Your goal and the education you'd need?

....

....

....

....

....

....

Your creativity: All of us are amateur creators. Not in the sense that we're all average, but rather, that we all love to create. The word amateur is derived from Latin **amare** which means 'to love.' Despite lacking creative encouragement, we secretly still would love to make stuff. Again, not artistic stuff, just making things that allow our identity to flow through the work of our hands. Most of us continue to put this inner drive on the shelf thinking it'll emerge in retirement. Which in my opinion is why most people want to retire early, so they can do what they really like as soon as possible. I say 'why not now'?

Start

by making a list of four or five things you'd love to make. Could be as simple as restoring furniture or cars, or as complex as building your own tractor or bakery oven.[61] Try to not think of what you could make today, but in the next five years or more. Stretch your imagination out a bit here by looking towards how the next few years could create the platform for this creativity. And it doesn't have to be something you make money at. One designer I've heard of helped a fully paralyzed graffiti artist with ALS (amyotrophic lateral sclerosis) communicate and paint again by creating a cheap pair of hard-wired sunglasses hooked to a projector. We've limited what we can make to what we can sell, and I think we're all losing out with this mentality. Regardless of the money, what would you like to make?

....

....

....

....

....

....

....

....

....

Next,

describe how those things you want to make could possibly change a small part of the world. Not the whole thing, just that local part of the community you could affect with something ingenious. I find that when I move past the typical view of creativity (making amazing things to impress millions, earn millions...) towards a beneficial perspective (making things that truly help or inspire people), something gets released inside. I believe true creativity hinges on this motivation. When I stop trying to earn or impress, I free up the internal bandwidth of my own intuition, and thus my creativity. Try and connect the five things you'd love to make with a beneficial effect on your neighborhood, city, or world.

---

61 Check out Marcin Jakubowski, the guy who created an open-source set of blueprints for 50 farming tools that can be built cheaply from scratch. He calls it a "civilization starter kit." More can be found at: opensourceecology.org.nyud.net/

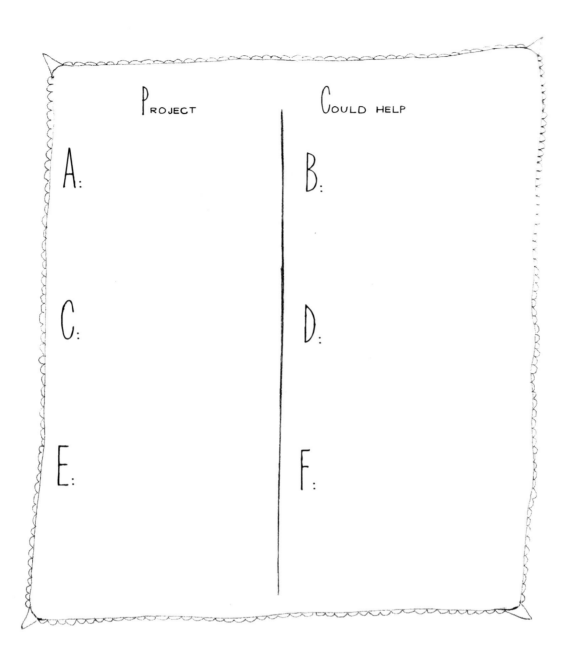

P ROJECT   C OULD HELP

A:

B:

C:

D:

E:

F:

Finally, try to visualize your creative environment.

Draw or collage (from mag clippings) the space you'd love to work in, and describe your creative process in that space. What does it look like, who's with you, what kind of music is playing, how much time are you spending there each day... Again, you're projecting what this space would be like in 5, 10 or 15 years from now; when you get to call most of the shots.

My Ideal WorkSpace

Making direct connections

Changing tack a little, let's develop another aspect of your story from a very different angle. Seeing this from a lot of different perspectives allows you to draw on more sources when it comes to writing your overall story. So stay with me, there's method to this.

- *Start out by taking three or four fairly random 'I am' statements from your identity map.*

- *Brainstorm three or four very different things you could do with the combination of those statements.*

- *Then, choose the idea you like best and grow that thing like a child. Meaning, what could you do in the next five years to develop it... Then, over ten years what could it become? And then in 15 or 20 years, what could that core idea grow into?*

Do this two or three times with very different 'I am' groupings until you end up with a good set of ideas that you really like. As you do this, you'll get a feel for how your identity stays the same over time, and yet your creativity matures... This is an important place to arrive at, where you're not held back by a lack of confidence but instead are giving yourself room to grow.

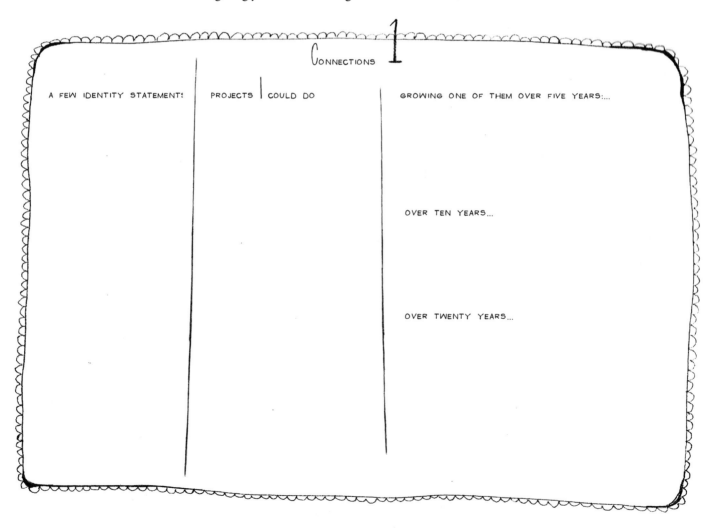

CONNECTIONS 1

A FEW IDENTITY STATEMENTS   PROJECTS I COULD DO   GROWING ONE OF THEM OVER FIVE YEARS:...

OVER TEN YEARS...

OVER TWENTY YEARS...

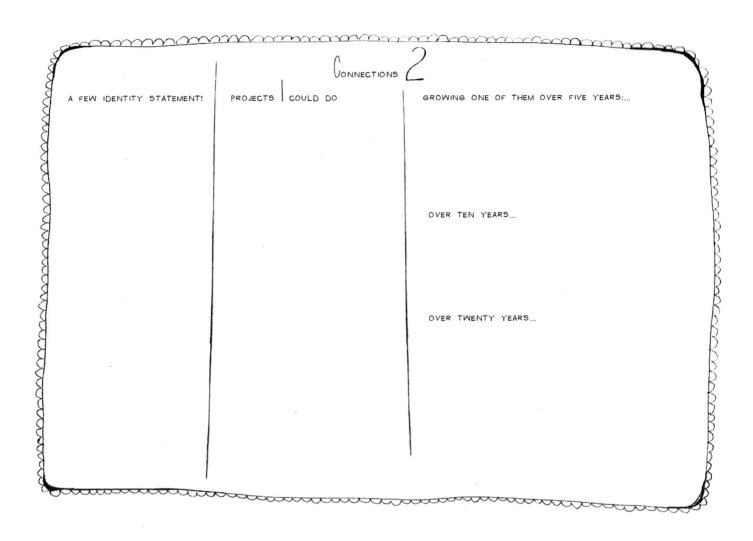

CONNECTIONS 2

A FEW IDENTITY STATEMENTS	PROJECTS I COULD DO	GROWING ONE OF THEM OVER FIVE YEARS:...
		OVER TEN YEARS...
		OVER TWENTY YEARS...

Mini checkpoint:

Facing the demons, removing the blockages

As you move through these exercises, you may get blocked from time to time. It could be a lack of imagination or practice, in which case you should enlist the help of some friends. But sometimes we just get blocked by issues that still need to be dealt with. For instance, a friend and I were working through some of the exercises above but whenever she tried to speak into her future, voices of the past kept popping up.[62] In this case, expectations spoken by her father were blocking the freedom she needed to project into the future. All of us have heard similar expectations, but for some of us these words become anchors binding us to the ideas other people have about our future. When this happens, we need to stop and process the issue to keep it from subverting our story. One way to do this is to write down the words spoken over us, or the expectations formed by those around us. There's often helpful advice or good intentions behind these voices but they're marred by the story they try to create, scenes from our future that don't line up with who we're trying to be. We'll start by listing the good values behind these voices so we don't demonize the relationships. One value might be that our parents want us to be able

---

62 I originally misspelled this which read 'voices of the past kept pooping up'. Same difference.

to care for ourselves... Fine. We can then list the negative bits, like the useless job descriptions or false identity statements our parents thought would create 'financial security'. Eventually, these will need to be countermanded with a better story. A story that you can gracefully explain to those projecting the false future. Often, it's not that key people in our lives think their idea of your future is the best idea, it's that **they've never really heard your view of the future**. You may not be able to tell them directly, but by articulating these stories, you'll have an internal narrative to move the anchor out of your way. Here's a way to workshop issues that block you:

1. Articulate the issue as described above. *(These will mostly be expectations placed over your life, but it could be anything. Just write down what you feel is stopping you.)*

2. Trace its roots. *For instance, my dad constantly told me to "get a job" because his dad was always looking for ways to get rich quickly. Therefore my father's hard working nature became a generational pressure to not repeat the problem. Somewhere along the way, our family lost the plot on identity. Where did expectations in your life come from and what motivated them? It's important to move past the expectations and see their roots because that's what we're really dealing with.*

3. Write out what your future *would look like if you tried to fulfill other people's expectations regardless of your identity. You need to see how this would affect you so you're motivated to work in the right direction.*

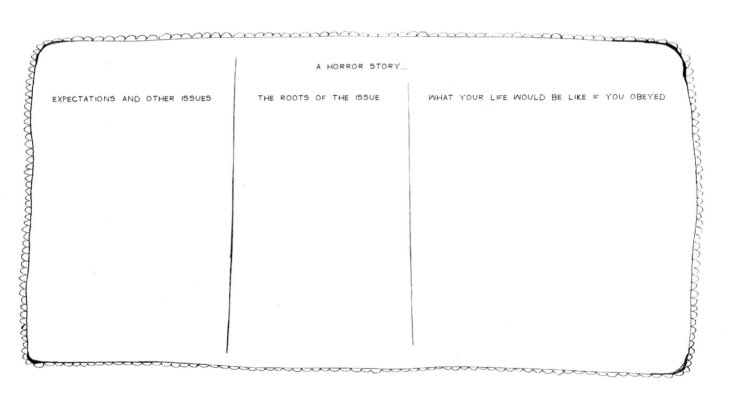

A HORROR STORY...

EXPECTATIONS AND OTHER ISSUES	THE ROOTS OF THE ISSUE	WHAT YOUR LIFE WOULD BE LIKE IF YOU OBEYED

4. Now look over your 'I am' statements again and find a way to celebrate the core themes you've discovered. This may require a party, a weekend with your friends, or anything you can do to mount a proper defense against misguided expectations. My friend and I went over her identity and the stories of her life that highlighted **the truth about her**, so she could see this inner strength shining through her best experiences. This allowed her to press through to telling her own story.

5. Then get back to the story telling, but with a renewed motivation and a commitment to not put lame expectations on your children, or theirs...

Meta narratives and making commitments

Now that you've had some time to brainstorm a bit and come up with a wide array of ideas about your future, let's get back to the power of story to put it all together. When you take the various pieces of your story; home design, relational hopes, projects you could invest in, etc., and put them all together, you're starting to form a **meta-narrative**. This larger story should define and inspire movement your soul can support over decades. To get there, lets look at the primal force that story can be for you and your friends. As I mentioned, over the millennia people have gathered around the fire and listened to inspiring stories that reminded them of where they came from, who they were, and where they could go. This primal force is the kind of narrative that calls our soul to action. These stories stretch us and move us out of our comfort zone into a place where only the strongest commitment to integrity (being your self) will bring fulfilment.

As I've mentioned above in the bit about scenario planning, I think these stories work best when they speak to and move the group forward. But sometimes to arrive at that we need a personal narrative that can connect with others as we go. This personal story needs to tie together all the sections listed so far into a **story arc**. This arc has a number of different elements to it, typically a beginning, middle, and end that's true to your identity and values. We'll break these elements down in the next chapter on planning but for now I want to focus on the reason why all stories have an arc and how those bits may help you move forward.

The meta-narrative or story arc of your life has **a beginning where the journey is defined**. This usually happens in the first act where a defining event challenges the hero (that's you by the way:-) into action. I like to think of this as our busted past, or wasted hours pinned behind a lame classroom desk, or the misused hours we spent on things that weren't based on our identity. The defining moment could also be when you're faced with a decision about education or work, and feel conflicted about the choice because you're not sure if it's you or not... So you have to make some choices and need a raison d'être to proceed. Sometimes the hero runs away from the challenge because they have no sense of identity and therefore purpose, but please don't do that, it always ends badly. Let the present dilemma move you into action.

The second act in this meta-narrative is the **forming stages that unfold identity in action**, which usually leads to another challenge, namely that the world will not play nice which makes it super hard for the hero to be themselves and achieve their goals.

This leads to the second act climax, or conflict, which requires something special from our hero. Something amazing inside has to emerge to overcome this barrier to growth or fulfillment. I often see this in my friends' lives where they have a dream or a goal and then get rebuffed by the world around them. This often leads to even more self-doubt. But if you're super motivated—hopefully by a story that's truly you—you'll press through this challenge and find something deeper. Something that calls together your mind, soul, and strength into a symmetrical attack on the problem.

The third act of your story arc sees you **pressing through those challenges and resolving the conflict** begun in the first act. You've now moved past the vague impressions of self into a realization of personhood. Your resolution often helps to solve the issues of those involved in your story and you form a community narrative that moves your whole crew forward. I've seen this in quite a few people who persistently stuck at their story until they established themselves. This doesn't mean a lack of further challenges, but rather an ability to face just about anything thrown at them from this stage on.

This meta-narrative is the story you tell about the next 15 years. It's not about the job you'll have, it's about the life you'll live. We're moving past the industrialized version of careers into a more holistic story about your home, relationships, creativity, etc. You can include your work but remember to see it as a vocation (spiritual and personal calling) where you earn by creating value vs. selling yourself to pay for the weekend. Looking past your future as a means to pay the bills and into a holistic expression allows you to put your whole self into creating value, which just so happens to have the pleasant effect of paying the bills.

A good example of this what Blue and Co. have done in creating the local cafe this book was written in. I'm including it here just to give some life to the ideas. Have a read and then get ready for your turn:

An example of my meta-narrative is a story about hospitality
and building environments. Years ago I set out to create a place where others can dwell in healthy relationships and hopefully discover more of who they are. For me, this functioned best by building or developing something with others, because at heart I'm relational and a pioneer. I would rather create and build something than maintain or manage it. And because I have **futuristic** in my mix (from Strengths) I can imagine what the future might look like and then make that a reality by putting key steps in place and walking them out over time.

So, following Patrick's model, the first act of this story would be when my wife and I met another crazy couple named Nigel and Cathy, who also loved providing great food, having people live with them, and creating community initiatives. We knew that living this way can be tough when you are doing it by yourself. So we started spending a lot of time together talking through scenarios and dreaming about the possibilities.

This leads to the second act. After talking about who we were, we asked what kind of community we would like to live in. Our combined story led us to settle in an eclectic old part of Auckland city called Kingsland. It had a raw feel to it with a strange mixture of down-and-outs and rich yuppies. It's become a hot spot for night life as well as boutique fashion shops, restaurants, and of course cafes (where there are yuppies, good coffee will soon follow). Along with the highest young adult population in the city, this neighborhood represents a great mix of diverse cultures with European, Asian, and Pacific peoples all living nearby. All these aspects connected with our story where communal hospitality was a high value. We ended up buying a building complex with two apartments on the first floor and a shared deck. We can shut the doors and curtains if we want (rarely happens) or open up all the doors and make one big living space. This works out great for the kids that need to run around, and we have great kitchens which is where we're presently running **The Kingsland Cooking Club** every week. Locals join in, learn to cook and meet other newbies while learning the craft, and eat amazing food.

At the rear of the ground floor there's a warehouse space where the kids built skate ramps and have friends over to play. We also utilized the space to run community garage sales and Texas hold' em poker nights raising funds for community initiatives. At the front of the ground floor were two retail spaces that sat side by side. One was an office space and the other was a pretty average café which was struggling to make it. I had my own commercial coffee machine (sits on my kitchen bench, 'cause I'm serious about hospitality) and Nigel had been into coffee in a big way for years. Like a lot of people, we always thought there would be a café somewhere in the future, so when both our tenants moved out the obvious thing to do was to move in and push the story forward.

We'd never built a café before and didn't really have a set plan of attack, but both Nigel and I have **activator** (Strengths) in our mix so we knew that the plan would unfold for us as we started working. We rebuilt the place from scratch using our community's identity (as pioneers, innovators, designers, and foodies) in the process which developed into a great collaborative effort. For example, a large part of our surroundings are businesses. We also have a lot of artists and students that we wanted to get closer to. Then, there's all those wonderful mums with push-chairs that need their caffeine fix... Design wise, there wasn't one style that was going to cut it so we kinda went by braille and created an environment as eclectic as the neighborhood. We did have a couple of questions in the forefront of our minds like 'what would make our community feel at home here'? and 'what would we want to use this space for when the café wasn't open'? We ended up with a mix of concrete, brick, native timber, and raw white plaster creating a number of different spaces like intimate areas with vintage couches, a combination of small to large tables, alcoves, and a massive community table made of recycled coffee sacks. People come in and feel right at home. Perfect.

There's a lot more to my story (the third act), from how I use **Woo** (winning others over) on a day to day basis meeting people in the cafe, chatting, coaching etc., to hunting with my kids and developing retreats out in the wild for whole neighborhoods of people. This overall narrative gives me the freedom to do some crazy day to day stuff, like blocking the road with a free BBQ so the people I don't yet know can stop for a bite and say hi. But my story also provides clues on how to be prepared for the longer-term implications, like running the next level of our huge (4,000 plus people) yearly youth camp, which is why I'm flying to London at the end of the month to see what similar organisations are doing... At the end of the day, if I know who I am throughout this story, I can join in with others and do some bigger things together. This kind of group identity is at the heart of any thriving neighborhood and it's exactly what I've been looking for. And by looking for, I mean speaking it out and making it happen.

Committing to your story

Your story should be about a life you'd be willing to die for. You want to rekindle the kind of passion required to make your story happen. You start by looking at where you've been encouraged the most and where you may have buy-in from those around you to gain some determination, which is both an internal and external thing. We need an inner drive based on our passion, but we also need a determined pull from our tribe. When these two things come together, you'll have a well rounded motivation to get started. And this is where commitment comes in. We all know how to daydream and plot ideas. But it takes a special kick to move that into action. I've found that making a commitment to our story requires the simple use of our free will. A will that's been retarded by confidence killing systems (like standardized school tests, grrr) but is still capable of making baby steps, which over time can change our lives. A good story will kick this simple force into action, but at the end of the day, taking the first step in starting a big project will always be going against our internal trends. So you just gotta suck it up and make that step. Practice will create confidence and confidence will inspire more steps, so give your soul something to work with and make some commitments. And tell other people, because that sort of forces the issue in a good way.

As you develop your big-picture story, don't feel like you need to be trapped into one narrative. You're only looking at the next 15 years so it's not like you're stuck to this one path. I think it's best to write out a few of these meta-narratives from different vantage points so that you see the diverse possibilities your entire identity can create. I encourage people to tell three very different stories spanning the next 15 years (including being in different cities or countries) and then either choose one or stitch various pieces together to create their best case scenario.

Finally, once you have the story down, you need to give it a little time to settle. You're about to make some pretty big decisions (which we'll look at in the next chapter on planning) so your heart and mind need some time to form an agreement. You don't need too long—as that may lead to procrastination—but just long enough to make a commitment you can share with others and then act on. Some people will need to enter a season of experimentation to make sure they really want to invest along certain lines. This is a really healthy use of your time, especially if you're going to build the next 15 years on that experiment. But again, whether you're experimenting or diving in, you don't want to spend too much time waiting for a confidence that will only develop once you gain some experience. Take your best shot and get moving. If necessary, you can diverge a bit on the way.

Practical steps in telling your story

So let's have a go, shall we? Here are some tips in telling this big picture story.

Review: Have a look over all the story exercises we've done in this chapter. See if you can see any symmetry (repeating ideas, stuff that keeps popping up). You're not looking for a simple path, but for how different 'I am' statements keep shining through the various story angles you've written so far. Or, you may catch a glimpse of some highlight that really inspires you so you may want to tease that out a bit. Let this review give your intuition another chance to speak to you. It's an art well worth developing. Note any highlights or inspirations here:

....

....

....

....

....

....

....

....

....

....

....

....

....

....

Outline: Using or adding to the part above on *Warmups*, do a simple outline of your life 15 years from now as lived over 1 week's time. So, 15 years from now you could look at one week of your life, and describe in outline form how you'd like to be relating, creating, living (your home), learning, and working. Think through each day of the week, how would you like to fill the hours of those days? Add as much as you need to fill that week with identity based activities and relationships.

MONDAY:

AM   AVO   PM

TUESDAY:

AM   AVO   PM

WED:

AM   AVO   PM

THURSDAY:

AM   AVO   PM

FRIDAY:

AM   AVO   PM

THE WEEKEND:

AM   AVO   PM

Essay or visualize: Next comes the hard work. I'd like you to write out an essay or short story based on the outline above. The idea is to add nuance, motivations, twists in the story... that allow you to see the real-life effect in these ideas. Remember, we're trying to move away from straight laced algorithmic approaches to the identity = job description equation. I want you to notice the colors on the walls of your future home or the sound of your children's voices when you teach them to take their first photograph. I want you to describe the way you take the natural world around you and form it into something even more beautiful / useful. The story version of this 'week of your life' allows other aspects of your soul to speak up, maybe for the first time, in an implicative way. And it doesn't matter whether you can write well, because that's not the point. You have a built-in gift, which is the natural ability to tell your own story, so just go for it. You're not being graded or paid for this either, so just relax. You may want to start out with visualizing the story by illustrating parts of your life or clipping a bunch of mag pics that show what you want to be living like or doing. Some people have done 'vision' boards like this which is also a good way to get those juices flowing, but at some point, you want to fill in the gaps with words. Words that will inspire and encourage you to step up and do something:

My Story Starts Here:

Variation: If you have the energy, or after a bit of a break, do it again but in a different way. Write another story of your life 15 years from now using different locations, or creative expressions. Look at your identity map again and take a different approach. If you can, do this a third time so you can start to see the broader possibilities all wrapped up in that beautiful soul of yours. It doesn't have to be a novel, just four or five paragraphs that allow you to see what that world could look like. The variation may lead to a new idea all together because you've moved past typical identity expressions into a deeper synthesis, which is where I think a truly creative life is found. We often start with the typical because our neural pathways have dug grooves into our brain. So the creative must paint and the math-head must be an engineer... But when you start telling different versions of your own story, it starts to move you out of those grooves into synthesis, and that's where you truly break out, like art therapy, or yoga based social work...

Communicate: Next, I suggest you share these stories with people you can trust to take you seriously. And by the way, if you think you don't have those people in your life you'll have to look harder. Often we're trapped by what we think people think of what we think... One guy said the fear of man is not being afraid of people, it's being afraid of what we think they think of us. So go and see who you can bounce these ideas off, because my hope is that this kind of communication will at least encourage your hearers to think of their own story. You may be happily surprised with the viral effect this kind of process can lead to. We're all very well versed in the discouraging, depressing ways of killing each other's dreams, howsabout being different?

Concerns?

As you let this story settle in, you may develop some reasonable concerns. I don't mean life stopping paranoia brought on from lies of the past. But rather, things you'd want to work on, like how to pay for this plan, the timing of it all, and the relationships you'd need to improve on or create... Don't see these as blocks to your path, but important issues to deal with as part of that 10,000 hour maturity process. Instead of becoming stuck, you can create a strategy to actually **do something** about them. For instance, if you want to do something that'll take some time before you get a return on the investment, you can work towards a financing strategy like a job you'd be willing to do part-time, or crowd-sourcing funds for your first album... In this way you can pay for the creative space needed to invent the next great energy scheme or a better way to feed your neighbors at a local market.[63] Having a process transforms these issues from obstacles to milestones of growth and maturity. All you really need to rock this process is a reasonable way to meet reasonable concerns. There'll be a lot of risk involved too, which is fine, but for those things you feel may kill the process, map 'em out and work them. The only thing that should change your story is if you come up with a better one along the way, which will happen if you're moving in the right direction; your direction. So, looking back at your story of choice, what are some reasonable concerns and what could you do about them?

---

63 I met a guy in Tacoma recently who managed the local street market there. Creating these spaces is such a fantastic way to get local growers, cooks, and crafters together with healthy food and cool stuff in general.

concerns:

....

....

....

....

....

....

solutions:

....

....

....

....

....

....

....

....

Telling this story is your opportunity to breathe again. Taking the time to allow your soul and imagination to connect is an amazing therapeutic process. Getting in touch with that child-like nature is the beginning of the needed healing in our lives, a healing from the abandonment of self, of the years seemingly lost trying to be something else. The healing slowly evolves as you validate your identity with real ideas you can actually live out. Ideas you can share with the important people in your life. Ideas you can plan and act on. As the story slowly becomes plausible, so do you.

Down to earth
with Kay Morten Aarskog

Long-term dreaming

I first started telling the long term story of where I wanted my life to go when I met my Hilde. I wasn't looking for a relationship at that point, so we spent three months hearing each other's stories and hopes without wrapping them in pink clouds. In that time I learned to appreciate the totally fresh angle Hilde had on my dreams, and was super excited about the faith she had in me and an enthusiasm for what I shared. She was also really honest in telling me if I was rushing into things which helped me slow down and realize that walking out my identity was more about leaning into things than knocking down doors. I still had to step out in faith and take a lot of risks, but leaning into things gave me the opportunity to mature. I learned to move forward with integrity rather than making my actions a means to an end.

Committing to the story

Telling the story of how I wanted to walk and work with young people in Norway and around the world has given me access to the resources needed to make that happen. I wanted to help these kids know their own passion and have a faith that could support it, but this couldn't happen until I clearly committed myself to making it happen in the unique way that I envisage. For instance, my wife and I both share a story about how we want our home to be a place where lots of young people can experience a sense of belonging and healthy modeling in how to deal with different challenges. But it took us both telling that story to others and making active choices to invite people in—being available when needed—before we were trusted in our local community. As I committed to and moved in my own story, the resources I needed to get things done, like trust, money, and people followed that commitment.

Money rules?

One thing I've found surprisingly hard is to know how money works within a passionate calling. I started out investing time and my own resources, apprenticing myself to gain experience and to develop some content. I want to develop my 10,000 hours of mastery in my field, but I find it hard to assess the market value of what I have, now five years into the story. I struggle to know what to give away and what to charge for in this service I'm creating. I'm choosing a bit of money making stuff so I have enough to create a bit more freedom. I want to continue developing my craft but it's not totally clear yet how to balance the content development (for youth work) and the marketable stuff. I have a plan for seven years of apprenticeship, ten to fifteen years of mastering and then five to seven of mentoring others, and the money side of this will be a challenge.

Risk and decision making

I am an adventurer, and I'm often willing to risk a lot to try to bring people into my story, or commit myself into developing theirs. But in the last two years I've been learning to protect my self, my dreams, my family, and my resources by making decisions to involve people in a team rather than do it by myself. It slows things down, but it also spreads out the responsibility to carry bad situations through. I'm not alone when things (people, situations...) get messed up and end up sucking up my time and energy. At times it's super challenging for me to share decision making authority in a team, both in the family, or in my leadership team at work. But again and again I'm thankful for the chance to share burdens and carry difficult situations through in a community so I'm not totally alone when it comes to dealing with ugly situations.

Chapter Fourteen

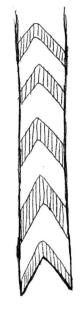

 Planning

There's a kind of no man's land between ideas and action. It's the place where we get stuck waiting, as though half asleep, for something to happen **to** us. All of us know how to dream. Most of us know the importance of planning. But there's a war zone between these two fields; where our apathy faces off against our initiative. From my perspective, there are two things holding us in the trenches. The first one is that we don't feel our dreams are doable so we never actually plan to make them happen. The second anchor is that we're often living under the expectations of others, and so don't have the energy to plan our way out. We end up cycling between daydreaming and reacting to other peoples' opportunities.

But...

...now that we have a story—one that's actually based

on our identity—we should have the grace, energy, and authority to put these ideas into actions. And this is the main difference between the sleeper and those who've excelled in their lives. The people who know their own story put the day's energy into making that story happen. They see a world, for instance, in which building after-market Harleys would be the best way to spend their time, and put their waking hours into creating a small business like West Coast Choppers, which ain't so small anymore. Or they see children being left to die in the hospitals of Kampala as an opportunity to create a better world for them, so my friend Annie gets on a plane and creates that world. And so with you, if you have a real story, or a story made real by your identity, you'll have real energy, grace, and authority to make that story happen.

Planning then, is simply mapping out that story into time-frames and choices so you can turn it into a reality day by month by year. At its core, planning is about defining the necessary steps to move your story forward. Reasonable steps that take you from where you are today to where you could be in ten years. Turning your ideas into doable steps is a very powerful force against the inertia of a reactive life. It takes all those fears of the future and forces them to deal with what you can actually do today, revealing what you're truly capable of. Planning shows you a glimpse of the road ahead so you can create an appropriate pace for yourself. Turning your story into milestones, goals, and day to day actions keeps you from racing ahead too fast, or walking too slowly. Here are some tips to set that pace.

Destinations define beginnings

One great thing about stories is that they describe a destination. This destination—whether it's a five year milestone or a long-term lifestyle you'd like to achieve—naturally defines the steps needed to get there. For instance, if my story's destination is about developing a community living-room kind of cafe where my family, friends, and neighbors can all benefit from an artistic, nutritious environment... then all I have to do is break down the steps needed to make this happen. These steps become my plan. If my identity defines my place in this story as the manager, or the chef, or the environmental designer... then I look at what I need to learn and develop in order to make that happen. Knowing my place sets out a series of natural steps to take and choices to make. Those choices also form a natural order which have to happen first, second, and third... And the coolest thing is once I outline all those steps, I now know what I need to do first—which might be an education choice, or business plan seminar. I don't have to run the cafe tomorrow. Each step I take slowly but surely turns my story into reality.

These steps don't become clear unless the destination is clear, or clear enough. If, for instance, I want to work in hospitality or education, then I need to clarify my story so I can better define the path to get there. Even 'being a teacher' is way too general a destination to know what I'm shooting for. Your destination comes from all the stuff we've done so far; a clear sense of identity, a rich brainstorming process, and an adequate experimentation period to settle on a story you're fully committed to. Once you have a story worth living for, my assumption is that this story will naturally define the steps needed to make it real. If it doesn't, write me (patrick@patrickdodson.net). Also, there are a lot of different ways to realize / plan out your story as long as you have a destination. The main thing is to plan and act so you don't get sidelined by inactivity.

Another aspect of having a destination is that it moors your life to long-term cause and effect. Connecting your story to where and how you'll, live for instance, anchors you to the land (home, place, neighborhood) which makes you think differently about how you're living today. Knowing what your work and creativity could look like in ten years helps you consider how to live a sustainable lifestyle now. Describing the kind of community you want to end up with gives you a sense of what you can be doing immediately to develop these kinds of relationships. All these aspects have a settling effect. They give us a sense of potential belonging and help us wrestle with our typical tourist mentalities. This is super important for a generation weaned on short-term thinking where flexibility has become a badge, when in reality, and over the long-term, it's a stressful liability.

Creating tribal buy-in

Once you have a simple plan / outline of what needs doing (which we'll leave room for at the end of this chapter) you can start sharing it with the right people. People who will hear you, encourage, and champion your ideas. People who will challenge you in a proactive way. As you connect with the right supporters, the ideas and steps in your plan start to gain some feedback. As ideas emerge from your friends and you synthesize them with their plans... you're no longer going it alone. After a while, the network effect kicks in, like a friend who knows a friend who can give you an internship in a similar business or art guild... Your plans should give others a sense of their place / context in your life, which creates a team over time. This team will support the longer-term process of achieving your overall story. This comes back to the idea we've mentioned before about finding your tribe. Your family, close friends, and those you want to collaborate with professionally are the basis of this tribe. Your story and plans give each person in that tribe an opportunity to connect with you in a healthy way. Instead of your family repeating the 'get a job' mantra, they may now know what kind of work they can support. Instead of your friends hanging about without a purpose, you guys now have something to do or learn together. Instead of workmates complaining in the lunch room about their lives, you can plan and brainstorm with them to constantly push your story further. Plans give everyone in the tribe a better way to connect - which should result in you being more intentional in their lives and their stories. As you gain this community effect (not by waiting around for it, but by giving people something to work with) and start acting on the first few steps in your plan, you start to see the power of being yourself in a group. This builds strength and a sense of momentum, which gives you grace to deal with the larger challenges your plan may present. Even if things don't work out as you want, you'll have enough momentum to work around the hurdles.

Your story and plans also help define the extended story and plans of the tribe (the people, location, and community models) best suited to grow that story. As your plans, and thus your tribe, unfolds you slowly forge into a committed group. This community has the potential to scale your initial story into something larger than originally imagined. There may be some compromises needed in order to achieve these larger plans together, but as your crew unfolds, you'll find your natural place and pace within this bigger story. I've often struggled with this bigger story dynamic, probably because I'm a bit of a rebel. I've always wanted to move faster than the group around me, but I've found that my rushed pace was usually based on a lack of patience. When I've moved at the pace of the group, I learned a lot more about my self and got a lot further in my plans than I could have working on my own. That's not to say that we shouldn't pioneer or explore where others may not want to go, it's just that we should know the difference between true pioneering and impatience.

Plans can change, but your identity doesn't

As you move forward, you may see a better way to express your identity. Or you may learn even more about yourself that you'll want to put into action. So you'll make some changes to those plans... But unlike those who do nothing because they don't want to invest in the wrong direction or are suffering from FOMO,[64] you'll have already been moving on the power of your original story and can now change directions if you find a better way to get there. Knowing this allows you to fully dive into your plans because those possible course corrections won't show up until you're moving.

So, your story may change or diverge and that's fine as long as it's still your story, or rather, still you. Your core identity has a kind of nuclear strength which can be expressed in a huge variety of ways. Giving yourself an initial story gives your soul movement in which to further express itself. And while you may continue to understand more and more about your identity as time goes on, your identity never actually changes. What changes are the ways you can express that identity. So feel free, and plan to be, as much of you as you know at this point.

Sometimes opportunities pop up that appear really interesting or more profitable, but they may not be you. Plans based on your identity allow you to say no to wastes of time, even the attractive ones. Having a story keeps you focused so that you're not vulnerable to any opportunity that comes your way. And as you walk out your plans on a day to day basis, you get some runs on the board which encourages the things you're saying 'yes' to. Each and every day you're being yourself is like a slow healing or strengthening process, which added to the skills you're developing, facilitates the fulfillment of your overall plans. Over time, this becomes a kind of security. It's way better to know where you're going than being 'open' to anything that comes along.

Five natural seasons of planning

Over the years, I've observed thousands of people walking out the plans of their lives. I've found that for myself, and for many others, there are usually five distinct seasons - or five phases - that help people move from their initial idea to a mature reality. They look something like this:

• *The season of experimentation* helps me to sort out my priorities by testing the waters of my story with intentional trials. Taking a three-month course, or taking a camera with me each day gives me time to see if my identity, passion, and timing is lining up before I make a longer term commitment. This naturally leads to...

---

64 My nephew Matthew just pointed this out to me, it stands for Fear Of Missing Out. Another disease fostered by a tourist culture.

- *The season of education,* where I commit to learn the things I need to know in order to make my story happen. It's where I educate my raw identity statements (like 'I am hospitable') into knowledgeable talents ('I understand creme brûlée') which I can build on through...

- *The season of apprenticeship,* where I turn my education into practice. Finding key people who are amazing in the fields I'm pursuing so I can learn and practice along side them. Over time, this will mature my story into...

- *The season of production,* where I am now hitting my pace and creating, doing what I envisaged years prior. Where I have the knowledge, practice, and means to be consistent in fulfilling my story. Over time, I will be able to share this in...

- *The season of multiplication / mentoring,* where I'm able to branch out, share with others, and co-create with even more people. Having learned so many lessons, I'm now ready to share with those who are just starting out. I can also build on this platform to break out and express other parts of my identity and write whole new chapters in my story.

Understanding these seasons gives me grace on a number of different levels: A grace that knows where things are going and where I'm at in the unfolding. A knowing of approximately where I'm at in these seasons as the years roll on so I can keep moving when things are slow. A knowing of how to pace myself when things seem like they're moving too fast. Knowing these seasons also gives me a patience which I can share with my tribe, so we all have a sense of what we're capable of over time. This will keep us from judging ourselves based solely on what's happening today. Finally, having a sense of seasons allows me to transform my time perspective **from present hedonistic to future creative**. We desperately need this grace and perspective to help us out of the short-term cycles.

Setting mature milestones

To start the planning process we need to break down your story into milestones, or key places you want to get to in the unfolding of your story. When you combine your milestones with the seasons mentioned above, you create a plausible way to make your overall story happen. Your story already has at least one milestone, that is, the place you want to arrive at. But using the seasons above, you can break down at least five milestones, each one a doable place to arrive at every few years in your journey. For me, some 'destination milestones' in my story would be:
- *become an amazing father / mentor / collaborator with my family and friends*
- *become a right of passage photographer*
- *become a writer of non-fiction books and inspiring screenplays*
- *master the art of hospitality in the home and community*
All of these tie into my larger story, but knowing these destinations helps me to break down possible paths that'll get me there.

Mature milestones have useful details that help me know what I'm really shooting for. For instance, instead of just being a good photographer, I want to learn how to capture important rites of passage, like the one-day-transformation of waking up single and going to bed married. Or, instead of just having kids, I want to be a world-class father / coach who helps his family discover their path in life... These details give me clarity when it comes to making plans, and then the choices within those plans. Like, if my photographic destination is about capturing human interactions, I may look at studying photojournalism or anthropology instead of fine art photography, or both if that's where my milestone leads me. So the milestone predicts the kind of details my path requires.

For instance:

Milestones...
• *I want to become a rite of passage photographer*
• *who captures amazing stories in a photo-journalistic style*
• *by visually connecting with real people and their deep stories*

...create a detailed path
• *so I look for opportunities that will train me to see human nature*
• *that teach me the craft and ability to capture that nature*
• *and practice each day, looking for pro-bono or paid projects in birth photography, weddings, or whatever.*

These milestones are derived from a mixture of my 'I am' statements and the creative ways I choose to put them together. This ties into my passion and my heart for responding to the world around me in a loving way. This final bit (the place of our neighbors in our stories) is essential to creating meaningful connections between identity and the real world. My experience has been that fulfillment only happens when I'm using my gifts in a beneficial way with my neighbors. Which I've seen mirrored in the lives of today's great photographers like James Nachtwey and Yann Arthus-Bertrand. Their gift becomes a challenging and inspirational way to see the world differently, and an attempt to heal its pain. I want to be like that when my photography grows up.

Authority v. Confidence

As your story develops into plans, you start to gain a kind of faith. Not a blind faith about being a superstar musician while having no real musical talent, but a grounded belief that you can achieve being your true self. This grounding allows you to see the authority you possess, based on what you can truly do with your identity. You get comfortable with not having any real confidence as you start out, because confidence, as mentioned before, happens once you've achieved certain milestones. You can't wait around for this, and need to move forward on faith, a faith based on what exists in your soul, and so you act...

When I started writing, I knew I was going to be less than average and had no real confidence. But I did have a sense of faith that the glimpses I saw in my soul (communicator, wordsmith, intuitive, theatrical) could be formed into expertise over time. So I called out a milestone and started working towards it. Eventually, I will gain confidence but I don't need that to have a go, to learn my craft, and put in my 10,000 hours. For that, all I need is the authority to be myself. Plans give me a positive way to turn those glimpses into action and that authority into confidence.

So yeah, that's the theory. Let's try putting this together for you. Using all the principles listed above and especially this idea of understanding life's seasons, I'll map out a story-to-plan scenario so you can see what I mean. Then I'd like you to do the same for your story:

THE STORY:

IN FIFTEEN YEARS I WILL BE MARRIED WITH THREE KIDS LIVING IN KENSINGTON. MY LIFE WILL REVOLVE AROUND MY HOME WHERE NEIGHBORS AND THEIR STORIES BECOME THE BASIS FOR MY PHOTOGRAPHY BUSINESS. MY POLITICAL ACTIVITY, MY CONNECTION WITH THE LOCAL ARTISTS, AND MY FAMILIES NATURAL TIES WILL PROVIDE A LIVING EDUCATION FOR MY CAMERA TO LEARN FROM. I WILL SHOOT ANYTHING AND EVERYTHING BUT FOCUS ON THOSE HUMAN STORIES THAT SHOW THE CHANGING NATURE OF LIFE. BIRTHS, BIRTHDAYS, MARRIAGES, MORE BIRTHS... WILL FORM THE PLATFORM FOR MY RITE—OF—PASSAGE EXPERTISE. I WILL JOIN OR FORM A PHOTO—TELLERS GUILD WHERE OTHER ARTISTS IN THE AREA WILL HAVE A FORUM TO GROW AND COLLABORATE WITH. I WILL HAVE A GOOD GRIP ON TRADITIONAL AND RECENT PHOTOGRAPHIC TOOLS—AS WILL MY KIDS—SO THAT I CAN CONTRIBUTE TO A LARGER DISCUSSION VIA TRAINING PROGRAMS I WILL DEVELOP FOR LOCAL YOUTH OF ALL AGES. WHEN THIS STORY IS GOING STRONG, I WILL BUILD ON THIS FAMILY BUSINESS PLATFORM AND START ENVISAGING THE NEXT TWENTY YEARS. SWEET.

268

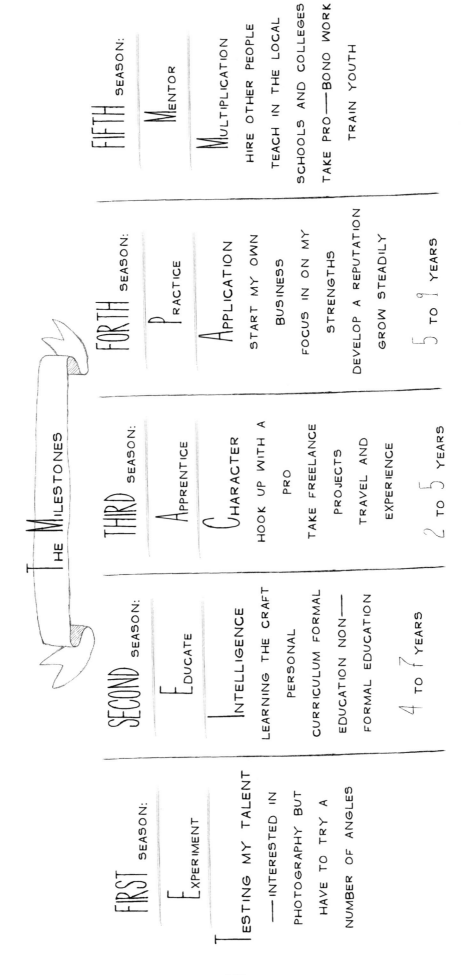

The Milestones

FIRST SEASON:

Experiment

Testing my talent
— interested in
photography but
have to try a
number of angles

SECOND SEASON:

Educate

Intelligence
learning the craft
personal
curriculum formal
education non—
formal education

4 to 7 years

THIRD SEASON:

Apprentice

Character
hook up with a
pro
take freelance
projects
travel and
experience

2 to 5 years

FORTH SEASON:

Practice

Application
start my own
business
focus in on my
strengths
develop a reputation
grow steadily

5 to 9 years

FIFTH SEASON:

Mentor

Multiplication
hire other people
teach in the local
schools and colleges
take pro—bono work
train youth

Your turn:

Planning - from the end of your story to today

(remember, you get to do this a few times in your lifetime, so don't freeze up on me here. Also, if you don't like the format I'm offering, just line through my headers and use the pages as you like...)

2 WRITE DOWN SOME MILESTONES TO ACHIEVE THAT GOAL

↓

EXPERIMENTS THAT NEED TO HAPPEN

EDUCATION I WILL NEED

APPRENTICESHIPS I CAN TAKE TO PRACTICE

3

—UNDERNEATH EACH SEASON, WRITE OUT HOW MUCH TIME THE SEASON MAY TAKE

↑

STARTING TO ESTABLISH MYSELF...

4. *What should you commit to first?* Do you need to experiment before committing? What would that look like (be specific about the experiment, give it some time frames)?

....

....

....

....

....

....

....

....

....

5. *What do you need to do in the next two years to reach the first milestone?* And how will your family and community be involved?

....

....

....

....

....

....

....

....

....

6. *What do you do today to prepare for this journey?* Communication with others? Education? Money and other resources?

....

....

....

....

....

....

....

....

....

Leaning into your future

You can make a number of different plans until you settle on the one you really want to follow. This is just to get you started. Once you have the plan and decide to move forward, maybe you should have a rite of passage party to formalize the commitment? Describe the perfect party / ceremony where you gather the key people in your life, explain the quest, and ask people to join you in this journey. We do this for weddings and big birthdays, why not for life planning?

At the end of the day, your stories and plans give you a sense of direction. It isn't fortune telling and you're not predicting everything about the future. There are some things you have no control over what so ever. But there's a lot you do have a choice about and these plans could help you see the difference. As you lean into your plans, you'll have real ideas to work with which will lead to other ideas, and the plan may change... Getting you moving in the right direction is the most crucial thing at this point, so don't worry if your plans are a bit messy or are overly detailed. Once you get moving, you can refine your plans as long as they're consistent with your identity. And as you take action on these plans, you'll want some extraordinary people, ideas, and wisdom to come along side your process... And that's what the next chapter is about.

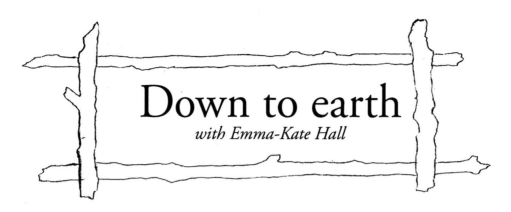

Down to earth
with Emma-Kate Hall

Our lives are often merely reactive, in a tragically unconscious kind of way. And it's the unconscious part that's the killer when it comes to actioning the stuff of our dreams. If we don't have a clear and accurate sense of who we are, how can we possibly engage with the world around us in any meaningful way? And if we don't have some kind of deeper understanding of the world around us, how can we possibly navigate the terrain in which our identity-born dreams will be lived? So yeah, I think we need to do two things. Unpack our identities with the rigour, courage, and tenacity of one whose very life depends on what's discovered (cause it kinda does). This includes coming up with some stellar stories based on the rich, raw substance of who we are. And also begin a process of coming to understand more consciously and critically the overall picture of our context—a complex mix of philosophical / scientific / economic / political / social ideologies, our national culture including our language and collective narratives, our family history, our personal set of childhood / life experiences, etc.—and how all that's affected the formation, or retardation, of our identities... as well as our resultant (in) capacity to not only have dreams but have a damn good go at living some of them.

With regards to planning, it seems to me that turning my ideas into plans and actually doing my plans are two very different things. And require very different skill sets/character traits. I think there is a place for planning and I find it helpful to come up with a strategic plan for how I might practically accomplish a concrete, short-term goal (say anything up to 2 years ahead). This might be a specific art project, business idea, or collaborative community venture... tangible ideas that fit with my longer term stories. Perhaps one of the biggest upshots of this kind of planning is that it helps me think through ahead of time any potential problems or risks and how I can either mitigate them at the outset or address them en route. It also helps me to set realistic time-frames and come to a decision on whether an initial idea is in fact really doable (or how I might enlist the help of others to make it so, or put my creativity to work in brainstorming other outta-the-box options). All these things give me a better chance of actually achieving my goal, which gives momentum to the journey of making larger ideas a reality over a lifetime.

But I also find I can have the best laid plans and still get horribly stuck. And that this is always a cue to re-engage more deeply with the two areas I mentioned above. It's a process, but I've been able to overcome even the most seemingly insurmountable roadblocks by choosing yet again to press into the truth about my unique identity, as well as the pertinent details of my context and its effects. At some of the harder junctures of my life it's been invaluable to have someone help me do this. I've also needed to give myself permission in certain seasons to take the time and space required to really wrestle this stuff through without the external pressures of having to produce something amazing too. It's work, for sure, but then what's a bit of intentional hard yakka if it means being able to live the incredible adventure of my very own bohemian dream?!

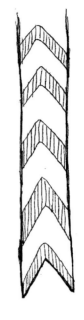

Chapter Fifteen

Help from above, or next door...

I believe identity is key to fulfilling our potential as people, but in itself, it's simply the raw material by which we can see that potential. All the 'I am' statements that are true about me need to grow into realities that can be seen and expressed through my relationships, the work of my hands, and my overall lifestyle. Unless I can find a meaningful way to draw these identity statements into those realities, they lie dormant as my potential self. So for me, listening to my soul and journaling identity was a crucial first step, but to reach my potential, I needed something more. Making plans gave me a roadmap for practicing my identity, but even still, it was a little daunting to take the first steps. Because, as we saw earlier in the book, a lot of us have grown up without either encouragement or much equipping which makes even well laid plans difficult to follow through on. What I needed was something extraordinary to kick-start my identity into development with some inspiration, and maybe even a bit of revelation.

I knew I was starting late and that there was pressure

from the outside to get on with something, anything as long as it paid the bills. So I had to respond to that pressure with a better way. I also knew I didn't wanna live a typical life or compete with the lame social norms that exalted talent over substance. So I needed to find extraordinary insights that truly equipped my 'I am' statements in a substantial way. Before I started acting on my plans, I developed a simple list of questions that I could research in order to find some revelation, or brilliant starting points. These questions emerged from observing how amazing people developed their gifts. Over the years, I've seen similarities in how they gain and apply wisdom to their process. It wasn't anything super complicated, just a consistent approach to seek out and apply what they learned (and a ton of discipline and hard work).

Firstly though, as I began to ask these questions and apply what I was learning, a number of things happened. A huge amount of ideas started popping up. Different ways of seeing photography, or marketing, or parenting... I started gaining a bit of revelation as to the root structures of my craft, like foundational approaches to education or community development. These five questions also became the sources of further research or education. Using a mind map technique, the core questions blossomed out into all kinds of useful branches. Which is exactly what I needed in order to counter the typical, narrow minded approach to vocational development. If I was going to beat down the pressure to survive in a harsh modern world, I needed tons of new ideas grounded in ancient wisdom.

Help from above - questions 1 & 2

I believe there is a spiritual component to where we've come from, or where our identities are formed, and therefore how we live out those identities. I'm starting with the hardest question (the spiritual side is kinda hard to explain and hard to apply) because I found that when I start my journey with a spiritual acknowledgement, I'm looking for ancient foundations instead of clever clues. The other questions listed below are super helpful too, but I want to start my search at the source. For me then, I wanted to know how the spiritual dimension speaks to my personal development and therefore my plans. If my identity was formed by God, and God is the source of all that I am, then God must have a clue about the things I want to do with my identity, like how to tell amazing stories or be a fantastic father...

I started with this question:

1. What is the nature and character of God like in the areas I'm pursuing?

So, for instance, if I want to understand communication/storytelling, I want to know **who God is** (nature) and **what God has done** (character) as a communicator. In asking this question, I'm stretching myself outside the norm of communication theory and technique into a very personal / spiritual approach. And not that basic theory isn't important, it's just that I want to add as much possible to my palette as I start developing my foundational views. What I'm looking for are age old principles, root structures I can build on.

This first question is a difficult one to ask. It's not like you can make a phone call or google the query. Like all questions about identity, you have to know the person you're talking to, and that comes of deep relationships. I've been getting to know God for over 30 years, so when I ask this question I'm drawing on thousands of experiences and conversations, meditations, and the stories of others. Having said that, I don't think it takes 30 years to understand God's nature in a particular field because I think everyone has an intuitive sense, built within us from birth. Simply by asking this question we alert our spirit to start seeing the answers, whether they come by meditative thought, a visual from a walk in the forest, or the work of our hands.

Ergo

An outstanding example of someone who has applied this first question is George Washington Carver, an American scientist, botanist, educator, and inventor. Immediately following the abolition of slavery, Carver set about discovering and teaching people about the hundreds of applications for peanuts, sweet potatoes, pecans, and many other agricultural means to help poor farmers diversify their crops and heal their land, namely from a devastating dependency on cotton. As a scientist, he would ask God to reveal the mechanisms by which the world and the universe operated. His assumption was that they were created intentionally and that he could discover those intentions by speaking to God about...

"the three great kingdoms of the world which He created—
the animal, mineral, and vegetable kingdoms—to
understand their relations to each other, and our relations to
them and to the Great God who made all of us."[65]

By knowing God in this way, Carver set a revelational foundation to his science through discovering characteristics of God which he translated into agricultural education and practice. As a result, I'd say he had a renaissance-like effect on his times.

Here's some stuff I've found when asking this question about writing:

Nature and Character of God - *what is God like?*
- Author and finisher of the story (overview, brings to completion)
- Love (the story is relational)
- emotive: Jealous (passion, purpose, redemption and judgement)
- challenger

I know it's a bit of a nebulous question and the answers are not necessarily authoritative. But if you ask the question, you may find intuitive responses open up a whole new range of ideas and cool approaches... I've often found that connections get made to other ideas or sources, and within a short amount of time I'm thinking differently and acting on these insights. Which should change the nature of the game, because now I'm functioning in my identity loaded with some wisdom from above.

---

65 *Rosa Parks* By Douglas Brinkley, New York, Lipper-Viking, 2000, page 18

For instance, I would apply the first question in this way:

If God is love then everything on the planet is a relationship. If I stay in touch with this attitude, I'll have a grid by which to measure everything I do. If I apply this core truth to some other attributes of God, like faithfulness, creativity, etc., I can develop a framework by which to measure my own story telling. This has been a huge help with the screenplays I've been working on. Since I'm a trainer and very philosophical, I tend to write in a didactic way. Knowing the relational nature of God as a communicator / story-teller (human, emotive, passionate...) highlights when my own work lacks an emotional strength. Over time I can bridge the gap between my approach and a deeper wisdom, which should result in better writing.

When I add these insights to my plans, I start to see some encouraging ways to move forward or to further educate myself which become a huge boost to my motivation. I also see some unique angles that differentiate me from the crowd while furthering my potential in the field. This means I'm not competing with everyone else on the same terms. So, this is a good start but I need to keep adding to my palette. So, I also ask the second question:

2. *What have ancient scriptures said about what I'm trying to learn and do?*

For instance, if I want to pursue the field of health care, I want to know what's already been discovered. A great starting point is to seek out the tested wisdom in ancient texts. Even in a world of constant invention, there's a lot of grounded understanding that needs to be applied in order to make sense of those inventions. Like, when you read the Torah, you see tons of instructions on basic health which focus on preventative care. This is a brilliant angle to approach a field now dominated with medicating or surgery after the fact. When you look deeper in these texts, there are some real gems which focus on relationships, community, and its impact on disease and health. A lot of this wisdom has been lost in what has shifted from communities caring and healing each other to mega industries with skyrocketing profits and salaries. Looking back and drawing on the wisdom of the ages helps you contrast and reconsider your place in this field and its possible redemption.

Now you may have mapped out a plan to study health care because that was part of your story. But once you start asking these questions and get some wisdom under your belt, you may decide to pursue that study in a more focused way. The benefit of these questions is that they help you connect your 'I am' statements with a broader wisdom and perspective, which actually helps you focus in on your particular angle.

Back to my question though (communication), here's what I get when I ask this second question:

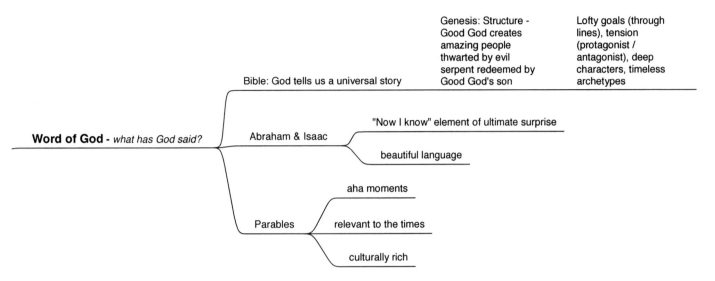

As I look through these examples I start to see more principles, ideas, and techniques that I can use to measure or add to my own work. And as I'm building a broader platform, I'll need to expand the search to other historical texts and stories. So I can then ask:

3. *What have others throughout history said about what I'm pursuing?*

I've never been much of a reader, but my children have done a great job of drawing my attention to amazing works like *Paradise Lost* and *The Brothers Karamazov.* As I read through these fantastic stories, and then about the lives of their authors, I start to see layers of their craft (like how revelation effected the work of Milton, or the incredible ability Dostoevsky and Tolstoy have in exploring human nature through their characters). These observations can go on the map, but if I look further I start to discover all kinds of stuff:

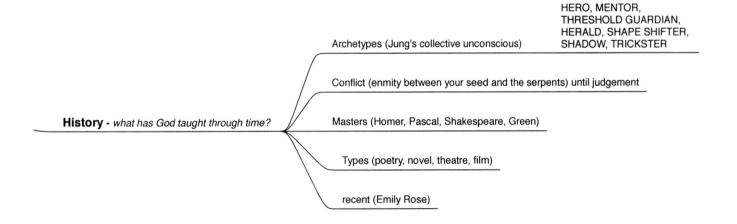

As these questions and my responses build up, I start to see even more connections. For instance, Carl Jung introduced the idea of a universal consciousness, and then others built on it by describing story archetypes[66] which can be understood by all cultures over all epochs. In itself, it's a super useful concept, but when you cross reference it to the other five questions (like what have ancient scriptures said), you start getting a real clue. Like how in the bible Solomon makes a statement that God has placed eternity in the hearts of man,[67] which confirms the idea that we not only have a conscience, but an eternal perspective on life and therefore stories. This ties in really well with Jung's ideas. Putting these two ideas together allows me to understand the structure, nuance, and effect of storytelling in a whole new way.

Again, as the research, sources, and then applications stack up, I can refer back to my plans and make alterations, or simply adjust my attitude. I'm also gaining a sense of momentum in my unique way of applying these ideas, which again means I'm not competing with everyone else on the same turf. Next, I want to build on this by asking:

4. *What can the natural world teach me about my field?*

For this question, we'll look at two areas: design and parenting. There's a tie-in here with question two because there's a scripture that says, "God can be clearly seen by observing the physical world around us",[68] or what Isaac Newton called "the book of God's works"[69]. So, in asking the scriptural question first, I start to look at the natural world with a different lens. For instance when it comes to design, a key principle to follow is understanding the design's form and function. The elements of design, whether it's graphic or industrial, need to work together to create a unified effect. This principle is beautifully displayed in the form and function of tree branches, honey combs, and how bubbles form together. You see a consistent geometry of 120 degree angles creating both structural strength and beauty. If you're doing industrial design, this is a foundational place to start. But as you dig deeper, you start to see all kinds of cool stuff which you can add to your designers palette. Like how giraffes have a special valve in their necks to restrict blood flow when they lean down to drink water, because without this the huge amount of blood rushing to their heads would cause them to nearly explode. Looking further still, you'd see how Woodpeckers have dual purpose saliva in their beaks which acts as both glue when their tongues reach inside trees for bugs, and then a solvent to release the bugs once back in the bird's mouth. Even cooler, their tongues wrap around the back of their brain to cushion the impact while pecking. Imagine learning stuff like this weekly and applying it to your design practice?

Now when it comes to parenting, I've had my eye on birds, I mean, I think penguins

---

66 A great example of this is Joseph Campbell's *The Hero with a Thousand Faces* which compares hero archetypes in mythology throughout the ages. Film makers, musicians, and writers have used his perspective to help them tap into the core elements of our human journey.

67 Ecclesiastes 3:11

68 Romans 1:20

69 *An account of Sir Isaac Newton's philosophical discoveries: in four books*, by Colin MacLaurin, Printed for J. Nourse, 1775, page 61

are birds? Anyway, if you've seen *March of the Penguins* you may have also been astounded at the incredible role reversal these brilliant creatures perform. The female goes out and does what they do best (hunt and provide) and the males stay home and protect the young. And I mean protect, as in covering and keeping eggs alive in minus 120 degree (Celsius) weather by wisely rotating as a group, buffering freezing winds, and keeping the flock alive. Are penguins flocks? Anyway, I can learn all kinds of things as a parent from these guys. Like how they play to each other's strengths instead of assumed roles. My parenting life can also be challenged at its foundations by observing how even crows mate for life and model an extreme commitment to their partner.

As a writer, here's what I've discovered in the natural world:

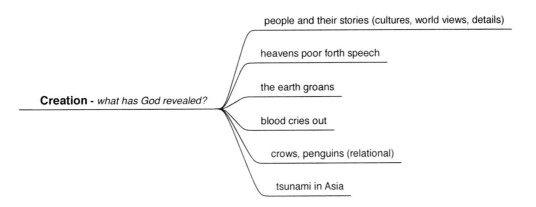

These initial impressions inspire me to understand anthropology, the natural sciences, and current affairs much more deeply. I want to understand the story behind each element which will change the way I write and live. As I put these things to paper (or laptop) and create practical ways to apply them in my life, I'm not only extending my identity's reach, I'm changing the way I live on a day to day basis. And since it's my life I'm developing, I need to ask this final question:

5. *What are my personal perspectives (from my soul, mind, and my experiences) in the area I'm pursuing?*

We often downplay our unique perspectives. Perhaps because, among other things, we have an under-developed sense of self. But the truth is that we all have a super unique way of combining our experience, neural routing, and dreams, etc. to create a whole new way of looking at any given area. Respecting our own way of seeing the world is a very important stepping stone in creating our small, but important, part of the future. And not just for ourselves, but to add our bit in collaboration with the creations of our tribe. J.R.R. Tolkien called his creative process (and that of all people) **sub creation**. Our opportunity is to create within a created world. We build on the creativity around us with our own world-view and particular process. Your personal view is an essential element in sub creation.

This book is an example of the way Blue and I see personal development. Our unique experiences and world-views allow us to add a dimension to the field that can only come from us. But if we're not asking the other four questions, our personal perspectives may end up pretty shallow. So, while I think we should take our ideas a lot more seriously, I also think putting these five questions together creates a really well-rounded approach to any given field of interest. Here's my initial response to the fifth question:

	life is complex, don't over simplify
Personal perspective - *what has God taught you?*	my story has seasons (chapters, trilogy)
	it doesn't come easy, write, rewrite, learn, learn some more

If you don't take your *self* seriously, no one else will

I mentioned in the beginning of the book that I'd come across a number of people who seemed to know, younger than most, who they were and what they wanted to do with their lives. One of the most interesting dimensions to these people was that **they took themselves seriously**. It's like they saw what they were becoming and acted like they were already there, or that getting there was simply a timing issue. I think the same thing will happen as you start to take your identity seriously by asking some serious questions and applying what you learn. Even the act of pursuing your story and plans with a bit of research will start you on a process of exercising your authority as you push that story into action, even if the action is a few baby steps.

For instance, I'd been taking pictures for years, but at one point I started taking my self seriously and did a bit of research. I looked back in history to see what some of the great photographers like Henri Cartier-Bresson or Ansel Adams shot and how they saw the world. I started paying more attention to the natural world, observing light and its effects... I took more notice of conflict and story in the scriptures to understand transitions and rites of passage, etc. Each question I asked was a step in taking my self, and therefore my craft, more seriously. As my internal conversation shifted, my photography improved, and my clients took the work more seriously. Not that we need tons of affirmation to move forward, we don't. All we really need is to make commitments that are essential to reach a level of maturity and skill in our field.

I was talking with a friend about this recently. She has real potential in being a producer (as in facilitating artists to produce their events and creations). Her identity statements, StrengthsFinder names, her experiences and passions, etc. were all pointing in this direction (among other things of course because remember, we're not just one vocation). As we were talking I suggested she makes herself a business card. Just a simple baby-step, that would push her over the line from thinking of her self in a certain way, to doing something that presented this self to the rest of the world... The research we do leads to ideas and revelations that help us formulate, and then communicate, what we're seeing. From there, we need to reveal ourselves to our family, friends, clients, and the larger tribe we may connect with over time. Any steps you can do to formalize—or in some way speak out what you're learning and becoming—will add to the momentum of your journey.

Identity unto others...

As your research spans out into libraries, cafe conversations, night schools... you'll start to interact with your neighbors in a new way. Instead of consuming community (which is what we do when we're identity-less) we start to see our place differently. This allows us to see others in a similar way. Like, seeing their place or helping them to see who they are and what they could do with some research of their own. Having a solid sense of identity, and then sharing the development of that identity, gives you the ability to treat others as you'd like to be treated yourself. The golden rule is a fantastic principle that compels us to walk along side our neighbor's process. And I love the idea of loving my neighbor **as my self**, because if I can see me, I can see the other. And if I can be me, I can give what I have to the other, or maybe work together on a common project, like the friends I mentioned at the Aurora Commons.[70]

I'm writing this book in a cafe (*Crave* in Kingsland) where I'm also curating the art space in which local artist are exhibiting monthly, where my son is working on a screen play right next to me, where they're gonna also start a film club, where my wife and other son work in the kitchen and as barista's, where the owners and I teach a cooking club, where we collaborate on other community development projects, where people show up every day and sit on these same couches to talk about life and love and the pursuit of liberty, or photography... This happens because I know a bit about who I am, what I'm looking for, and to a large degree, so do my neighbors who are becoming my tribe. And as a tribe, we can love and contribute to our larger community in a way I simply can't by myself.

By asking these five questions, my growing revelation over the last ten years is that my identity grows to the degree I engage with it in the community. As I research the human effect of identity and practice being me with others, more of me gets drawn out... The same goes for those I'm practicing with. When I show up at the *Screen Writers Guild* meetings, I find another guy with a good script who needs a producer. As a facilitator, I naturally want to help him find that producer, so in the same evening hook him up with another friend who's now working to get that script made into a film. Being my self moves the group forward and I move forward with them. Doing the research gives me at least a clue about the whole process.

Starting out with this whole identity / future development is hard because you feel the need to spend all your time on yourself, your education, your money... But when you find ways to love, connect with, and facilitate those around you, you avoid that cyclical self absorbed state. For instance, a few of my friends in Seattle (mentioned above) have rented out some space in their neighborhood to act as a community living room. They play chess, read, discuss, and live a part of their days along side both the hipster and homeless. They collaborate on music projects, the baking of a decent brownie, the philosophy of the day... all the while being themselves and

---

70 Check out these crazy kids: The Aurora Commons: http://www.auroracommons.org/

honoring the other selves around them. The wall is lined with portraits of the street and its people. It's a beautiful space, which I think is the natural result of people finding extraordinary ways of loving their neighbor with their unique identity. And it's not like there's a huge org. behind them, or that the hosts are super established in their own lives. It's what they know about themselves today that comes through the door each morning. And most of them are pretty young, so all they've done is act on what they know of their values, sense of style, and love for the street they live in. Simple eh?

Doing the research mentioned in this chapter
can add another dimension to the raw material of your identity. And when I look at the world and how it's developing, I know that for myself I really need something extraordinary to not only get by, but to make an impact. I want the radius of my life to create a beneficial effect on the world so my kids and their kids have something better to work with. I'm hoping these five questions help me do what Heather's (my wife) grandma always told her; to leave the place you visit better off than the way you found it.

Checkpoint:

You are here

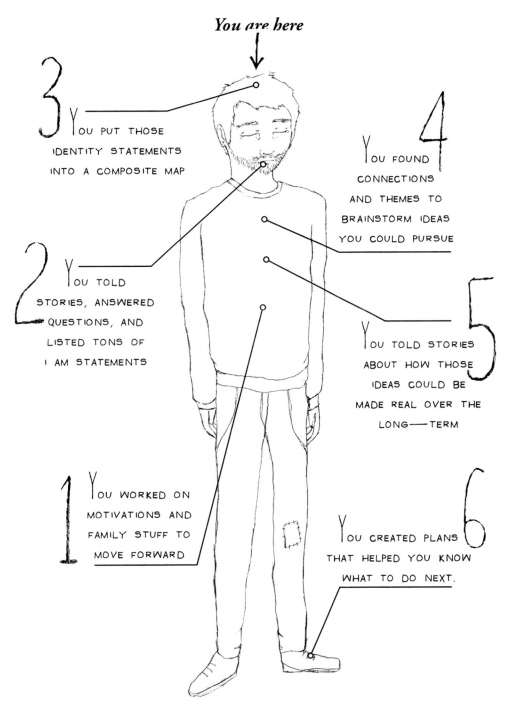

3 You put those identity statements into a composite map

4 You found connections and themes to brainstorm ideas you could pursue

2 You told stories, answered questions, and listed tons of I AM statements

5 You told stories about how those ideas could be made real over the long—term

1 You worked on motivations and family stuff to move forward

6 You created plans that helped you know what to do next.

You ready to get going?

What's next?

What's stopping you?

Chapter Sixteen

Putting your identity to work in the really real world

You still here?

At this point, you're all dressed up and ready to go to the party, but then you stop and notice:

- *there's no gas in the car (economic hardships seem too difficult to proceed)*
- *your mom STILL wants you to clean your room (family situation feels like an anchor)*
- *what you're wearing looks terrible (you're too afraid of what others will think, or that the thing you want to do will fail)*
- *your friends forgot to pick you up (not enough community support for what you want to do)*
- *you've lost the address (not enough information or resources to proceed)*
- *you are 'Le tired' (not enough energy to get off the couch)*
- *your kids won't go to sleep and are racing around the house on the babysitter's back (too many needs, too much distraction at home to pursue your dreams)*
- *it's too late and you've missed the party (all your energy is being spent on the 'part-time' projects)*

So far we've talked about what you want and who you are. We've told stories and planned out brave new worlds for you to explore. You've put in all this energy (you have, right?) and are ready to do something, to move forward... And then you wake up, or go outside, and you notice that outside of this book, the real world is exactly the same as when you started. Or, even worse, now that you see things a little more clearly. For instance, you really start to notice all the distractions out there eager to eat up all your free time. Or you feel way too alone to step out and try something new. Or that you just don't have the money... All these roadblocks. What to do?

A day in the life

In the blog we had going while writing this book, I asked a few hundred of my friends to let me know what they find hard about pursuing their own story. Here are a few comments from the days of their lives:

Kate wrote:

It's a relief to see that I'm not the only one struggling, as clichéd as that sounds. I really plugged into the concept of identity when I heard you in '07. I think there are two major roadblocks I am facing right now: 1. Money, and 2. Courage. First, the money: I have school debt that feels like a noose around my neck. I am glad I chose to get an M.A., and I did think through the ramifications before I chose to take out the loans, but since the recession, in my field, the only options for recent grads seem to be unpaid internships or mid-level jobs that require far more work experience/skills than I currently have. So, I feel a bit stuck. I'm trying to look at it as an opportunity to reconnect with my other interests, but the clock is ticking financially. I guess I feel like I have to put financial solvency over striking out as an entrepreneur. Second, courage. After two years studying and working in the field, I've got a problem—I'm passionate about human rights law, but the field (as of now) completely leaves out the artistic side of my personality. I can imagine hundreds of ways to incorporate the two, but I feel like I am duty-bound to pay off the loans first. Additionally, trying to break into the writing/publishing world (which is how I would like to connect art to human rights) seems completely overwhelming. The thought of querying major publishing companies with something I've written—and then dealing with the rejection—eh, it's a lot to think about. Again, maybe it's a question of timing. I also identify with what others have said about needing support/encouragement from a community that gets your soul. I have wonderful friends and family, but we don't share similar life/faith/identity goals yet...

Gert Jan wrote:

"Why would you?" I think that question covers a lot of my obstacles when people ask it either directly or indirectly. If they only asked "How could we do this together", "How did you get this dream" or "What's gonna be your next step"! It's so hard to start anything when people give you the idea that it's not worth trying and that you're all alone if you do. So many people think you should be normal, just like themselves...

Sam wrote:

Money, fear of 'what ifs' such as how much of an impact I can really have and thus settling for something a bit more simple than my ultimate dream. I think one thing that's holding me back is that I'm having a hard time finding good community and support - let alone people that can share my ideas. My motivation fluctuates like a roller coaster...

Claire wrote:

If I did not have the support of my parents I never would have started pursuing my identity and translating that into a career. Having the personality I have I would've done the 'right thing' and did what I was told and gotten a job. I think the big factor for me was money and the fear of ending up poor and having to rely on family for financial support when I desperately wanted independence. So not putting the money first is big. I find that going through this sort of journey has taken A LOT of my head space. Between family and identity, I have zero head space left and I'm single with no kids... hmmm so I can't imagine having that on top... craziness would probably ensue.
So I would say to walk out my dreams I need:
1. Somewhat of a stable family base
2. A bit of cash
3. To get rid of wrong ideologies (that's where you come in... thanks for the podcasts) cause it feels like swimming up stream
4. Someone to bounce ideas off

Andrea wrote:

This is very topical for me right now. Next week I finish up in my current job which is very corporate, high pressure... I have a great role in lots of ways but I feel like the real me has gotten lost and now has no desire to be there. I'd then have to find the next job which in the world's eyes should build on this last role, but every seemingly appropriate job description that's sent my way makes my heart sink and my stomach feel sick... So what's stopping me following my dream? I'm still not entirely clear what 'the dream' looks like and there's a huge pressure to sustain current levels of income to pay the mortgage, etc... At this point in time I'd gladly give up my home to do a job I feel truly passionate about. Just need to figure out what that is! Been trying to figure that out for a long time....

Martin wrote:

I've been dealing with my own identity since the Spring of 08, that's when I first heard some of your podcasts. Now at 24, I look back and do see a definite change... Really working through certain issues and then getting ready to apply them has been hard in a world that's always telling you to move forward. A part of this is finding an education that's brought me to a more specific direction... but now I feel it's crunch time and I need to choose something I can really focus on. Also, I guess I can put fear, dealing with money, and other people down on my list... but from where I am now, I would say headspace and the need to clarify are at the top of this list. I've been experimenting a lot, and the things that are me I've followed up with. But the way I see it now is that I have the opportunity to do some clarifying and to remove myself from a lot of distractions...

Sara wrote:

For me, there is an underlying spirit of comparison that holds me back from really going for the dreams that are inspired by my identity. I find myself fighting thoughts like 'If I really loved God I would sell everything and move to Africa.' Ironically, the christian culture around me is trying to help me be effective but it's somehow holding me back instead. I really have to consistently remind myself to get excited about who I am and that living from that place can be more powerful than comparing my life to the 'perfect' christian ideal. Spending the money to go to college is an important (however expensive) part of my long-term goals and plans. But sometimes I doubt whether the time and money is worth it. I think the most important thing for me is encouragement—more people saying 'just go for it'—and less people questioning the motives of my heart and if my ideas will succeed...

Jess wrote:

There is a big gap between the 'dreaming' and then how this plays out in reality. For example with us, it seemed like in the large youth org we worked with 'All things were possible' and dreams came into being easily. But now outside of that system, it's up to us to pull off our dreams. So yeah, things like needing to do part time jobs to fund the dream slow things down because so much energy and time go into those things... Also coming to grips with the question: 'Are these dreams really what God is calling us to do or are these just fancies in our own imaginations?' We want to live a life that's extraordinary, but the ordinary life sometimes seems hard enough...

Ann-Helen wrote:

It's really scary to go out there and go for my dreams. What if I fail? Sometimes it's easier to just dream about it because in that way I won't mess it up. As long as my dreams remain in my head, they're perfect...

Dino wrote:

Several challenges come to mind. One is a lack of confidence that if I take the step I won't have what it takes to make it work, and if I do make it work, will I be able to sustain it past the initial stages. Second, can I make the critical distinction between what I want to do, what I really want to do, and what's the flavor of the month. Third, doing the hard work of doing the work. These might be a bit too simplified, but put together they can carry a lot of weight...

Alexine wrote:

I'm in the middle of listening to your identity series online... Something that's come up really strong, and that I am totally grieving right now, is about what life could have been like if I'd been given a chance to dance from an early age. Looking back and remembering my life, it's all over me. I wanted to dance, I loved dance, I've always had a fascination for it, and as soon as I had a chance, at 14, I did some. Then got to high school where it wasn't offered anymore and stopped, until college, where I discovered ballroom. Back then, the obstacle was money, so I danced off and on. Then I had kids, and my back got really bad, so I had to stop because of that. Now I'm 37, have injuries, a bulging disk, and two kids, and while I could pick up dancing again, and probably will after listening to your podcast, it's going to be a lot harder to get good at it than had I been given the chance when I was little. Now time is a big obstacle, and physical ailments... I know I can still dance and feel tremendous joy when I do it. It just doesn't feel like it can / will ever be at the level that I would have liked...

Taylor wrote:

I guess for the longest time the struggle has been trying to fit perfectly into everyone else's ideas or plans for me. Not really my parents so to speak... but those people I wanted to impress. I worry that it'll never change and I won't be accepted. I've taken others priorities and tried to make them my own... Elevating them above what should have been my priorities to accomplish the great dream bubbling within me. Being at the front end of my 10,000 hours and comparing myself with someone at the end of theirs, or even the middle of theirs... Thinking, not only will I never make it, but there's no way I could make it in time. I just need a few people to see me for who I really am and encourage my embattled soul onwards. Someone to speak truth to me, someone to just take the time and listen to my heart.

Kath wrote:

I'm currently making notes on Harville Hendrix's Giving The Love That Heals... *it makes me think a lot about Kate's comment (from the book blog) on your 'What do you really want?' Especially regarding family... and how so much pain is carried from one generation to the next, that people often spend so much of their 20's/30's/40's dealing with childhood stuff. I / we want to be conscious enough to give our kids a head start in the pursuit of being who they want to be with minimal headspace taken up by how we messed them up...*

Emma-Kate wrote:

My concerns: Fear about what other people will think of my unconventional choices / approach to life... and on certain days, a fat dollop of self-doubt. I need encouragement from friends and family, especially those that really 'get' me. A cup of tea and a long walk by the river also seems to help :-). I think I also need to just keep going, to keep applying the little I already know even (perhaps especially) when I'm feeling scared and shy or wondering what's the freakin' point 'cause a regular day job would be sooooo much easier? So, let's say persistence. I'll also add that I find this less of an issue now (a number of years into the process of living from my identity and having a go at doing some of the things I really love), than it was initially as I was finding my feet in the process. Maybe it's because I've experienced a few small wins, or I now have a growing community of like-minded friends to share the journey with, or I've got a taste for life so I'm willing to fight harder to overcome obstacles. Perhaps my shoulders are also getting broader as I just grow up a bit, and I'm more ok with the fact that life is full of tensions and there will always be a degree of resistance. I think our creativity is a remarkable gift for finding ways forward where there seems no way... even if that creativity is simply put to work finding a way to hang in there at times (cup of tea anyone?).

What's real in your world?

So, let's look at these concerns from the perspective of what's real. I say this because when talking about identity, people will often say something back like, "yeah sure, but in the real world..." And I hear this. The concerns listed above are super valid and I would not diminish them by offering simple solutions. But the question I have is this; is the world around us a static environment we have to respond to or is it something we can shape? And if so, what may be stopping or facilitating our shaping the really real world? So yeah, there's no easy answers to living as yourself in a complex world, but here are a few tips to change what you can...

Clearing the decks

Everyone has a perfectly valid reason for not pursuing their own story. Only some of these reasons, however, are actually worth considering. After you take away any fear or laziness from the equation, what's left is something you can really work on. For instance, if someone is working in a job they hate for fear of not having a job at all, that fear will dominate the reasons why they can't study or take the time to write more songs... If someone looks at the seemingly daunting amount of time and effort it takes to pursue their story and decides they'll do it later, then that laziness will become a dominant part of all their future choices... But if you face these two ugly brothers and remove their presence from the situation, then what you'll be left with is a reasonable problem that your identity can actually cope with.

The key is to own our internal roadblocks before we can tackle the external 'realities'. If I can acknowledge and remove my internal fear of failure or my obsession with financial security, then I can use my real energy to face the actual difficulties of an economic downturn or a market seemingly saturated with people all wanting the same job. In fact, when I get that distracting fear out of the way, I can actually focus on my distinctive response and may just find a niche. The nature of fear is that it blocks all prospective solutions by predicting disaster on all fronts. Once its annoying voice is dealt with, you can sense and deal with the real situation. Because when people say they can't do such and such because it's simply not realistic, what they're often meaning is that from their perspective they can't see a way ahead. Remove the penny (the true weight and size of a fear) from in front of your eye and you'll see an entire ocean of possibilities.

Here's how I deal with my fears:
- *acknowledge them (speak them out, look at their root structure, like where they came from or what they're based on...)*
- *process the reasonable bits (what's true or actual about the concern)*
- *use my identity strengths to do what I can with the reasonable bits (and leave the results up to time and more effort as needed)*

Dealing with laziness is much easier. It's obvious (at least to your mom) and has a simple solution. You just speak out what your trading your future for and own the consequences. Like, 'Instead of creating the best skate park in the country, I choose to work this average job, because for now I get to buy a few toys along the way...' Or, 'Instead of working really hard on my dreams now, I'll wait until I absolutely have to before I make any significant changes to my life, even if at that point I may have forgotten what my dreams even were.' As you acknowledge the choices you're making today and own the reasons why, you'll give **cause and effect** the best possible chance to speak to those priorities before they work you later (as in mid-life crisis). If you're making choices today to just get by because getting by ain't that bad, then know that the slow suffocation of your identity will have a life destroying effect in the long run. You may have subtle reasons as to why you're not trying harder, or pushing yourself further, but if you can be completely honest your true self might have a chance at fighting for its own life.

The results of properly owning and working through fear and laziness will be living in the really real world. Not the perceived one of social pressures and internal confusions, but the actual place where your identity and hard work can make a difference. The real world is messed up, but malleable at the same time. Don't use 'reality' as a cop out for inactivity. Instead, call out what's truly difficult in the world around you, and what you're truly capable of in terms of changing that world.

Here are some tips of working the real road blocks:
No gas (petrol) in the car!
The old axiom still holds true; that if you don't work, you don't eat. This is a good pressure. It makes you find what you're best at and work hard at turning that into value for others who will then pay you in return. So far, so good. Money usually becomes a pressure when you're not working from your strengths. It takes way more labour hours to earn when you (or your product / company) are only average at what you're doing. If you worked 40 hours per week at things you loved and were really good at, you'd have too much money. But who gets to do that, right? Well?

The money side of life is hard, but you can deal with this over time. As you work hard on building your strengths, you'll also be building a good financial foundation. Our identities are wired to multiply stuff, in a world that's wired to be multiplied. So, if you work hard by putting your identity to work, you will pay those bills and have something leftover to be generous with. Oh, and read *Rich Dad, Poor Dad*.[71]

Your mom STILL wants you to clean your room!
A lot of people live under the constant expectation of their families—which isn't necessarily a bad thing—but the way these pressures are communicated or transferred can be debilitating. Other negative experiences from our upbringing can add to these internal pressures. These take up a lot of the headspace, or the bandwidth, we need to get on with being proactive. And you can't just ignore the pressure, it has to be relieved.

---

71 By Robert T. Kiyosaki, Business Plus, 1 edition, (2000), 207 pages

We've looked at this stuff in previous chapters, but I just want to say that as you progress, one way to release some of this pressure and get the headspace back is to look at a really long-term process. There's no way all this stuff (often generational) can be worked through before you get on with your dreams. You have to communicate, interact, change, and heal over time all in parallel with walking out your dreams. In fact, I've found that I have the grace and ability to clear my headspace best when I'm winning a little more each day through the exercise of my talents and gifts. When I get to be me, maybe for the first time in my life, I have courage to face the other. The other family member, or neighbor, or boss[72] who may want me to be something else gets to reckon with the real me. Over time, those big giant problem relationships become manageable. You just have to work it all in parallel.

Does this color look good on me?

Another thing that messes with our headspace is a fear of what others will think about our plans, especially if our story is kinda out there. Often, the mean spirited response we hear from those around us doesn't come so much from the fact they don't like your story, it's that theirs is being confronted. Like, 'why do you get to pursue your dreams?' And while I'm tempted to just say 'lose the lame friends', the truth is that you need those around you to be part of your story. And they need you for theirs.

The trick is to turn those mutual fears and expectations into a conversation. Do a better job of encouraging your friends while sharing your next steps and enlisting their help. Often, these peer based fears are only in our heads and aren't what our friends are thinking at all. But either way, communicating what you want to achieve gives everyone something tangible to work on. And if you do fail, or do get judged, then learn to be okay with this because these two things will be part of the rest of your life anyway. Failure will teach you to improve and judgement will teach you what you need to ignore. And by the way, doing nothing about your dreams does not make failure or judgement go away. You have to grab ahold and work them to your benefit.

Where's my ride?

Sometimes it seems impossible to find a few people who will just listen closely, and maybe even throw in with us. But it's super easy to connect with all kinds of people who'll be more than happy to waste your time being typical. And it's amazing how we can live surrounded by people and yet feel so alone and disconnected. You don't need to move city or dump all your friends to change this scenario. But you do need to consider how you relate to each other. Thoreau once said that most of us

---

72 I love the blurb on the back of Tom Peters book *Re-Imagine!* that describes the epitaph he dearly hopes to avoid: "Thomas J. Peters 1942-2003. He would have done some really cool stuff but his boss wouldn't let him." He also writes a quick epitaph for Mozart which reads: "W.A. Mozart 1756-1791. He changed the world. He enriched humanity. He was only around for 35 years. Think about it".
Re-Imagine! Business Excellence in a Disruptive Age, DK Publishing, 1st edition, 2003, page 33

"lead lives of quiet desperation"[73]... where we keep quiet about our identity and our dreams. It's like we're all lobotomized. I say we end the silent desperation by being bold enough to change the dynamic within your existing network. Tell them the story you want to pursue and ask them about theirs. Take the risk of rejection, mocking, or skewed glances, and just let people know who you really are and where you want to go with that. You'll find a bit of resistance, but you'll also find comrades. If you do this over the course of a year or two, you'll find that even in a small town in Switzerland, there are enough people to support your process. If you think these people are meant to come to you and pour time and money on your story, you'll be waiting forever. You're designed to be proactive, and proactive people create the kind of relational support they need. That support does exist and it's closer than you think, but you have to call it out.

You lost the address, again!

I run into a lot of people who jump into university because it 'seemed' like the right program, only to change degrees within the year. Or they just stick it out anyway, get a job, and force that education to pay their bills... Not cool. Others will get stumped with all the options available and go into an info-coma, then end up doing nothing at all. When you start really pursuing your story, you'll need to break out of simplistic approaches by getting all the details required to make the best possible choices.

Two words of advice then: RE SEARCH. In an outside-in reactive approach to life, no one puts in the time needed to really search out the details that will inform a personalized decision. As you start to outline plans, take the time to do A LOT of research. Each important step should be really well considered by drawing all the information you can into the fray. Especially if your path is gonna be tough. Most people check out because there's not an obvious open door, or because a solution isn't immediately clear. Some of the things you may want to do are going to be really hard and will take heaps of imagination, thinking outside of the box, and ferreting out the angles everyone else gave up on. And, if your world has been overly mini-van-mom'd, then you're gonna have to work extra hard at kicking doors open and finding solutions. Just sayin.

I'm 'Le tired'

(If you're lazy, read the previous section under **Clearing the decks** over and over again until this is not longer an issue:-). Nah, kidding, kinda. I understand a lack of energy based on a tired spirit. When you have tried and the efforts you've made haven't been rewarded, it sucks the energy away from future endeavors. Finding a second wind is the work of your will and that will needs a reason to kick back into gear, despite the past. My hope has been that your identity / story / plans will give your will a much better reason to find this strength. But I also know that a lot of you will have put in some years doing your best to get this far, and the wall you now need to get over can still seem very, very high.

---

73 From Henry David Thoreau's *Walden,* which reads: "The mass of men lead lives of quiet desperation. What is called resignation is confirmed desperation. From the desperate city you go into the desperate country, and have to console yourself with the bravery of minks and muskrats. A stereotyped but unconscious despair is concealed even under what are called the games and amusements of mankind. There is no play in them, for this comes after work." T. Y. Crowell & co., 1910, page 8

The first thing to consider is properly pacing yourself. In terms of rest, are you getting what you need daily (most sleep experts recommend 6 REM cycles, or nine hours per night), weekly, and yearly? Is your life balanced, because if it's not, you'll never have the extraordinary energy required to be yourself. The second thing to look at is where you're presently wasting time, and you know exactly what that means. Put that time back into research, inspiration, and feeding those parts of your soul that need it. Finally, have a look at pacing yourself so that you reach your goals within a reasonable amount of time. I want to write seven books in seven years. If I do that in ten I'm still happy, but in either case, I plan my 'life attack plan' over a doable period of time so I have the grace to actually get there.

The kids are crying!

Some people live in family environments where most of their energy bandwidth is taken up by those commitments. Just keeping the machine going leaves very little time to finish a good book, let alone attend night-school or develop a small business on the side. But the real tension, as Kath mentioned above, is that if you can't function out of your full identity, how can you help your kids see theirs and not get stuck in the rat race of education, work, taxes, and then…

I totally relate to this and want to write a book on the subject, 'cause it's huge. But for now I would say that you need to put a stake in the ground. If you don't arrest this process it'll drag you through the rest of your life, living under the tyranny of the urgent. The 'stake' is a set of attitudes and priorities you want to foster while you're in the thick of it. Meaning, you're already doing a million things, so make each one count. Firstly, don't waste time on amusement. If your free-time isn't doing things that inspire you, you're squandering that wealth. Secondly, make all your choices line up just a little bit better with your identity. My friend Hailey spends quality time with her two girls by taking pictures together (she's a photographer) and helping them to make their own unique creations. Her articulate and humorous husband Andrew takes those pictures and makes miniature newspapers (as in 5x8cm) for the kids featuring their own stories. Instead of complying with status quo roles in the home, we can transform that same environment when we make each choice line up a little bit closer with who we are. So, whatever you have to do each day, make it a little more like you and it'll add up to a slow transformation over time.

It's too late, I've missed the party

The average age of 'successful' people seems to be getting lower every decade. Pop stars coming out of grade school and software stars coming out of college give the impression that the rest of us have missed the boat. But I think we're looking at the wrong indicators. The people who've nailed life's real issues (love, lasting creativity, sustainable community) are way past their 20's. In fact, some studies I've seen suggest that those that burn brightly in the beginning hardly ever burn for very long. Especially young artists who tap into the pop milieu, they seem to peak in their 20's and then poof. I suggest we reconsider our metric for how old is 'too old' to pursue any given dream.

What we should consider is whether we're spending the time we do have in the right way, or if we're redeeming everything we've learned so far. Some waste tons of time pursuing the right dream from the wrong path. My son Jordan had lots of opportunities to work various jobs on film sets, but he knew that if he spent all day being an AD (assistant director) he would have zero time or energy left to actually direct. So he took the guerrilla route of making his own shorts films, music videos, and TV commercials so he could create a more direct path to his goals. We can capitalize on our experience and develop our talents at any stage of our lives if we're willing to set our own metric for success; which I define as being myself in a loving way to those around me. I can do that at 20, 40, 60... Especially given that each year exploring identity gives me a wisdom I can't get in any other way.

Don't forget what you've been given

The human spirit is an amazing thing. It can succumb to 'affluenza' or overcome the meanest obstacle. What causes it to do either seems to be the stuff of poetry. Why does one person with all the opportunities in the world squander their life, while the other—the poorest of child soldiers—spin that adversity into gold? What's that mechanism which changes our entire world and forms it according to either our strengths for good or our weakness for our demise? The great battle between your soul's will and the fear of failure determines the rest of your life. But it's not just a matter of 'positive thinking', it's about putting the fear of failure in its place.

For instance, when J. K. Rowling was in her 20's, she felt her life had "failed in an epic scale".[74] This is how she described it:

> *"An exceptionally short-lived marriage had imploded, and I*
> *was jobless, a lone parent, and as poor as it is possible to be*
> *in modern Britain, without being homeless. The fears that*
> *my parents had had for me, and that I had had for myself,*
> *had both come to pass, and by every usual standard, I was the*
> *biggest failure I knew."*

While this was a horrible time, with no clear light at the end of the tunnel for the young woman working at Amnesty International, the experience of **true failure** "[...] meant a stripping away of the inessential. I stopped pretending to myself that I was anything other than what I was, and began to direct all my energy into finishing the only work that mattered to me". She regained her focus and passion for storytelling by darting off for lunch writing in a cafe, and the rest is history.

Our fear of failure is largely the fear of an **assumed failure**, or an assumption that we will not live up to the expectations placed upon us. Fine, the sooner we lose those expectations the better. But we have to differentiate between assumed failure—where the world's criteria sets the bar—and true failure which strips away the dross revealing the self and its real potential, even in crisis. Rowling continues: "You might never fail on the scale I did, but some failure in life is inevitable. It is impossible to live without failing at something, unless you live so cautiously that you might as well not have lived at all – in which case, you fail by default."[75] True failure will happen

---

74 Transcript of Rowling's Commencement Address, "The Fringe Benefits of Failure, and the Importance of Imagination," given at the Annual Meeting of the Harvard Alumni Association in June 2008.

75 ibid

as you pursue your identity, but so will the discovery of deeper strengths, stronger relationships, and a clarity you can gain in no other way. The only way you can know the difference between assumed failures and the truly helpful ones is to be true to your identity as you move forward. Let real failure have its effect on you and keep the assumed ones out of your head by forcing them to face the real world of your soul's making.

The resilient quiet strength of our souls is the source of a life well lived. That place in us, where our identity lives and connects us spiritually to God and humanity, is a seed that longs to create the really real world around us. Not the world we see today, but the one we can create. The shadow of what's to come is brooding inside of you, waiting for its chance to get into the light and do some good. But if it stays suppressed for much longer, it will turn in on itself and become need, stress, and loneliness. This nuclear force within us can only be unleashed if we say so. The simple yet powerful switch is our will. We will to do one thing or another, choose one path or another. Circumstances do affect us, but at the end of the day, our will has the majority vote. There's a proverb that says "the power of life and death is in the tongue."[76] What you say yes or no to will create one world or the other. Amazing isn't it, that for most of our lives we thought someone else was actually in control while we've actually had this internal force all along. Our will, what we do with it, and what we say has the power to transform the rest of our lives—and by extension, the lives of those around us. Use it well.

---

76 Proverbs 18:21

Postscript:

I'm still learning how to write. In terms of those 10,000 hours to master something, I'm somewhere in the 1,000-2,000 hour range. I'm a little embarrassed to publish this book such as it is. On top of this, I've made it my habit to write the first three drafts in a crowded cafe next to Blue and 30 other people. (As I write, there's a gorgeous curly-haired 4-year-old practicing the most shrill, horrible scream I've ever heard.) While not at the cafe, I'd be writing in my living room where the wonderful dysfunction / creativity of my family kept slamming into my thoughts. I wrote in this environment to stay in context—or in the flow of real lives—but man does it make writing hard. My kids are in their late teens and early 20's and drive me nuts most of the time. And right now, my wife isn't really happy with me. On top of all that, the year so far has been a financial wreck and that's following 28 years of just getting by. During the last two years, I've had nine operations for skin cancer, two of which were malignant melanomas. Fun.

Now, I could still counter each statement above with 10 other things for which I'm very, very thankful. But if I can write a book, the hardest one for me so far, in the midst of all this, I wonder what you can do? I mention these things simply to encourage you. Don't wait for things to get better before you launch out. You make things better by putting in the next 1,000 hours, then the next... alongside whoever's willing to walk with you.

Multiple Intelligence Assessment[77]

1. On a scale of 0 - 3, please rate how you feel you most identify with the following statements by recording your numerical answers in the square adjacent to the statement number:

0 = Never - 'This is not me at all!'
1 = Seldom - 'Only unless I have to!'
2 = Sometimes - 'Well, sometimes!'
3 = Often - 'This is me

1.		like to write
2.		compute mental arithmetic problems quickly
3.		spend free time engaged in art activities
4.		play/or have a desire to play a musical instrument
5.		do well in competitive sports
6.		have a lot of friends
7.		value a sense of independence and strong will
8.		tell jokes and stories
9.		enjoy using computers
10.		report clear visual images when thinking about something
11.		easily remember the melodies of songs
12.		move, twitch, tap or fidget while sitting in a chair
13.		socialize a great deal around the neighborhood
14.		react to strong opinions when controversial topics are being discussed
15.		have a good memory for names, places, dates or trivia
16.		ask questions like "Does the universe end?" or "What happens after death?"
17.		find it easy to read charts, maps or diagrams
18.		notice when a musical note has been played off key
19.		engage in and enjoy physical activities like swimming, biking, hiking, etc.
20.		keep up to date with the latest gossip
21.		tend to live in your own private, inner world
22.		enjoy reading books in your spare time
23.		enjoy playing and winning strategy games like for ex. chess, checkers, etc.
24.		tend to draw accurate representations of people or things
25.		like to play music while you study
26.		like to touch people when you talk to them
27.		enjoy being involved in several group activities
28.		enjoy being alone while pursuing some personal interest, hobby or project
29.		find it easy to spell words accurately
30.		reason things out logically and clearly
31.		enjoy movies, slides and photographs
32.		collect records, tapes and/or CDs
33.		enjoy scary amusement rides
34.		find yourself serving as the "family mediator" when disputes arise
35.		have a deep sense of self-confidence
36.		appreciate and enjoy nonsense rhymes and tongue twisters
37.		devise experiments to test out things not understood
38.		enjoy doing jigsaw puzzles or mazes
39.		sing songs to yourself
40.		demonstrate skill in crafts like woodworking, sewing, carving, etc.
41.		enjoy playing games involving groups of people
42.		tend to go against the norm in dress, behavior and attitude
43.		enjoy doing crossword puzzles or playing word games
44.		enjoy working on logic puzzles such as the Rubik's cube
45.		daydream a lot
46.		keep time rhythmically to music
47.		cleverly mimic other people's gestures, mannerisms or behavior
48.		have a lot of empathy for the feelings of others
49.		tend to be self-motivated to do well on independent study projects

[77] This assessment is drawn from Thomas Armstrong's *In Their Own Way* Tarcher; (2000)

2. Fill in the following Score Sheet by entering your score in the square next to the relevant statement number and then by adding up your totals:

1.		2.		3.		4.		5.		6.		7.	
8.		9.		10.		11.		12.		13.		14.	
15.		16.		17.		18.		19.		20.		21.	
22.		23.		24.		25.		26.		27.		28.	
29.		30.		31.		32.		33.		34.		35.	
36.		37.		38.		39.		40.		41.		42.	
43.		44.		45.		46.		47.		48.		49.	
Total A		Total B		Total C		Total D		Total E		Total F		Total G	

3. If you want, list your top three or four intelligences back in chapter 5 as part of your journaling process.

What the letters represent:

A. Linguistic Intelligence
• "Life is words" • highly developed auditory skills • think in words • may love reading, writing or storytelling • good memory for names, places, dates, trivia • learn best by verbalizing/hearing/seeing words • motivated by talking, providing books, tapes and opportunities to write

B. Logical-Mathematical Intelligence
• "Life is patterns/relationship of ideas" • think conceptually; like abstract patterns and relationships • reason things out logically • like to devise experiments to test their theories • enjoy using computers and doing math in their heads • motivated by opportunities to experiment and ask questions

C. Spatial Intelligence
• "Life is a picture" • think in images and pictures • high awareness of spatial arrangements, location • like drawing, designing things, building, daydreaming • easily read charts, diagrams, maps • motivated through media and opportunities to create visual images

D. Musical Intelligence
• "Life is a song" • often sing, hum, whistle to themselves • may show talent or high appreciation of music • good sense of rhythm • sensitive to non-verbal environmental sounds • learn through rhythm and melody

E. Bodily-Kinaesthetic Intelligence
• "Life is movement, touching" • process knowledge through bodily sensations, "gut feelings" • need to move, engage in physical activity • need to touch people when they talk to them • may have skills to athletics, dance, mime or fine-motor co-ordination • communicate well through gestures, body language • learn by touching, manipulating, moving • motivated through role-play, dramatics, physical activity

F. Interpersonal Intelligence
• "Life is a party" • understand people (motives, feelings, etc.) • often leaders with abilities to organise, communicate or manipulate • enjoy many social activities • learn best by relating and co-operating, group projects

G. Intrapersonal Intelligence
• "Life is a special place" • posses strong personalities, deep sense of self • seem to live in own, private, inner world • self-motivated, strong-willed, independent, self-confident • certain quality of inner wisdom, intuitive ability • learn best when left to themselves, need private space

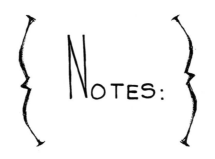

{ Notes: }

CPSIA information can be obtained at www.ICGtesting.com
Printed in the USA
BVOW050448250412

288611BV00006B/2/P